FOREWORD

I wrote this book to share my journey and inspire hope in those who may need it. I made many discoveries along my path from grief to grace, pain to peace, and sorrow to serenity.

I received pearls of wisdom from my Soul, wrote them down, trusted their guidance, and share them in this book.

This is a story about the love between a mother and a son, and more than that, it's a story of moving through grief and staying connected at the Soul level where the connection began, always was, and always will be.

It's a story of dreams and possibilities, of love and support, of holding on and letting go. It's a story of wonder and mystery and trusting and sharing.

It's about contribution and reaching out with a light into the darkness. It's about gifts hidden in tragedy and lives forever changed. It's about joy and sorrow and expanding to include it all.

It's about commitment and persistence and courage and life-everlasting. It's about you and me and us.

My hope is that those who read this will discover that even in the depths of unspeakable sorrow, there are gifts to be discovered and healing is possible.

Legends say that hummingbirds

float free of time,

carrying our hopes for love, joy and celebration.

The hummingbird's delicate grace

reminds us that life is rich,

beauty is everywhere,

every personal connection has meaning,

and that laughter is life's sweetest creation.

Author Unknown

DEDICATION

I lovingly dedicate this book to

Resh Michael Ortego,

my precious, beautiful son.

You continue to inspire me...

Resh Michael Ortego
April 17, 1977 - July 25, 2013

TCONTENTS

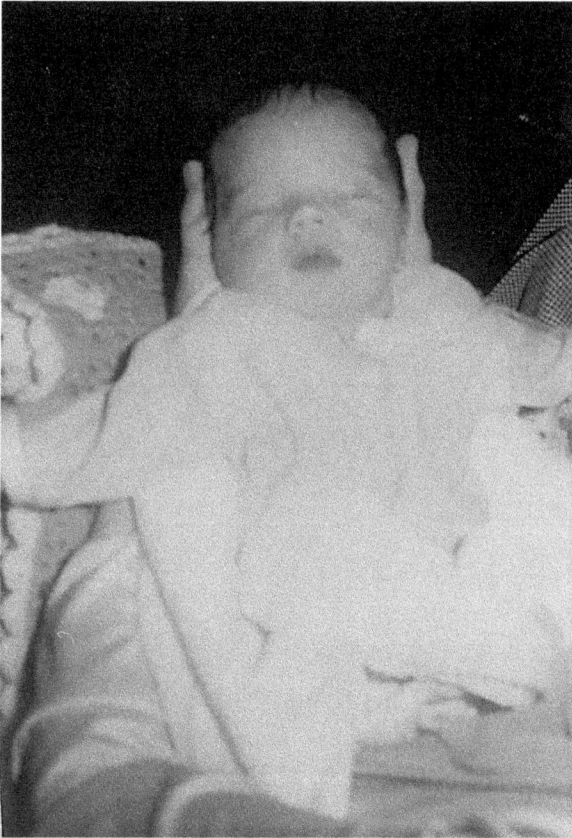

Our little Mikey Buddha baby

Introduction

Resh Michael Ortego, entered this world on a Sunday morning, April 17, 1977, nine months to the day after he visited me, his mom, in a dream asking me to join our family of four. I wanted a girl, but even prior to his birth, he was irresistible. His brothers named him Mikey after a cereal commercial. His silent monk guru at Mount Madonna gave him the spiritual name of Naresh, at age 22, and he became known in his professional life as Resh Michael.

On July 25, 2013, I received a call no parent ever wants to receive—that Michael had been killed in a tragic accident. I began posting on Facebook late that same night so I could reach out to his friends, especially his girlfriend Sammie. I needed to let my friends and his friends know of his death. Facebook quickly became my town square for sending and receiving news, as well as for sharing our collective grief and posting sweet memories.

Five days after his passing, Michael's celebration of life service filled our 200-person capacity sanctuary to overflowing with as many listening to audio outside the church as those squeezed inside. Over 400 people showed up to honor his short life. I realize the term "short" is relative but 36 years seems short to me.

This book is our story—a promise fulfilled to myself and to Michael. I have included poetry which rose up from me as I opened to all of the pain and the love. I have included what I call the "raw footage excerpts" from my Facebook entries and my personal journals.

Soon after I began keeping a "Michael journal," I received what I've come to refer to as treasured observations. These tumbled out in the first three to four weeks, like pearls of wisdom from my soul. I squeezed them into the first few pages of my journal as they arrived and trusted their guidance. I felt like I was being instructed, and I paid attention.

In pulling this book together, I kept asking myself, "What is the best way to assemble three distinct sources?" I wrote poetry which poured through during the first nine months. I also wrote down the story as a narrative, inspired by what occurred and by each of the pieces of guidance I received. In this second edition, I've blended the poetry into the narrative.

Lastly, there is the "raw footage" consisting of Facebook posts and personal journal entries which also contain the bread crumbs of the journey itself. I debated about including the raw footage, but my heart said to include it. I've edited some of the material for brevity's sake, and also have removed personal surnames from my journal entries. I have learned to listen to my heart so much more now, and my heart says most of these names are not necessary to the story being told.

I was inspired to write this book in order to share my journey and the guidance which helped me navigate the oceans of grief that threatened to drown me. I made many discoveries along my path from pain to peace to joy, all of which I am sharing. I also have a strong desire to inspire hope in others who may be suffering—hope that the deep love and connection to our loved one is still very present and accessible, even though their physical presence is gone from our sight.

For me, writing from my heart has become a way of healing and staying connected. I share and my load lightens. I feel the love and support of those who knew and loved Michael and those who may only know of him through me. I also have discovered how truly close we are to our loved ones on the other side, and I am learning the heart frequencies for communicating with Michael whenever I need to.

He awakens me in the morning with song and touches my soul with joy throughout the day. My story is unique to me, and yet in sharing it, I suspect many will see themselves within its pages.

Michael helped me write the last part of this introduction. When I listen in on just the right high frequency, I can hear him and he will dictate to me what to write. This is one of those instances when I asked him, "If you were to write an introduction to this book, what would you say?" Here is his answer:

"This is a story about the love between a mother and a son, and more than that, it's a story of moving through grief and

staying connected at the soul level where the connection began, always was, and always will be.

It's a story of dreams and possibilities, of love and support, of holding on and letting go.   It's a story of wonder and mystery and trusting and sharing.

It's about a voice—a most beautiful voice—and music and healing. It's about joy and sorrow and expanding to include it all.

It's about contribution and reaching out with a light into the darkness. It's about gifts hidden in tragedy and lives forever changed.

It's about commitment and persistence and courage and life-everlasting. It's about you and me and us."

I trust you will be touched and perhaps inspired or even healed from your own grief by some of the stories that follow. May you feel the love being poured into these pages as you read them. You may also find that I repeat myself. I sometimes need to hear something more than once in different contexts. I've made every attempt to have the material flow smoothly. I've also included photos of Michael at different points in no particular order just to give you a flavor of who he is. Many are not "high resolution" so may appear grainy. They are, however, highly charged with love.

Since I published the first edition of this book, I've written a companion book that includes a guided journaling experience. I've also created a very gentle, self-paced, online, transformational healing program, also in book form, designed to move those who are willing to take the journey from grief to grace to transformation. It is called: *From Grief to Grace to Transformation—Living Joyfully from a Broken-Open Heart.*

I have learned first-hand how rich the soil of sorrow is for growing and transforming our relationship to grief. I have also learned that when our hearts are broken open, it's good to leave them open, even though our natural tendency is to close and protect.

Living joyfully from a broken-open heart is not only possible, it's transformational. You'll discover there is a power and a presence available to you in each precious now moment. If you allow your broken-open heart to teach you, you will see it makes you more available for life and love. Demand your blessing from grief, and let it give purpose and meaning to your journey.

You may find, like I did, that we truly are spiritual beings having a human experience. We are all on this journey together and we are walking each other home. Now we see through the veil just barely, yet death can open our eyes to life and to love and to the mystery of the grand overall design.

Michael and proud mama after his performing
for her lawn party

Treasured Observations

These came to me in the first three to four weeks of my journey. I felt like they were being downloaded for me to share, so I wrote them all down.

1. *Feel what I am feeling—fully. Stay open to all of it.*

2. *Joy and pain are in perfect balance. I just have to pay attention and notice how deeply the love matches my pain.*

3. *Numbness is a safe resting place—not a destination.*

4. *Hugging and being hugged are essential to my healing.*

5. *The salt of my tears mixes beautifully with the sweetness of laughter—savor each moment.*

6. *Regrets, blaming, anger, shoulda's, coulda's, what if's, wish I'da's are all signs for dead end roads filled with land mines—do not enter.*

7. *If I notice myself already on one of those roads, do a U-turn immediately, grab a happy memory to hold onto, and pull myself back.*

8. *Say "yes" to helping hands. Let them feed, cook, clean, sort, and hug.*

9. *Life marches on—I get to choose the cadence that I can handle.*

10. *Revisiting the pain only brings on more of it. Learn to focus on the now.*

11. *Capture the stories while they are fresh. Write them down and share.*

12. *The only right way to grieve is the one that feels most right to me.*

13. *Give myself as long as I need. Listen to my heart.*

14. *Choose which thoughts I want to spend time with. Healing thoughts lift my spirit and help me connect to my loved one.*

15. *Stay in my heart space, listen to its wisdom. Let it guide all of my decisions.*

16. *Some words carry more comfort than others. Listen for the love behind the words.*

17. *Forgive everyone everything. It's a gift I give myself.*

18. *Watch for signs from my loved one—listen, feel, sense— serendipitous coincidences, alignment and perfection of timing—and especially hummingbirds.*

19. *Sleep when I can. Time loses its grip and calendars are of little interest.*

20. *It's okay to cry and it's okay to laugh—all at the same time.*

21. *Focus on the beauty all around me. Don't miss it by being sad and wishing things were different.*

22. *Know that my loved one is right here with me all the time, in every moment, just a heartbeat and a loving thought away.*

Dressing up in his big brother John's Indian Guides outfit

A dear friend sent me this writing by Davies, and I found it so helpful. I do believe that all is well, even when outer appearances would have us feeling otherwise.

When Sorrow Comes

By A. Powell Davies

"When sorrow comes, let us accept it simply, as a part of life. Let the heart be open to pain; let it be stretched by it. All the evidence we have says that this is the better way. An open heart never grows bitter. Or if it does, it cannot remain so. In the desolate hour, there is an outcry; a clenching of the hands upon emptiness, a burning pain of bereavement; a weary ache of loss. But anguish, like ecstasy, is not forever. There comes a gentleness, a returning quietness, a restoring stillness. This, too, is a door to life. Here, also, is a deepening of meaning— and it can lead to dedication; a going forward to the triumph of the soul, the conquering of the wilderness. And in the process will come a deepening inward knowledge that in the final reckoning, all is well."

Big brother Troy's football gear doesn't quite fit

Getting the Phone Call

The call that forever changed my life came in at 7:35 a.m. on July 25, 2013. I heard my cell phone chirping back in my bedroom as I puttered about through my morning kitchen routine of emptying the dishwasher and brewing my single cup of coffee. I dashed down the hallway to my phone and just made it in time to catch the caller ID as I punched "answer" on my phone. I wondered, "Why am I getting a call from Placerville this early?"

I hear an unfamiliar female voice. My ex-husband's wife identified herself and began telling me what felt like a very long story about my youngest son Michael and a car and something about "he jumped," and I'm feeling the alarms going off inside me as I ask, "Where's Michael? Is Michael okay?" My first thought is he must be injured.

I hear her say, "I don't want to tell you this."

"Tell me what?"

She repeats herself, "I don't want to tell you this." And then I hear her say, "Michael's gone."

"Michael's gone? Gone? Gone where?" I ask, as I begin to wonder if he's run away, which makes no sense. My mind cannot grasp the meaning of these words, "Michael's gone."

"He jumped in front of a truck, and he's gone." This first version of what happened came from his step-mom, stating that Michael had deliberately jumped in front of a truck on Highway 50 in the middle of the night. This is so far from any reality I have about my son that it only added to the already horrible story unfolding. I later learned from the officer on the scene that he didn't jump in front of the truck, but was running away from perceived danger and tried to cross the highway a second time. He didn't make it.

The sinking in of the meaning of the words, "Michael is gone," called forth a sound from the depth of my soul screaming "No! No! No! No!" and repeating with a guttural noise that I had never heard before and never want to experience again. I came to describe it as wailing or keening accompanied by a shaking that penetrated into my very cells. I tried to listen to the words from the phone as I began to pace. I asked to speak with my ex. He gave me a phone number and an address for the morgue. I scrawled it on a patch of paper.

I was alone in my Sacramento home that I shared with Michael, the home that he'd left three days earlier for a visit with his dad in Pollock Pines to get some help from his step mother for insomnia. She's trained in Chinese herbal medicine and acupuncture. I desperately tried to piece

22

together what I was being told and was feeling helpless to get to the bottom of what really happened.

Yet, how it happened didn't matter. The bottom line was Michael is gone. He's lying 29 miles away in the Green Valley Mortuary at the end of Bass Road which serves as the morgue for Marshall Hospital in Placerville. There is no undoing or fixing what has happened. No turning the clock back. Even now, as I write about this moment, which requires a remembering and a revisiting of that phone call, even now these words carry an echo of a grief so intense that my eyes flood with tears.

I had no place to put this news. No reference or framework to minimize its impact or hold back the tsunami of emotions crashing over and through me. I knew I needed to call my family, and that I must drive the short mile to my mother's home to tell her that her beautiful, precious 36-year-old grandson had been killed in an accident. I called my sister in Marina del Rey. She heard my sound and added her own "No! No! No!" as I groped for comfort through the 400 miles separating us.

"I need you," I wailed. "I need you now."

She held me through the phone saying, "Let it out! Scream it out! Don't hold it in." I obeyed.

I climbed in my car still clutching my sister to my ear, asking her to find the woman who helped her prepare my brother-in-law for burial when he died 12 years ago. We hung up. I told myself that I must pull myself together enough to operate a car and get to my mom's. I barely remember the drive, but the moment of shaking her awake from a sound sleep is imprinted forever in my heart. She cannot comprehend this news I am giving her.   I try uselessly to explain what has happened as we clutch each other. I don't have answers, only more questions.

I am plunged into making impossible decisions and engaging in unprecedented, unwanted conversations. I still needed to speak with my two older sons and tell them their baby brother is gone. I called my minister and each of my sons. Troy was alone in Idaho, going through a tough divorce. His dad had already called him with the news. John picked up the phone at his office and knows from the agony in my voice that he is about to get news no one wants to hear.

As I waited for John and his wife Michelle to arrive at Mom's, the numbness began to set in. I could not make room for this. I could not make it go away. There was no place to hide.
Mom and I held each other in tears and silence trying to make space for this horrible, unthinkable news about Michael.   All I knew was he left for his dad's Tuesday morning for treatment to help with five days of insomnia which had been bringing on some frightening on-again, off-again hallucinations of being chased. He had been unable to sleep. He called me Tuesday night and said he was going to stay another night at his dad's.

As a musician and entertainer, Michael often stayed up until the middle of night and would sleep during the day until maybe noon.   His creative juices flowed at two or three a.m., and he flowed with it. Recent dental work with appointments at eight in the morning had interrupted his circadian rhythms. He had been visiting his cousin, Kurt, in Santa Rosa for 10 days, and drove home late Friday. He shared with me that someone was following him. I knew it wasn't true, but his fear was very real. He tried unsuccessfully to sleep.

On Saturday, he drove to a friend's for a massage and side swiped another car on the way. Never one who loved being behind the wheel, Michael came home and told me he shouldn't be driving. Michael would not take sleeping pills, and he was desperate for a good night's sleep. He tried meditating. He tried to sleep again Saturday night and Sunday morning, reporting to me that he'd get close but couldn't make it over the edge. I drove him to another massage session on Monday evening and, after sharing a pizza, I left him with his friend. It was the last time I would see him alive.

I've since learned that sleep deprivation can trigger hallucinations. I've tried piecing the details together of what happened after I left him safe and sound but still tired at his friend's house Monday evening. His friend gave him a ride to see his step mom at her office in Cameron Park the next day, Tuesday. Michael didn't have a car or his cell phone and couldn't call me or drive himself home when he needed help.

It is my deepest sorrow that I wasn't there to talk him through whatever was terrorizing him. I know others have received knee-buckling news. I've witnessed television broadcasts and watched movies where actors vividly portray these tragic moments. Seeing it, even when it's very real, but happening to someone else, never prepared me for the experience of shock, the shaking in every cell, the disbelief and denial, the feelings and soul-wrenching sounds of having it happen to me.

My sister called me back at my mom's with a phone number for a home funeral director who could help me through this heartbreaking process. All I wanted was to be with Michael. While on the phone, my sister told me that a hummingbird flew into her living room, circling and finally flying out an open window. She was convinced that it was Michael, letting her know he is okay. This is the first of many signs and sightings of hummingbirds and amazing coincidences and synchronicities that began appearing. They brought on another feeling—a tiny ray of hope. I began to feel connected and able to believe Michael is gone from my sight but not from my life.

Looking back at the first five days, from hearing the news to sitting with family and friends on my patio after Michael's celebration of life service on July 30, 2013, I see that I ran through the full complement of emotions—despair, fear, anger, confusion, regret, shock, pain, sadness, numbness, vulnerability as well as hope, laughter, joy, love, compassion, tenderness, gratitude, awe and wonder.

One of my first treasured observations that I wrote down in my journal was to *"Feel what I am feeling—fully. Stay open to all of it."* I continued to learn the importance of staying open to all of it, because any attempt to close off my pain would also close off my joy—and I really needed the joy.

What is the Sound of a Heart Breaking

What is the sound of a heart breaking?

I remember the shock and denial

My guttural "NO! NO! NO! NO!

Echoing through my empty house

Repeating and repeating

Slowly replaced by a

Ripping, splitting, tearing open of my heart

And then an animal sound

The same sound of birthing and pushing and bearing down

This time to deliver myself and my body

To relieve myself of the intense pain of my son's death

No baby to swaddle and hold when the screaming ends

Only emptiness and a sound forever branded on my soul

The sound of my heart breaking

If I Knew It Would Be the Last Time

Waving to you as I backed the car out

What if I'd known it was the last time to see you alive?

Hearing your voice on the phone,

"Hi Mom. Staying another day or so."

What if I'd known I was hearing your voice live for the last

time?

Simple goodbyes

Gestures performed thousands of times

Taken for granted

"I love you, be safe, see you soon"

Assumptions that life goes on

Always another day, another smile, another hug

If I had known

I would have held you to my heart and refused to let you go

No one and nothing could have pried you from me

I could not have surrendered you, released you,

Poured enough love on you to last me forever

What if I had known?

I Will Be Blessed

I will be blessed

I will wrestle with the angels until my gift appears

I will climb from the well of grief, not drowning,

And command it to teach me

I will turn from the horror and

Seek the light shining through the cracks of my broken heart

I will be blessed

I will learn and grow and teach and heal and

Find my way to be the blessing

Not someday

Now

I am blessed

A Mother's Tears

Tracing back the times I've cried my mother tears

Each child so special

So delightful

Temptation to just eat them up

They were so deliciously precious to me

Crying at graduations and weddings

At their mushy cards for my birthdays and Mother's Day

Sentimental tears and big proud Mama tears

Tears when they moved out and left the nest

Each time a flood of letting-go emotions.

Relief tears when I learn all is okay

They are safe

And the tears of a broken heart,

Grief stricken

My child is gone tears.

These tears come unbidden and flood me with memories

These tears are now blended with sadness and joy

And fill the crater in my heart

These mother's tears comfort and connect me

Forever to my child.

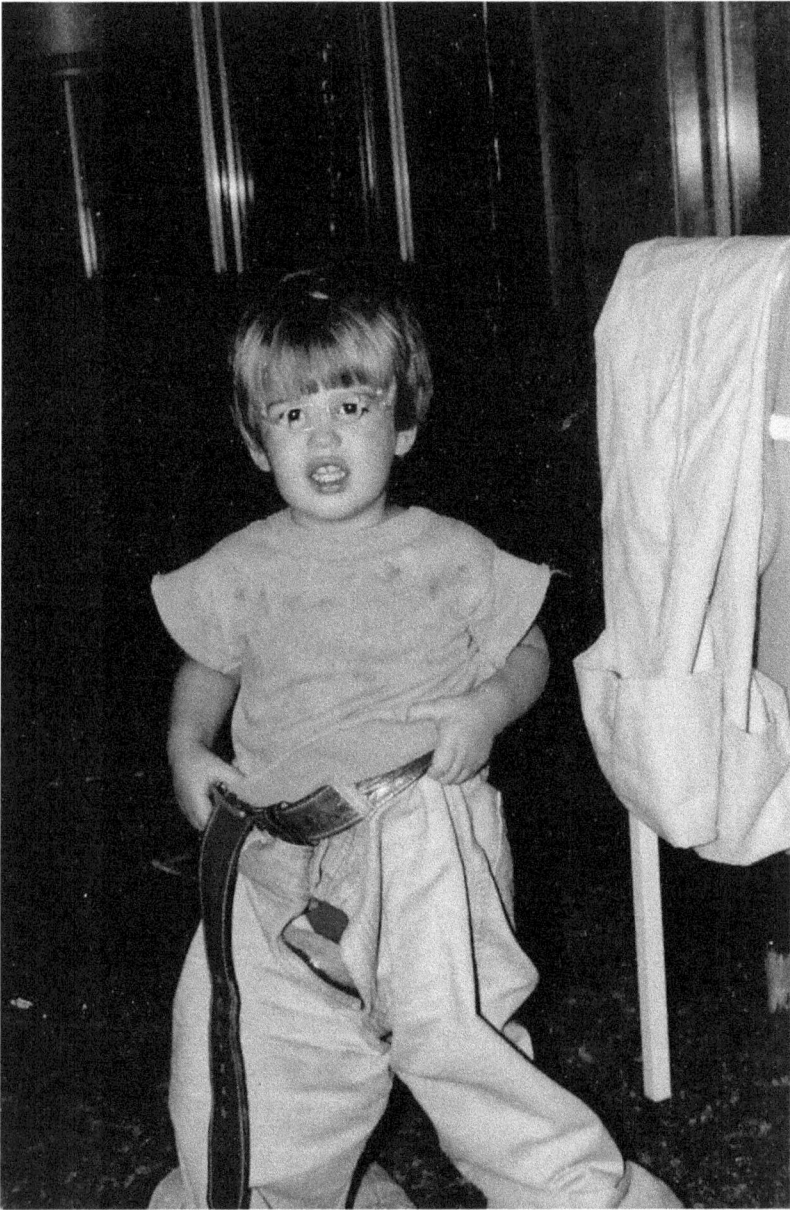

Putting on his big brothers' clothes and his
Mr. Potato Head glasses

Making Impossible Decisions and

Bringing Michael Home

"I cannot feel anything," I remember saying to my son John on our drive home. "It's like I'm completely numb. No more tears. Nothing."

John nodded in agreement. We are both quiet. It's now 5 p.m. Thursday evening, commuter traffic is heavy, and John is focused on driving. Following behind us a van is transporting Michael's body to my home. It's been a long day and many difficult decisions getting to this point. Silence and shock, nature's bandage, wraps us both in an emotional gauze, protecting our wound. The silence is welcome.

In the nine and one-half hours between getting the news and this drive home, I have received a crash course in funerals and mortuaries and laws and time frames and release forms. As a mother, all I wanted to do was get to my son. I had one burning desire guiding my decisions—get to Michael's side. My first call to the morgue was placed at 8:45 a.m. I tell them that my son is there, and I need to come and be with him. To me it seems a simple and reasonable request. I am told they must perform an autopsy, and I cannot see him until his body is released which could be a couple of days. No other options are given to me.

When I make that call, I am still at my mother's home with my son John, his wife Michelle, and their Rabbi. When Rabbi Taff learns that the morgue is holding the body for two days, he places a call to the coroner's office and explains that Michael's brother is Jewish, and Judaic laws require a family member to be with the deceased at all times and that the body be buried within three days. Even though my son Michael is not of the Jewish faith, because his brother John is, Rabbi is able to get the time frame for the autopsy and release of Michael's body shortened from two days to two hours. One of many miracles to follow.

That hurdle accomplished only brings up the next one—to what mortuary will the body be released? Since receiving the news, I have been asked to make decisions I am completely unprepared for. I am drowning in pain, and my rational logical brain is off-line. All my heart wants is to be with my son, to touch him, connect with him, tell him I'm here.

Decisions had to be made quickly, shock or no shock. Burial or cremation? Casket? Cemetery? Mortuary? My family doesn't have a burial plot. My parents are both still alive. My grandparents are interred in southern California. Rabbi is asking me if Michael will be buried or cremated. After some discussion, I decide upon cremation, and then learn that the recommended funeral home won't let me see him unless I have him prepared for burial, i.e., embalmed. They might let me sit in a nearby room, but not actually be with my son. My heart knew what my soul needed, and I quickly learned to tune in for its guidance more than I ever had previously.

I knew that my sister had been able to bring her husband home after his death. We all were able to spend private time with his body before he was cremated. I had asked my sister who to call and she had started those gears moving. Meanwhile, I only wanted to get to Michael—an option no one was giving me.

At 12:10 p.m., I received a call back from funeral director Cari Leversee who specializes in home and family directed funerals, the referral that came through my sister. After introducing herself to me, Cari explained that she would be able to help me make whatever arrangements I wanted. She also reinforced what I had already been learning—main stream funeral homes have systems in place and are not known for being flexible.

Cari asked me what I would like to have happen. I couldn't even formulate an answer before she intuitively said to me, "Would you like to bring him home?"

I could feel my entire system completely relax. My whole being and every cell in my body said, "Yes!"

"I can make that happen," she said. And with that, Cari took the phone number of the morgue and told me she would take care of everything. I just needed to wait for her next call.

That "yes" was a pure heart decision, and I continued to make the rest of my decisions about Michael from that same place. No more wondering about anyone else's opinions. I now knew how to check in and listen, and from that centered place, I could easily field whatever questions came. I just listened for that heart-felt "yes" or "no" and handled one decision after another. Since that time, I have continued to recognize the power of that guidance, and to defer to and trust my heart's wisdom more than ever before.

After several phone calls and many challenging discussions with the coroner's office, Cari and her knowledge of California laws and the rights of the bereaved prevailed. Now she and her husband Richard are following John and me in their van carrying precious cargo—Michael's body. I have yet to touch or see or be in the same room with him since receiving the news early this morning. Every ounce of my energy has been directed toward bringing him home and now we are almost there. I am stepping into another unknown. John became my rock, staying steadily beside me, ready to do whatever I needed without question. Cari and Richard are our guides.

I remember little about the four hours between Cari telling me she would take care of everything and our 29-mile drive to meet her at the morgue. Was John with me the whole time? When did my Mom come over to my house? When did I reach out to find Sammie, Michael's girlfriend? When did I call my best friends Darlene and Sue and Kelly? I knew we were all in shock, and that, for now, the numbness was welcome. Somehow I connected with key people in my life, but I remember very little other than being in the motions of what do I need to do next?

I think there was a brief time here at my house, before the numbness set in, before my home became very full of people, when I was finally by myself, when I curled up on Michael's bed, hugged his unlaundered smelly shirt to my cheek, and sobbed. I have learned I prefer the weeping, the aliveness of pain, to the cotton-headed, insulated, disconnected experience of numbness. And I rode my way through the shock and the numbness, knowing somehow not to linger, even if coming out of it meant feeling a depth of pain and sorrow and longing for life to be as it was—before the news no parent wants to hear.

I noted two more treasured observations in my journal...

Stay in my heart space, listen to its wisdom. Let it guide all of my decisions.

Numbness is a safe resting place, not a destination.

Bringing You Home

You are my child

Woven from my very womb

I remember your first moment at my breast

Your first wide-eyed look at this world

I remember bringing you home

Two older brothers taking turns holding you

So full of life and love and wonder and joy

Always my child, my delight, my prince

And...

I remember bringing you home one last time

My beautiful handsome prince

Uncertain what I'd see as we unzipped the body bag

And folded back the white cloth

Washing your face and untangling your hair

One last time to be able to kiss you and hold your hand

I remember bringing you home

To let them take you from my physical presence

Flesh and blood now cold and lifeless

To flood you with my tears and my prayers and my questions

To allow others to say their good byes

I remember bringing you home so I could let you go.

Cocooned

Seems like being cocooned

Is a wonderful way to heal.

Safe from prying eyes,

Tucked in, protected

Sometimes I wonder.

The caterpillar dissolves inside the cocoon.

Melts into a gooey mess.

New cells start following a new blueprint—

A complete tear-down, not a remodel.

No posts and beams left standing.

A blank canvas,

A miracle.

And—when the butterfly must fly,

The cocoon must go

And the wings are only strengthened

By pushing through the cocoon.

Working and resting and sensing a new freedom.

Breaking into the light

And flying free.

A wonderful way to heal.

Temptations of the Mind—

Noticing What I Am Noticing

Healing thoughts lift my spirit. Drama stirs stuff up and is unnecessary. I realized almost at once that my key to any kind of inner peace was to be found in how I chose to manage my thinking. This life-long, ongoing, never-to-be-completed assignment of managing my thoughts turns out to be the most powerful antidote for pain. I learned to step back and watch how the mind wants to revisit a hurtful incident, play it repeatedly, pull the scab off of the wound, make someone wrong. Why keep hurting myself over and over again with these mental forms of self torture?

This practice of noticing what I am noticing began long before Michael's passing, and it became my most powerful ally. I must recognize futile lines of questioning and the hot coals of resentment and anger when they arrive. If I am too asleep to notice, too gripped by automatic programming to pay attention, I lose access to choice. My willingness to tune into the hurt and listen to my trains of thought helps me participate in and direct my healing process rather than fall victim to and drown in my grief.

I committed to choosing compassion over righteousness, because when I don't, the only person who suffers is me. This requires alertness, so that as soon as I notice I've slipped into judging or blaming, I can make a different choice. I'm learning to dial into the higher vibrational thought patterns over the lower ones. I also discovered that those are the best channels for connecting with Michael.

I found that my feelings of grief had their own rhythms and waves. I had no way of managing that ocean, only riding it. However, I could see that spending time with thoughts of how much I love Michael, how he lived a life of simplicity and unconditional love, how he would stay calm and listen deeply from his heart—these thoughts inspired me and filled me with joy.

If I added the thoughts of "why" or dwelled on how much I miss him, my level of peace would plummet and my sadness would rise. I could direct my thoughts to those areas where the emotions that followed were of a higher vibration. It was a practice of noticing and choosing, noticing and choosing. As I was riding these emotional waves, over which I had little control, I learned the art of being present in the moment. I could see that going into the past or out into the future took me to places that didn't serve me. Fear and regret do not live in the present, unless I go and fetch them.

Temptation knocked on my door constantly at first, encouraging me to go down the blame and anger road especially towards Michael's dad at whose home he was staying. If only someone had called me. If only his dad had just called 911 from the house. He should have known better, should have listened better. His dad should have turned around when Michael asked him to. His dad should have called me. If only I had kept Michael from going. If only I had driven him to his dad's myself. I should have sensed he was in trouble from not sleeping. He should have had his cell phone. His dad should have stayed by his side and never left him. The list goes on and on and on.

None of these futile cross examinations made anything different—nothing changed the fact that Michael was gone, deceased, passed on, lying in a morgue. Nothing could turn the clock back and have it not happen. I kept turning away from these thoughts again and again. I knew in my heart that his dad was in just as much pain as I was--that he adored Michael and was most likely fighting his own battles with blame and anger and regret. Finally temptation quit knocking as often and eventually just gave up on getting my attention.

What I notice about any of those beginning sentence stems of "if only" and "should haves" is that if I allow them to percolate and simmer inside of me, they add to my sadness and anger and render me powerless. They make it unsafe for certain people to walk the streets of my mind.

Perhaps the finality of the situation made me more aware of the futility of those lines of questioning. Not so in previous times of losses where some other outcome was perceived as possible, where some argument could turn the events in my favor. No! This one was final, and the only thing changing by my even considering these questions was my inner state— from sad to more sad, from despair to more despair—from grief to more intense suffering.

I am now seeing that in all matters of the heart, wishing and second-guessing, and giving in to anger and blame do not serve me. They drop my vibration, and I lose my calm center. Do I find myself heading down dead-end roads? If I am not paying attention, yes. And, when I notice my surroundings, I turn for the light and head back. I find having some sweet memories and happy joy-filled images to call upon pulls me back quickly.

Somehow a part of me, a wise woman deep inside, guided me gently away and reminded me to focus on what I could do now, in this very moment that would help me move forward and heal. Often it was finding a loving memory and holding on tight. Getting a photo, playing a song, hugging his shirt, and once he was home with me, for those 24 hours, just sitting beside him, holding his hand, talking with him, and sending him love.

Michael's time here, his 36 years plus 99 days, gave me so many happy memories to pull from, including our last weekend together. We spent time talking, cleaning his room, sorting through boxes and microphone cords and piles of papers, getting organized, and also just hanging out.

He treated me on Monday to a massage with his friend Big Al and assisted him, so I have a beautiful memory of being kissed on my forehead and gently caressed on my face and shoulders by Michael while receiving a wonderful massage. I have a sweet memory of him sitting on the sofa next to me, his right arm holding me tight, and his head resting on my shoulder, telling me how glad he was that he got me as his mother.

I have DVDs and CDs of him acting on stage and singing and giving us his creative playful energy. These are the roads I enjoy going down if I need an energy shift. These are the sweet memories that sustain me. And I am learning to create fresh now-moments from the new dimensions I find myself in.

I know blaming isn't what Michael would have me do. Today, if temptation knocks on my door to blame those who didn't do what I would have done, instead of filling myself with anger and resentment, I check in with Michael and feel his presence. I listen as he guides me back to love and forgiveness. He tells me to trust that this was his time to go home. My thoughts can resist or embrace this reality. I can choose to suffer or surrender to a higher possibility.

I continue to walk this path of noticing and choosing and listening to the wisdom I receive from within. I believe Michael has added his voice to those I hear on my own internal wisdom channel. I dial in as often as I remember to. Noticing and choosing, noticing and choosing. More treasured observations...

Choose which thoughts I want to spend time with.

Revisiting the pain only brings on more of it.

Regrets, blaming, anger, shoulda's, coulda's, what ifs, if only, wish I'das—all are signs for dead-end roads filled with land mines. Do not enter!

If I notice myself already on one of those land-mine roads, do a U-turn and grab a happy memory to hold onto, and pull myself back.

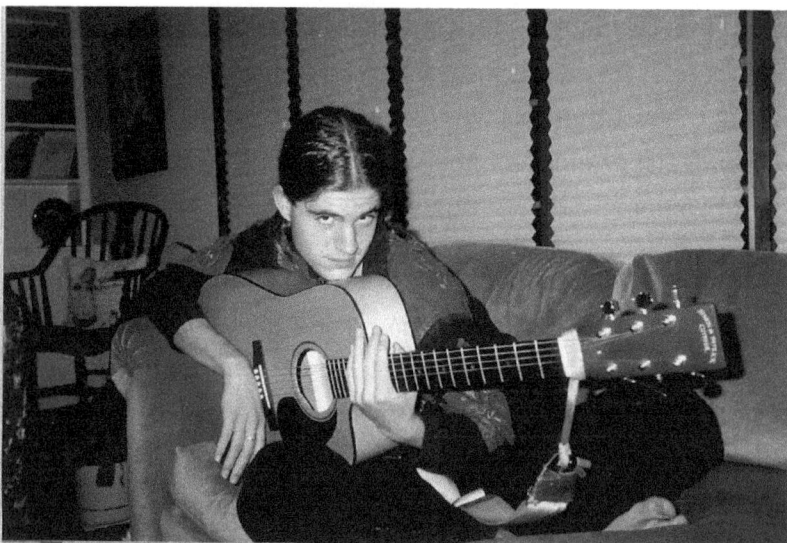

Angel Clouds

Soaring spirits dancing

Trailing wisps

Playing across the skies

I love angel clouds

I drift with them

See angels dancing and playing

I imagine those I love

Now freed from Earth

Waving to me

Puffy clouds awake my imagination

Clear skies with a single puff

Perhaps an errant angel on a grand adventure

Dark clouds and

Rippling clouds

Thunder clouds

And clouds reflecting sunsets and rainbows

And my favorite—angel clouds

Wispy soaring dancing angels

Telling me there's more—much more

Amazing

To step fully into a broken heart

To feel the jagged edges

To notice how deep the chasm

To fall without grasping for why

Some say amazing

To explore the softness

Live moment by moment

What's showing up now and now and now

Amazing...To let in love

Let her pour her healing waters

Into and over all the broken pieces and parts

To welcome the flow, the rush, the currents

Sent to fill and soothe

Some say amazing

To find joy in the midst of pain

Courage to stand steady

Faith that all is well

To trust in a Divine order

Amazing

Where else could I go except

To follow the light I could see each moment

Some say amazing

I say Sweet Spirit, Amazing Grace,

Guiding and holding my hand all the way.

Moments Out of Time

Moments out of time

Sweet silence

Spirit wrapping me in wonder

Touching the veil

Learning to listen

Feeling the energies

Hearing the guidance

Embracing it all

Knowing nothing separates us

As close as our love

As immediate as our thoughts

My connection to the Divine

To my loved ones beyond

Standing in blessed gratitude

My sweet silent moments out of time

Precious Unrepeatable Moments

Michael's passing felt like a meteor crashing into my heart, creating a bottomless crater of pain the size of which I had never felt. I had no place for this new reality—this explosion within my known world, a force I could not control, and an impact I could not make space for—a reality I was powerless to change.

My healing began when Cari delivered Michael's body to our home. I was finally able to touch him, see him, tend to him, wash his face, wash his hand, kiss his brow and cheek and head, talk to him, and feel the peace that surrounded him. In our home, a back bedroom with its own entrance, served as both my library and Michael's massage room for when he saw clients at home. He also used it for recording and meditating. It took no effort to create a beautiful sanctuary for spending private time with him in one of his favorite spaces full of his loving energy. His simple cardboard coffin fit perfectly on his massage table. We draped it with one of his beautiful massage table covers and lit candles. I brought his music and kept it playing in the background.

The first thirty-six hours remain a blur except for key memories, mostly of sitting with Michael while he was here with me at home. Holding his hand and talking to him. Several times throughout the night, I returned to the sanctuary we had created for him and just sat quietly next to him—not wanting it to be true, knowing my life had changed, grateful to have him home.

That evening Sammie arrived with her mother, as did Ben, one of Michael's best friends and fellow musicians. Over the next twenty-four hours, a parade of friends and family streamed through his room taking a moment to write notes and paint on his "box" and share their favorite Michael stories. We celebrated his life, surrounded him with our laughter, and flooded him with our tears. We put his favorite black felt fedora hat at just the right angle upon his head, and wrapped his Sammie-hand-knitted purple Christmas scarf around his neck. We covered him with flowers and poetry and some of his favorite meditation symbols.

It may seem strange to speak about savoring grief, yet there were so many moments when I became aware of this rare elixir—tears and laughter—and sweet memorable moments occurring simultaneously. I'm grateful that others captured many of these moments in pictures. Taking photos wasn't going to happen if left up to me. I seemed to know, at a deep soul level, the importance of me staying in the moment, fully present to the laughter and the tears we shared, as we said our goodbyes to Michael's physical presence in our lives.

Almost as if in chorus, the healing waters of love and caring and compassion began flooding in from everywhere, soothing the agony I was feeling. My church created a novena in our small chapel for anyone who wanted to light a candle or spend a quiet moment of prayer or meditation. Cards and flowers began arriving. Emails and phone calls were made by my close friends to let others know what had happened. I let myself surrender and lean into the love sweeping into my life filling the ache in my heart.

My family and friends somehow knew just what was needed, and food magically appeared, people were fed, Michael's bathroom drawers were emptied, his clothing sorted through, errands run—all while I moved slowly through a fog of emotions I had never faced before.

I remember homemade muffins, delicious chili, freshly baked apple pie, a whole turkey with the works, trays of pasta, cookies, and coolers filled with water, sodas and wine. My friend Vicky even bought me clothes to wear to the memorial. I learned to say "yes" and "thank you." I needed and welcomed all of the hugs and the love pouring in to fill and heal the wounded chasm in my heart.

I began to refer lovingly to my home as being in a state of "Divine Chaos," especially as we prepared for Michael's memorial. My sister Christina, niece Holland, nephew Kurt, and his girlfriend Thandi all moved in for the week. They arrived Friday afternoon and spent some time with Michael before we bid him goodbye. Flowers and plants and cards and well-wishes continued to pour in. All counter tops and flat surfaces were laden with something. In the middle of it all, I wandered and helped where I could.

Kurt worked through his own sorrow of losing Michael by getting the slideshow and musical put together for his celebration of life video. Almost from the moment he arrived, Kurt began creating the tribute to his cousin, who was also his best friend, mentor, and partner in creating music. He dealt with his grief by pouring himself into creating the most beautiful memorial slideshow, canvas portraits, collages, and memorial cards to give to all of those who were attending the service.

Sitting by his side, I experienced the joy and heartache of pouring through thirty-six years of photos. Albums and boxes of loose pictures were sorted and scanned to capture the essence of my beloved son. We listened to hours of his musical recordings to pick just the right songs, knowing that this was truly his last performance here on this side, and that he was going to be singing at his own service. We hovered together on the sofa over Kurt's laptop computer, holding each other, sometimes sobbing, sometimes laughing, remembering all the times depicted in the images. I felt so grateful to have such a beautiful collection of pictures and music from which to draw, not only for his memorial service, but for our own healing and the mending of our hearts.

Intuitively I knew these were precious, unrepeatable moments in my life and in Michael's. I experienced and welcomed them all. We shared so many stories about him. The telling of them brought Michael even closer in our hearts, filled us with joy and then sorrow, more joy, more sorrow. We each spoke from such a deep love for him—a celebration and recognition of his legacy—realizing with his passing how much he had blessed every one of us. We all deeply mourned, shared our profound feelings of loss, and thanked Michael for sending us, even now, new ways to connect with him—tears and laughter, rainbows, gentle breezes, hummingbirds, songs—all reminders of his presence.

I wrote almost daily in my journal, posted status updates in Facebook, and welcomed each card and email, each comment, personal visit and phone call. I walked through my days slowly, willing to let others take care of the "doing." I breathed in the love and joy and hurt and sorrow, and somehow knew it was important to savor it all.

I kept noticing this balance of pain and joy, resolved myself to feeling both fully, to hugging and being hugged, to letting the love pour in—friends coming by to see Michael, sharing their hearts, their stories, bringing with them food and flowers and cards and help. So many loving hands comforted me, and my broken heart open to receive it all.

In the first couple of weeks after his passing, I was struggling with the intensity of the loss of his physical presence and learning to listen for him on new channels. Often the communication would come as I was writing in my journal and asking him questions.

On day twenty, I was on my pre-planned Alaskan cruise, struggling with not having his CDs to listen to, and finding that recalling happy memories of him made me cry. I needed to know how to connect. I didn't want to shut down, yet staying open seemed so unbearable. On that morning I asked him, "How do I communicate with you, my dear sweet son? What is the best channel?"

I instantly heard, *"Listen in your heart Mom. I am right here. It's okay to cry. It's okay to laugh as well. You are still the best mom. I love you."* Michael really shows up as my wise teacher so often. His letting me know I could laugh and cry all at the same time truly helped.

This juxtaposition of joy and sadness seems to be a balance point for staying centered—perhaps somewhat like a tight rope walker with a balance bar holding a focus on each next step moment by moment.

I hear from deep within a voice, my wise woman part, saying "Let it all in—let it all in. If I try to avoid the pain, I will miss the joy. Stay open. Stay present."

More additions to my growing list of treasured observations...

Joy and pain balance each other perfectly if I stay open to them.

It's okay to cry and it's okay to laugh—all at the same time.

Savor each moment—the salt of my tears mixes beautifully with the sweetness of laughter.

Riding the Waves

Surfing—not something I've ever done. Not really.

A little body surfing as a pre-teen

And some riding on the top of an inflated raft.

I know the idea is to make my way

Out beyond the crashing to the swell

Watch for the right moment

Catch the wave and let it push me to shore.

True surfers make a show of it

Riding in tubes, cutting up and down the edge

And breaking away before the shoreline to catch the next big one.

I can only imagine the feeling of working such powerful forces and

staying engaged

Not pummeled and pounded.

Yet, I feel I've been surfing my own waves

Those that came with sudden loss

A loss so huge that riding it without crashing seems impossible.

I took it on

Staying engaged with waves of pain and sorrow

And finding my way to ride them

Only to resurface when they pulled me under.

I learned not to fight them

To let them roll through

To feel their force

And use it to move me forward...riding the waves.

Living from Love and an Open Heart

Broken open—no way to close the fractured pieces

Closing from the pain

Would shut out the light

Best to stand in the shards and feel it all.

No separation

Between the pain and the joy

Only my mind can choose which I focus on

My heart just feels it all

And wonders

I check in for what's next

Not with my logic,

Only with my heart

Living from this new expansive awareness

And a heart broken wide

Every day is a Gift

Words to be written or a truth to be lived?

Every day is a gift

A platitude or truly gratitude realized?

Breath of life, eyes to see, ears to hear

My hands to touch and my tongue to taste

Every atom and cell in my body alive

Working to keep my unit working

So I can enjoy and participate in life

I can communicate

I can listen and I can love

I can go to sleep, unaware, numb to it all,

Busy, busy with circumstances

Or I can awake to the realization that each moment is precious

Each day lets me shine my light and be a blessing

Each day I get to choose to see life as a gift

Thank you for this day

Mother Love

To be a mom is

To be love's channel and expression

To hold gently

To nurture and nourish

To delight and be a light

To protect and encourage

To guide and listen for guidance

To let go and hold on and know when

To listen for dreams and fears and

To be a soft place to land and rest

To build the nest and

Push them from it

To see their essence

To reflect their beauty

To cherish and treasure their presence

To realize they are gifts and hold them as such

To forever stay connected heart to heart

Sons and Grandsons

What is it about sons and grandsons

That lights me up

Makes me smile

Warms my heart

Today I watched my sons playing soccer with my grandsons

A pick-up game across the street at the park

The park where my sons all grew up playing with their friends

A perfect day—sunny, warm but crisp in the shade

A field blanketed with fall leaves

Laughter and shouting of the most fun sort

A six, two sevens, and a ten in grandsons

Plus two forty-something dads

I know Michael was running around with them in spirit

I took my time just letting it all in

Savoring the moments

All of my progeny together

Don't know what it is about sons and grandsons

But I sure love it

The Language of Love and Hugs—

Finding the Right Words

Sometimes I was the comforter and sometimes the comforted. Hugs—heart-felt, all-in, full-of-love kinds of hugs—made such a difference. I often couldn't find words to speak or even hear the words being spoken, but the love being exchanged through the physical and even virtual hugs gave me such joy in the midst of the pain.

Hugs are different than words. Some words are more helpful than others. Knowing what to say when someone is in deep grief—that's not so easy. I heard so many predictions. "You'll never be the same." "Your heart will never heal." "The pain will never go away." "You will always have a hole in your heart."

I knew not to take these words in, and to bless those who said or wrote them, because they were meant to be loving. I could see the projection onto me of their own belief system, and I saw that I could choose not to buy into it, while still sending them love and appreciation for reaching out to me. Most helpful were those who gave me no predictions or phrases, just, "I don't know what to say, but am sending you love," or "I feel your pain and I'm sending hugs."

When I received the news of Michael's death, I was by myself at home. I started pacing and uncontrollably shaking and hearing sounds from my grieving soul that I had never ever heard before. I had no one to hug or touch except by phone. As I gathered myself enough to drive to Mom's, I clutched my phone to my ear and held on to my sister, 400 miles away.

When John and Michelle arrived at Mom's, we stood in a huddle of grief and shock and clung to each other. My son Troy, 800 miles away in Idaho, stayed on the phone with me. He needed hugging and was physically alone himself. I've experienced hugs sent over phone lines, through texts and emails, in cards and in person. All are welcome, all are healing, all are ways we connect heart to heart—sometimes as the comforter and sometimes being comforted, and most times both happening at the same time.

One of my sweetest memories of Michael is of him tenderly hugging me and kissing me on my forehead the last time we were together, just three days before I got the fateful phone call. More than once over our last weekend together, almost like a part of him knew, he told me, *"I love you so much. You are the best mom. I'm so glad you are my mom."* And we talked about one of our favorite stories, the one about him coming to me in a dream nine months to the day before he was born, asking permission to join our family. I'm so glad I said "yes!" I'm so grateful for all of the hugs from Michael over the years, and the feeling that he is still wrapping his arms about me from the other side.

I remember hugging and holding Sammie when she arrived, bereft, in agony, wanting, as did I, for it to not be true. We hugged and walked together into the sacred space where Michael's body lay, wrapped in a white cloth, zipped into a white bag, packed with dry ice, in a card board casket, with his beautiful face and his right hand the only parts accessible. I had never met Sammie's mom before, but we hugged. For anyone who came near me, a hug was my greeting and my deep expression of love's presence.

Words that encouraged and words of love and affection made me smile and were soothing. Any stories shared with me about someone's experience with Michael were ever so welcome. Photos of Michael that I had never seen before showed up on Facebook and filled me with a bittersweet joy. Those words that added images of pain and predictions—not so helpful, but I understood. I let them all inform me of a process that I had never asked for and was completely engaged in. I learned first-hand about choosing my responses and guarding the portal to my mind.

Even the terms we choose to use to refer to death carry a certain frequency. A friend at my church recently used the term "change" instead of "passing" in referring to the death of her brother. "Death" has a finality to it, where as the term "change" is simple and inclusive—his change and my change and everyone who knows and loves him—all of us, experiencing unwanted change.

We get to choose how we will work with the change—resist it, deny it, resent it, accept it, embrace it, let it teach us or torment us. I'm reminded of a song dedicated to Michael at one of the first Spiritual Life Center Sunday services after his death. *"Everything Must Change."* I mostly cried through all of it. Yet, I also loved the lines that brought a smile to my face, *"There are not many things in life you can be sure of, except rain comes from the clouds, sun lights up the sky. and hummingbirds do fly. Winter turns to spring, a wounded heart will heal...and music, and music makes me cry."* Michael continues to teach me, and I feel so grateful.

Three more treasured observations...

Hugging and being hugged are essential to healing.

Say "yes" to helping hands. Let them feed, cook, clean, sort, and hug.

Some words carry more comfort than others—and they are all meant to be loving.

Listening intently to make any corrections to his music recordings

Death and Dying and Passing On

Moving on, changing, dropping the body,

Singing with the angels,

Back to the All That Is, Here in Spirit

Forever in our hearts

Resting in peace with God in Heaven

Words, words, words—concepts and images

Explanations to myself

To my family and to my friends and to anyone who asks

Communicating the most intimate, heart-breaking

Open painful letting go of what was

Finding a way to be with the new what is

Finding the words to go with the change

Holding the images that allow me to heal

Discovering the nuances and new ways of connecting

Beyond the words and the concepts

Beyond the longing for a return to what was

Somehow touching the edges of a new reality

New languages and new ways of knowing

Beyond the doubts and fears and pain of loss

I find you at the end of the rainbow

In the beauty of being, in the domain of Love

I feel your presence. I find words

Pick them up and put them down

Experiment and return to the land of feelings

The place of no words—and there I sit in sacred silence

When Love Comes Knocking—Say "Yes"

A compliment—say "yes" and thank you

An offer to help—say "yes" and thank you

A smile, a kind word, a gesture—all love knocking

Say thank you

When pain comes—open wide the door

Love will flood right in

To ease the hurting

Say "yes" to helping hands

Let them feed and cook and clean and hug

Their gift is in their gifts being received

Our gifts cycle from giver to receiver

To giver to receiver

Ever expanding the love pulsing at their core

When love comes knocking

No matter the guise

Say "Yes"

Managing Grief and Comforting Myself

I am not an expert on grieving—only a committed student of my own process. Early on I found I needed to write in my journal and also share on Facebook what I was experiencing. I could feel everything and nothing all at once. My circuits were fried. When decisions were being asked of me, real estate clients needed to be taken care of, details about services and cremation needed to be attended to, I turned inward to my heart and stayed there, moving at a snail's pace, and finding I could not or would not push myself.

I believe this helped strengthen a powerful witness within myself who, along with Michael, was wisely leading me. I continue to observe what is unfolding, and find that sharing what I'm noticing about my experience helps me heal. Those who have read my postings on Facebook comment that the posts touch them deeply, and, for many, they are finding their own healing through what I've shared. I believe it is a heart thing—messages from the heart are powerful and healing.

For me, talking about Michael was very therapeutic. I also feel that because I was able to have him in my home for 24 hours, my grief was quite different than it might have been if I had gone a more traditional route. I was able to spend unlimited time with him in a very private and sacred setting that was familiar to both of us. Friends and family were able to come and be with him. I got up several times during the night to go and hold his hand and speak to him. When the mortuary came to pick him up on Friday evening, we gathered around him for our final farewell. I tucked him in one last time. Kissed his face. Told him how much I love him. Cari held the lid until we were ready, and then we closed his beautifully decorated cardboard box filled with our love and our tears, and carried him out to the waiting mortuary van. It was finally okay to let his body leave. We waved our goodbyes, and I felt complete with that part of the process.

That night I slept on the now empty massage table cradling a pillow I made by tying together the sleeves of an unlaundered shirt that was one of his favorites. It smells of his body odor, and it still comforts me. I held it to my heart and remembered holding him as an infant. Many of my tears have been soaked into its fabric. I have various places in my home that are mini-altars to his memory, including the massage room where his music stand, harmonica, bandoneon, and dancing shoes still occupy a special corner. His two acoustic guitars went home with his brothers. I suppose someday most of what I have will be packed away, and only a few of his things will remain, along with all of the sweet memories. I'll know when I'm ready. I feel the joy of his presence when I can see him in photos and listen to his music.

I quickly noticed that I was out of step—moving very slowly if at all. I wanted to stop strangers in the grocery store and say, "Don't you know my son just died!" I felt like the world had stopped for me, and no one else noticed. Not that I didn't have friends and family tending to me, just an experience of extreme slowing down and noticing the world moving at a pace I could not match, nor did I care to. I picked places to venture out where I felt safe and loved.

My first outing was to church on Sunday, three days from receiving the news. Michael gave many beautiful performances at Spiritual Life Center for Christmas candlelight services, and Evening in Tuscany fundraisers. He made monthly recordings for the choir's tenor and bass parts. We shared this community, and there I could feel both the love for me as well as the love for Michael. I couldn't make myself sit in my regular pew up front. Instead, I sat in the farthest row back, opposite side, near Stu, the sound engineer who was also my son's dear friend and musical collaborator. They had been working on a Broadway Hits CD album. Everyone who knew me made their way to the back of the church to give me a hug. It was safe to just take it all in and let them come to me.

My next outing was to my Rotary club lunch, eleven days after his passing. Many of my Rotary friends had attended his memorial service. I spoke a brief thank you to everyone for all of their support. Hugs were again enveloping me in their healing energy. Two days later, I wandered into my office at Coldwell Banker for our weekly Wednesday morning meeting. I showed a brief photo slideshow Kurt created with "When Angels Whisper," the song written and sung by Michael to a tune written by Stu. Michael had performed at a couple of Coldwell Banker events over the years and was loved by all who knew him. I stayed about an hour before needing to head home.

On Sunday, 17 days into the process of adjusting to Michael's death, I was boarding an airplane to Seattle with my friend Diana, and soon we were checking into our suite on a Holland America Cruise ship, and sailing off for Alaska. This turned out to be brilliant timing of an already planned event. The quiet and peaceful waters of British Columbia and the Alaskan straits offered me quiet and serenity.

My grief became background noise to a much more interesting study that connected me more and more deeply to Michael. I could feel Michael guiding me through my grief with his music and morning songs and wise words when I needed them most. My built-in immune system of love became activated. I could feel hope and trust growing as Michael tended to me. Because I am open to messages from him, I believe those new channels opened quickly and have strengthened and widened as I have used them. My joy and gratitude continue to open new pathways to my soul.

People suggested I seek out a support group and read books about the stages of grieving. I knew their intentions were pure, and I also felt no pull to go or do what was being suggested. I learned to listen to my heart and do what felt right to me. I could tell what activities I was ready for and which needed to wait. I could listen to others tell me what I would experience, and know it was not my own truth, but was theirs. I could feel them projecting onto me their own grief, and it was all okay. I just sorted it through knowing it all came from love and from wanting to help.

One person noted how I seemed to be finding intuitively what she went to a therapist to hear when her son was killed by a drunk driver. She wrote this to me, *"When a painful event lands on our timeline, we can try to go around it, over it, or push it in front of us—all of which take a lot of effort and emotional energy. Or, we can step into it and walk through it to the other side. Then it becomes something in our past that we can choose to visit. As we do, most of the pain has been replaced by the happy memories."* I held onto these words as a road map and a confirmation of a path I had already chosen as being the best one for me to follow.

The image I had several times during these early days was one of being broken down on the side of the road. I could see and hear all of the speeding cars, and I could not even fathom going back on the road, even on the slowest lane. Today, I still enjoy bumping along with the less aggressive drivers, and seem to prefer the country lanes and city roads to the rush of freeways.

At first I had little need for sleep. I noticed naps were helpful, and curling up in bed with one of Michael's smelly shirts comforted me no matter what time of the day or night. For several weeks, I wandered through my days and let time have its way with me. I calendared very little, and stayed in the land of "no time"—not like I had no time, more like time didn't exist. I notice I still bend time to my heart's needs. No more slavery to a list of to-dos or rushing.

I have learned to listen and give myself what I need. For example, if I have a day with no appointments scheduled, I may spend the morning reading, doing some research, and writing. I may give myself permission to stay in my jammies until noon and then shower. I may treat myself to a pedicure. I find this quiet time very peaceful and restorative. When I have moments of feeling like a slacker, I let it go. No driving me with that bit of guilt anymore.

I am learning to listen to my heart and trust what is my next best activity. I committed to myself and to Michael that I would write something every day. Completing this book is part of my commitment. Each day is a new day, and I intend to live it with an open heart and a willingness to trust that I am being guided to whomever needs my services, either as a Realtor or a coach or a friend. There is no rushing me or pushing me or guilting me. I am being gently led, almost like a child.

Four more treasured jewels...

The only right way to grieve is the one that feels most right to me. My grief is as unique as my fingerprint.

Life marches on. I get to choose the cadence I can handle.

Sleep when I can. Time loses its grip and calendars are of little interest.

Give myself as long as I need. Listen to my heart.

Living List-Free and Love-Full

Calendars and to-do lists

Schedules to meet

Squeezing life between demands

No more

Trusting a heart opened to moments

Now moments

Time celebrating the beauty

Recognizing the swiftness and

Choosing to see life frame by frame

Really see it—feel it—smell it

Knowing in a flash of change

All could end

Living list-free and love-filled

Creating new channels, side eddies, pools of reflection

Letting feelings lead and

Trusting to-dos to be done

My heart rules

My mind and body follow

All could end in an instant

Savoring each moment

Living list-free and love-full

Plans and Goals

I make my plans and set my goals

Learn to intend and then let go

I dance between my linear make-it-happen side

And my open-hearted, let-it-flow because I don't know side.

Always on my list—growing my connection to Spirit.

Not on my list—losing a son.

And it showed up with all of its choices and lessons.

Learning to communicate beyond my established channels—

Not on 2013's list, but firmly established for life

Now and forever.

Pay Attention to Signs and Synchronicities

I am a voracious reader when I have a passion for a particular subject. The books written on the subject of afterlife communication present an array of evidence from triple-blind scientific experiments to anecdotal stories of contact with those who have passed—evidence piled so deep as to be undeniable except to the most hardened and committed skeptics.

I had an interest in this subject before Michael passed, but became a serious student when I knew of no other way of connecting with him. I needed to learn all I could, as quickly as I could. I would order a book from Kindle, read into the middle of the night, during the day, and any slot of available time I could carve out, until it was completed, and then order the next one. Sometimes I had two or three waiting for me.

I followed the trail of inquiry like a bird after breadcrumbs or perhaps a hunter discovering the next footprint. Video interviews from AfterLifeTV.com led me to many of the books I've researched. Each book would bridge me to the next. I think this all helped me to pay attention to the signs and synchronicities that were occurring.

I began noticing signs from Michael and feeling his energy within moments, and synchronicities kept happening. I could hear and feel and sense his presence—more sometimes than others—and even that became a teaching for me. I noticed wavelengths where communication flows and others where it cannot get through. I could feel new patterns being created, new channels opening, and I could notice how my focus dialed me in or not.

Scientific brain studies point to the reticular activator portion of the brain as that place where we file what's most important for us to notice. Since so much data is firing at us all the time, we will miss what we are not looking for. A more spiritual way of saying this same thing is, "What you focus on expands."

Both tell us that we get more of what we are looking for and focus our attention upon. Another phrase from one of my spiritual mentors, Mary Morrissey, is, "The universe reads your intention by where you place your attention, and it is perfectly designed to give you what you focus on." I have a keen interest in staying in communication with Michael. This is all the more reason for me to pay attention to signs and synchronicities and perfect timing.

I felt from the beginning that Michael was orchestrating events from his side to help us bring him home. Five minutes here or there, and we would have failed. His musical timing was always impeccable. I believe he helped us get our timing aligned. One of my first calls after receiving the news of Michael's death was to my sister Christina. Just five minutes later, and I would have missed her. Instead I caught her just heading out the door. Five minutes later, and she would have missed Jerri Grace Lyons, founder of Final Passages, who was leaving to teach a class about family-directed funerals. Jerri was our link to Cari Leversee who is the angel who brought Michael home to me.

My sister, Christina (aka Alorah) also reports two signs that were very important to her in these first moments. First, Michael died early in the morning on July 25th, a day which is considered to be the Day-Out-of-Time in the Mayan calendar—a calendar system which my sister has lived by for 20 years. It is the day that marks the change from one year to the next—the most important and magical day in the year.

Additionally, one of the first actions she took after hearing my news was to search on YouTube for a visual of Michael to show to the six women who were convened at her home ready to go wind-dancing on the beach with her. The song which came up at the top of the YouTube list was his performance of the song, *"This is the Moment,"* from his starring role in the musical Jekyll and Hyde. She reports that listening to him, and hearing him sing, felt to her that he was telling her directly that the transition he had made had landed him in joy. The lyrics that stood out to her most were, *"When I look back, I will always recall, this is the moment, the greatest moment of them all."* These are also the lyrics I hear him singing to me most often on my inner channel where I connect with him. He awakens me with song and sings me to sleep.

While I was speaking with my sister, a hummingbird flew into her Marina del Rey home and circled for several minutes until she was able to open a window and let it fly out. I held onto her words telling me, "I believe this is Michael here with us, telling us he's okay." Ten hours later, at my home, as Cari was sitting with Michael's body, she decided to pull a card from the Native American Medicine Cards specifically for Michael and his journey. I remember her saying to me, "I hope you don't mind, but I saw your deck of cards, and pulled one for Michael." Out of a possible forty-four cards, Cari pulled the hummingbird—the symbol for joy in the Native American tradition.

I knew Michael was confirming the connection to our experience with the hummingbird. Later we began to realize, as we shared stories, how many unusual hummingbird sightings family members and friends were experiencing during these first few days, each sighting bringing an experience of joy.

My beautiful hummingbird stained glass window has been hanging in our family room for over 15 years, a hummingbird garden stake welcomes visitors to the front door, and a hummingbird weather thermometer greets us at the back door. I now realize I already had an unconscious affection and attraction to this tiny winged miracle, so Michael chose to use this as an early sign that he is with me. If I'm talking to anyone about Michael during the day, almost always I will spot a hummingbird feeding from one of the many feeders that I now have. I believe he is letting me know he's listening in on our conversation.

There are many other signs and instances of ways that Michael has individually chosen to connect with loved ones. On the morning of Michael's memorial, his brother John's phone suddenly began playing *Ripple* and, moments later, *Little Wing* started on its own—two songs that connected him to Michael. The lyrics to *Ripple* were significant to him*: "There is a road, no simple highway, between the dawn and the dark of night, and if you go no one may follow, that path is for your steps alone."* The phone was in John's pocket for the first song, so the rational scientist in him figured maybe he had accidentally bumped it to set it off. The next song happened minutes later when his phone was sitting on the kitchen counter where nothing and no one could have jiggled it or set it off.

Older brother, Troy, who lives in Idaho, told us of experiencing the soothing comfort of a five-minute rain storm as he was walking around at midnight, by himself, talking to Michael, trying to grasp the reality of Michael's death—news he had just received that morning. Troy said the temperatures had reached 100 that day, and hadn't cooled down much. He couldn't sleep, and was on his fourth trip around a long country block feeling as sad and lonely as he could ever remember feeling. He heard a rustling of leaves in the distance and felt a cooling breeze filled with raindrops coming his way. It lingered over him for about five minutes. Troy says he knew it was Michael. He hadn't yet heard Michael's lyrics in his song, *When Angels Whisper*, where he says, *"Anytime the rain comes storming, I'm there, you can't miss."* Girlfriend Sammie experienced a soft breeze that same night coming through her window as she tried to sleep, and felt it was Michael's presence comforting her.

When Michael's body arrived at our home, I wanted and needed to know his spirit was also present. I felt it to be so, but longed for something a little more reassuring. Cari suggested using a pendulum. I was grateful for the suggestion. Pendulum communication during hypnosis is something I was already familiar with, so I trusted the process. We established a "yes" and a "no" answer by holding the pendulum over his body. With Michael, a swinging back and forth straight out from my center is a strong "yes" and swinging in a circle is a strong "no." As soon as I established this, I began asking questions. "Are you here with us?" "Are you at peace?" "Was this your time?" "Are you singing with the angels?" His answers were clear and were "yes." I also asked if he had felt any pain and got a clear "no." One of the decisions I needed to make was how long to keep his body at our home. Cari suggested I ask him using the pendulum. It was very informative. "Your brother Troy is arriving on Sunday, do you want to stay until then?" I got a big circle telling me "no." "How about staying until Saturday?" Another big circle saying "no." "How about tomorrow at 5 p.m.?" This time it was a big back and forth "yes." I laughed. So, we made arrangements to have him picked up the following day. I still enjoy using a pendulum to check in with him on a regular basis.

Amanda, his dear friend and co-star in Jekyll and Hyde, tells of him showing up on her birthday as a dancing dolphin in the surf of southern California, waving to her with flips and dives. She also began seeing hummingbirds. When she visited me a few weeks after Michael's death, we sat and watched the video of his memorial service. As she looked up and out my family room window, we could both see my dolphin wind chime and hummingbird stained glass framed together in my window, followed by a hungry hummingbird showing up to feed. We both cried and said "Hello Michael." On her way out to her car as she was leaving, she spotted a newspaper on the curb with just "Michael" showing on the folded banner of Carmichael Times. "Now he's just messing with us," she smiled as she handed me the paper.

Two and one-half weeks after Michael's passing, I left on the Alaskan cruise. Michael had been creating a cabaret show with his friend Scott, another musician, and they had sent an audition tape to a cruise line booking agent hoping to get a gig on a cruise ship. Instead, here I was taking some of Michael's ashes with me, as he accompanied me in spirit. We connected by "accident" with the cruise line's piano bar singer early one morning, and his lounge became our favorite place to relax in the evening, listening to him sing. One of our excursion guides for whale watching and our rain forest hike was named Michael. He was working for the summer so he could pursue his real passion of performing as a musician. I would randomly end up sitting next to musicians at our dining table. I kept sensing Michael's presence.

On the one month mark, August 25, I was reading article by David Kessler about who and what we see before we die. He reports it's usually our mom who comes to escort us when we are ready to pass, and I was feeling sad that Michael didn't have me there to greet him. Then I remembered that my dear Aunt Betty gives the best hugs ever, and so I stopped reading for a moment and checked in with Michael. I asked through my tears if he was now with Aunt Betty, my favorite aunt. Michael had sung at her funeral service over 10 years earlier. As I returned to reading the Oprah article that had prompted the question, Michael's clear answer made me laugh. I turned the page, and Kessler was explaining that if our loved ones in the dying process start to talk to people who have passed, don't tell them they are hallucinating, instead encourage them to tell you more. For instance, he wrote, "If they are seeing or speaking with someone like their Aunt Betty," say, "It's great that Aunt Betty is here with you." I chuckled, and thanked Michael for giving me such an obvious sign. Kessler could have used any other name as an example. He chose "Aunt Betty!"

Numbers began to catch my attention when I realized and connected the dots for Michael's birth number of nine. When I began looking more closely, I recognized that his age, 36, adds up to nine (3+6=9). He had nine leap years in his life. He was born nine months to the day from the day he visited me in my dream, asking permission to join our family, the day I woke up knowing I had conceived. He passed in his nine year (4-17-2013 = 18 = 9) which is a completion year, on the 99th day after his 36th birthday, and his total days on this planet Earth equal 13,239 (1+3+2+3+9 = 18 = 9). I cannot make these things up. I looked up the number nine, and it is considered by some numerologists to be the most tolerant, least judgmental, and most conscious of all the birth numbers. Fits Michael like a glove.

I continue to read and learn about and study all of the channels for communication with those who have passed from our sight. I have seen a few mediums, and continue to use my pendulum to check in with Michael. I am committed to learning how to increase my ability to recognize signs and speak with Michael in whatever ways I can, and in whatever language he is teaching me. It has helped me to move on into new ways of being with him, and has eased the agony of losing my most familiar channel, that of his physical presence here on Earth.

I began capturing my experience on Facebook and in my journal. I would get very still and listen. I'd ask myself, "What did I notice today? What am I feeling right now in this very moment?" I knew if I waited too long to write anything down, it would be lost. I wanted to remember it all.

I wrote about the many ways I felt Michael was reaching through to us—all of the coincidences lining up. I loved hearing stories from Michael's friends, especially girlfriend Sammie, of the ways they were connecting to him now. Sammie had a couple of dreams shortly after where he seemed so real that she got worried about how they were going to get all of his things back to him, because we had given them away to family and friends. He had so many hats—at least ten of them. Michael told her he was fine and not to worry. Another time they were in the car heading to my house to see me and almost made it before she woke up. She said it was so real.

Kurt had a dream where Michael was doing stand-up comedy to a huge audience and just having a great time. These signs and dreams and stories help me pay attention to the good and move toward wholeness.

Friends and family gathered in our back yard after his memorial and pulled angel cards from the deck that Michael and Sammie used on their first date (my deck which now lives with Sammie). We pulled *harmony, music, signs, Archangel Michael, soul mate, truth and integrity, divine timing, spiritual growth, meditation, and healing*, all qualities connected to Michael.

Michael loved violet and purple. These colors showed up in the gifts of flowers, candles, hydrangeas, wrapping paper, and Peter Pan agapanthus plant, purple lily of the Nile. I got hummingbird cards from people who had never heard the hummingbird connection.

The unusual leafy fern pattern in the fabric that we wrapped him in to send him on his way showed up again wrapped around a music box Cari gave to me at his memorial. It was the same fabric—design, color, exactly alike. At first I wondered if she had cut a piece from his blanket before we sent him off, but no, she had it at her home. It was a tie to a curtain. What are the chances?

Two more take aways...

Watch for signs from my loved one—listen, feel, sense— serendipitous coincidences, alignment and perfect timing.

Capture the stories while they are fresh.

Feeling my Way

Feeling my way

Listening on new frequencies

Higher, sweeter, softer

Stillness

Anticipating a note, a word, a phrase

Then following the images

And listening for more

Feeling my way

Guided by love

Michael and James Neal ready for a camping trip

When Angels Cry

I'm sorry. I'm so sorry.

Don't cry for me

I'm here. I'm safe. I'm home.

Listen through your tears

I am here—right here

Do angels cry when they cannot reach us?

Sending signs

Whispering

Arranging miracle coincidences

Hoping we'll notice

Hummingbirds and gentle breezes

Songs out of nowhere

Saying "Now here"

Dream channels

Openings between worlds

When angels cry...

Can you hear me?

I'm here—I'm safe—I'm home.

I love you.

From Broken Heart to Open Vessel

Pain. Will I work with you or fight you?

Labor pains, contractions to open a pathway for new life.

Death of my son,

Contractions pulling on my heart

Opening new ways of being.

Pain, physical and emotional,

Pushing me through to the light,

Pointing the way.

My broken heart becomes an open vessel,

The lotus blossom emerging from the mud of darkness

I can learn to trust the pain and its promise

To see it as my friend, not my enemy.

I can refuse to hold onto or fight this sacred friend of my

becoming.

I can embrace the breaking

Knowing that pain and joy each arrive bearing gifts,

Teaching me to expand and include

And to trust this Life Force that is breathing me,

Beating my heart, breaking it open,

That I might be an open vessel

For healing love to pour through.

Learning a New Language

Subtle clues of Spirit's presence

Soft breezes and unexpected alignments

Timing of events and happenstance meetings

Birds and butterflies catching my attention

Lyrics in my ear or over the air waves

High frequency ringing in my head

Pay attention to these new symbols

A new language...

Like learning to read the nuances of a newborn

Our language—our way of connecting

Teaching sounds and words and meanings

Now I am the one who is being taught

I am the infant in this world of connecting in Spirit

Teach me—stay patient with me—I am learning

Gentle Whispers

Gentle whispers

Soul to soul across the veil

Sweet hellos and soft nudges

"I love you"—a smile and tears of recognition

"I am here" always present carried in your heart

As you are in mine

Learning to listen and see newly

Senses beyond the physical

Tapping in and staying connected

Heart to heart, soul to soul

Beyond time and space

In the ever present now of knowing

Learning to hear

Gentle whispers and "I love you's"

Tuning In

I remember dials on radios

Automobile dashboards with big numbers

Turning the knob to tune in

To line up the dial with the call number

To pick up the signal

In a car, driving across country

Finding a signal then losing it to static

Then looking for another

In the desert

Through the mountains

Along the highways from here to there

Tuning in, grateful to find a signal

My heart tunes in to frequencies as well

I listen and receive and respond and scan for the signals

Signals from my precious son in another dimension

Signals from those still here with me

My connections to those I love and

To those I have perhaps tuned out

My heart scans the frequencies and chooses

I listen—I speak

I write—I wonder

And I am grateful for the ability to tune in.

No Regrets

No regrets to steal the joy or lay waste the memories

I celebrate each flash of remembrance

I sing his songs in my heart

I feel the fullness of the love we shared

We honored and respected each other

We trusted and listened

Grief cannot steal the joy or lay waste the memories

I turn instead to a knowing deep within

We come from Love—we return home to Love

And, if we are awake enough to see it,

We realize Love's presence holds us while we are here

I celebrate this Love

Learned from my angel son Michael

I cherish each memory, each "I Love You,"

Each "Mom…," each good night kiss, each hello hug

No regrets, only gratitude

It's Okay to Heal—Grief Doesn't Keep Us Connected to Our Loved One

When I realized I was perhaps through the worst of the sadness and grief, and that I was having "normal" days, that tears were more gentle, and further apart, I found a curious notion presenting itself. I noticed the thought, "If I get over this, I won't be feeling as connected to Michael." And, even more than that, "If I get over this grief too soon, does that mean I didn't really love him as much as I thought I did? What will people think?" Almost like suffering was a badge of loyalty and love and caring, and the burden of grief could not be lifted without losing the badge.

I am not an expert on the subject, only a mother who was thrust into a situation not of my choosing which, never the less, required me to make choices and taught me about grief and healing from the inside out. I found that grief isn't the best or only channel for feeling Michael's presence. It is not a measure of how much I loved him. Longer grief does not mean more or greater or deeper love. I know the depth of the love I feel. Yet, the temptation to compare showed up.

Holding onto grief also kept me locked into an intense feeling mode. I had never experienced the depth of pain I felt with this shocking change to my life. I had been through a divorce after 27 years of marriage, betrayals, affairs, and other relationships that didn't work out. Those were painful and shocking, yet this was on another level altogether.

By comparison, my normal state of emotions was feeling flat next to what I had been experiencing in the early weeks after his passing. Numbness was just a notch below what I was calling normal. It all frightened me until I saw through it. It is okay to heal. I can still stay connected. Holding onto grief is not the way to hold onto my loved one.

"Moving on" is a phrase often coupled with grief—like there is a place to arrive. I see in my linear brain that this appears to be the case—Points A to B to C, etc. I've read about the stages of grief and also about the fallacy in this theory. I chose not to study grief from a book, but to observe it in myself. I believe it is a unique experience for each person. And, I believe we will each need to deal with our feelings, the way others relate to us, the thoughts that present themselves, and how to comfort ourselves as we move through the process. There are healing and helpful ways to do this, and ways that prolong the pain. Grief has been my teacher on how to embrace a most difficult experience and discover a path through the pain to an unshakeable peace. It's a place worth arriving at.

When kind, loving people told me my heart will always have a hole in it, a part of myself rose up, defiantly raising my internal stop sign, and silently saying "NO" to that suggestion. My heart was indeed cracked open and my perception of the sacredness and fragility of life forever altered.

The "cracking open" revealed aspects of myself I had not encountered so forcefully before. I found courage and strength, vulnerability and deep compassion at levels I didn't know were possible. Friends would call me "amazing," and I didn't know how to respond. I wanted to understand what they were seeing and experiencing as "amazing."

I believe what they were seeing and responding to arose from this cracked open heart and my intuitive knowing that if I looked for the blessings and trusted the guidance I kept receiving that I could hold all of the pain and all of the joy and my incredible love for my son all at once. My heart didn't have a hole. Instead, it had no boundaries, no limits, and an expanded capacity for living and loving and giving and receiving.

I hold on to the memories, the joy, the gratitude, and continue to find new ways to stay connected through new channels. It's all new territory for me, and I'm trusting the path of peace, not pain, grace and not grief, and serenity over sadness.

"Focus on the beauty of what's here right now, not on what's missing." These words came directly from Michael. He spoke them to me on day twenty-one when I was deeply grieving. I woke up in my cabin on the Holland America cruise ship, looked out at the Alaskan waters that we were sailing through, and saw that the sun was just beginning to light up the sky in the most beautiful rainbow colors.

I headed for the top deck, sobbing yet determined to see the sunrise. Michael spoke to me over my right shoulder, *"Mom!"*

I literally stopped in my tracks to listen. *"Focus on all the beauty all around you. Don't miss it by being sad and wishing things were different. I'm right here."*

He certainly got my attention. The sunrise was spectacular, and the colors bathing the waters were vivid reds and oranges, yellows and blues. I stopped my crying, wiped my eyes, and took it all in. I remembered his promise, *"I'll meet you at the end of the rainbow."* This radiant display of light certainly had the rainbow colors, and Michael was right there with me, reminding me to pay attention.

That was the second time I had heard his voice as if he was standing at my right shoulder. The first was on the day he passed—within moments of my learning of it—and his words were, *"I'm so sorry Mom. I love you. I'm so sorry."*

Being able to feel his presence when I'm quiet and tune in has made such a difference. I've asked him questions when I'm writing in my journal and received clear channeled answers. I hear him singing always in the morning in my left inner ear, and the songs vary across the lyrics he recorded on CDs and those he performed on stage.

His reminder to stay in the moment and focus on what is beautiful and joyful right in front of me continues to bless me and teach me. Whenever I catch myself missing him or wishing something was different, I can change my focus.

23. One of my favorite pearls of wisdom... *"Focus on all the beauty all around you. Don't miss it by being sad and wishing things were different.*

Wonderment

A feeling of wondrous joy pouring through my every cell

And spilling out of my tear-flooded eyes

A beholding

A moment so sweet it lights me up from within and I glow

My sons, no matter how grown, fill me with wonderment

Watching them, beholding their joy, feeling my own gratitude

That they chose me as their mom

Beautiful music and natural vistas

From God's paint pallet

Fill me with wonderment

Simple acts of kindness and love, witnessed

Fill me

My prayer—to stay open and bear witness

To behold the love

To say thank you for it all

A Temptation

Holding onto grief

Hoping to stay connected through my tears

Revisiting and rekindling the pain

Of shocking sudden loss

Replaying memories hooked to extreme emotions

This gut-wrenching form of aliveness tempts me

Fearing if I surrender to healing

Release myself from grief's bondage

I will lose any connection to him all over again

Dull flat numbness cannot compete

And grief tempts me to stay stuck

Yet, I'm awakening to the joy

Hidden in and beyond the grief

I follow the lightness of my heart

Trusting it to guide me

The path opens and grief

No longer my jailer

Becomes my teacher

In letting go, surrendering, allowing grief to speak,

To sit with me for awhile before moving on,

I am learning to follow the light

And listen for the voice of my loved one

Beyond the grief,

Whispering to me of love and angels.

Forgive Everyone Everything

My mentor, Mary Morrissey, emphasizes in her teachings the power and importance of forgiveness. Whether I am holding onto feelings of anger or resentment or disapproval of another, or of myself, I am creating my own suffering. No one else gets to think my thoughts but me, yet the thoughts I think have everything to do with the quality of the life I am living.

The practice of choosing my thoughts and noticing when I'm holding onto judgment and anger became vitally important to me when the news of Michael's death reached me. As I have moved along the journey of healing, I keep running head on into forgiveness. She reminds me to let the judgment go. Drop the resentment. Find another way to perceive what is causing the anger and pain.

Just when I think I have put those negative emotions behind me and my heart feels at peace, a memory or an event stirs up pain or anger and reminds me, once again, that I still have forgiveness work to do. The same names pop up whenever I am presented with the question "Who do you need to forgive?" I thought I had whittled the list down, but when I look with an open heart and an honest eye, the same names reappear. All of them, I notice, in my opinion, seem to have inflicted harm or pain onto one of my children. And, the most challenging for me are the ones Michael spent his last hours with. The ones I feel could have listened and prevented the tragedy from ever occurring. Twenty-twenty hindsight is always perfect, or so the saying goes.

The last time I was struggling with the anger that erupts when I dwell on what I feel a more nurturing situation could have prevented, I received a message from Michael that made all the difference. This was thirty-six weeks into my journey, and I had just received a copy of the police report, so the sadness and anger had been thoroughly triggered.

A few days passed, and I was still feeling the sting of it all. I decided to ask Michael for support. I tuned into his wave length, after preparing myself in silence to hear him, and I asked him, "Michael, why did you leave the way you did?" His answer, "*It was an opening in time, and I had an appointment to keep. If I had stayed home with you, I couldn't have gone. I actually needed Dad to not listen and to leave me so I could take my exit. Try to let him off the hook. I know you carry anger towards him.*"

And with that, I vowed to do my best. So, whenever the conversation in my head tempts me to blame his father, I remember this message from Michael, and I turn towards the light of acceptance, trusting that Michael's soul was calling him home, and he was listening, even though my human awareness cannot fully understand this.

I do my best to remember to "forgive everyone everything." I do it for me, not for them. I do it so I can move on. I look under the anger and find sadness—a deep ocean of emotions that this loss has added to. I say "loss" because I miss Michael's physical presence so much. I miss his laughter and sweetness of spirit and his amazing beautiful voice. I miss his messes and his music. I grieve for what he still had to bring to the world.

And, I celebrate what he did do in such a short time. I know he never uttered an unkind word or intentionally harmed anyone or anything. He would gently take spiders outside and literally wouldn't kill a mosquito or a fly. So, when I feel the pain of unforgiveness in my heart, I turn to Michael for inspiration and support. I remind myself of the power forgiveness graces us with, and I do my best to "turn the other cheek"—to find another way to see it, to cast a kind eye on the perceived perpetrator. I take myself by the hand and gently lead that part of me that has forgotten back to grace, to love, to healing energies and expansive thoughts.

Mary Morrissey tells a story I love about her conversation with the Dalai Lama that illustrates the power of forgiveness. She wanted to understand how he could generate compassion and exude happiness when his home country of Tibet and the people of Tibet were being destroyed by the Chinese government. When she asked him how he has been able to keep this experience from dominating his daily awareness or affecting his daily happiness, he had the following answer. "Everyone of us has friends. Friends easy to love. Friends make mistake, even easy to forgive. Then we have what we call sacred friends. Oh, sacred friends. Very difficult forgive.

Very, very difficult. Chinese government my sacred friend. I would never have developed compassionate heart absent Chinese government. Chinese government makes so difficult to forgive that I had to get very, very big heart and have to keep very, very big heart and it's a big challenge."

I love that story, and the lesson it has for me, as I run into my own sacred friends. Are they safe to roam the streets of my mind? Do I want to attack them? It's quite a practice and it does develop the heart muscle. I know my heart has expanded and grown in my capacity to love because of my sacred friends.

I have also learned the power of letting myself off the hook for all of the shoulds I've placed on myself over the years. Am I safe to roam the streets of my own mind? Forgive everyone everything includes me in that circle. My life is what it is today because of all that has happened here in this earth school. Another Mary Morrissey-ism, "The circumstances of your life are the curriculum for your spiritual growth." My life is sweet because of my adversities, not in spite of them. It's sweet because I have learned to look for the seed of what's possible and good in that which doesn't appear so on the surface. My life is sweet because I ask, when I remember to, "What have you come to teach me? What is the blessing in this?"

Wanting to Blame

Really, it's a reasonable train of thought

I can see the evidence right before my eyes

It all adds up to his and her fault

Why didn't they listen

Why didn't he turn around

Why didn't he stay and stand guard

Is this litany of "why didn'ts" changing the "what's so?"

I know better

I recognize the futility of it

Wanting to blame, to make another guilty for my pain

Justification for holding them outside of my heart

To resent and judge and feel better than

And these are the poisons I have learned to recognize

So I ask myself to forgive

To give for myself a new perception

To give for myself some healing thoughts

To give for myself a turning away from blame and toward love

It is a process

Done moment by moment

As each temptation arises

Wanting to blame

Learning to forgive

Underneath the Anger

Someone told me long ago to look

Underneath the anger

So I'm looking

An ocean of sadness and

Unanswered questions

Impossible rewinds

How could you leave him?

Why didn't you listen?

The anger is easier

It has a righteous force and puts blame on another

The pain beckons me to swim in its depths

And drown if I flail against it

Can I learn to float on its surface?

Teach others to swim above the pull of its undertow?

Will I make it to shore

And see it from a new space?

What are its gifts?

How do I forgive?

Where is my comforter?

Are there any answers or just more questions?

Looking underneath the anger

Creating a New Normal

How have I changed since Michael's passing? I feel more connected to my heart. I cry more easily. I listen more carefully. I feel like I love more deeply. I am present to the fragile nature of life, how precious it is. I am attentive to what I feel are signs of Michael's presence, and very drawn to anything I can learn about life after life.

Michael seldom leaves my thoughts, and I notice I am so used to it, that if I go awhile without thinking of him, I feel an urgent need to call out to him. The reality of Michael's physical absence echoes in the background no matter what I'm doing. Day by day I am learning about the nuances of joy and sadness and pain and healing. I am helped by my belief and faith in life after life, and I am learning to talk to him out loud or in my heart whenever I need to.

Some days are easier than others. I've journeyed quite a distance. I am finding ways to honor his memory and see the blessings in all of it. I've never felt stuck in this process—I've felt sad and my heart has ached for wanting to hold Michael and be with him for an in-person conversation, but I have always felt like I am moving forward and in doing so am helping others to do so as well. I've learned to keep telling Michael I love him and let the tears flow.

I am aware of a contrast to the intense emotions of the first few weeks and now. I'm experiencing more gentle tears, not the sobbing ones. These gentle ones well up and spill over from a sweet memory or the lyrics of a song. I feel more peace than pain. I am learning to integrate new ways of being with Michael, as I let go of the familiar ones which I so often miss. Gentle tears help.

There is an intensity in the attention from others surrounding the immediate loss, and then it all quiets down—less attention, less intensity of feeling—more "normal." I experience living more from love and an open heart, and I find moving back to a left-brain focused activity is not as easy for me. I feel less connected when I do. I associate the right brain with heart-centered.

The rawness has scabbed over, and I have been very good about not picking at it. I feel its tenderness and feel the scar is a beautiful reminder of how much love we shared as mother and son. Deep love, sweet memories, experiencing the wave—the sadness-joy elixir—even though I know he's just a thought away, it's still an adjustment. I don't know how the idea of "getting over it" got connected to matters of deep love and swift endings. I don't even like calling it an ending. Really, it's a new beginning.

I especially enjoy listening to Michael's Broadway Hits and appreciating the mastery he achieved with his voice. Each song speaks to my heart in its own way. I always cry when I listen to him, wanting to hold him so much, missing him and feeling connected at the same time. No one can choose my thoughts but me. I choose to remember how much joy is in my life right now, even as I embrace the reality that I am still grieving. Interesting mixture—joy and grief.

I love the silent, still moments. Healing doesn't have to mean silence, yet there is a peacefulness in my life that is quiet. I'm still very aware of his presence in my life and of the many ways he winks a "hello" to me during the day.

My routines look the same as before, yet feel somehow different. My house is very quiet. I've shared this home with Michael for the last six years of his life. We joked that he came home for six months, six years ago—it was to be just long enough to get some bills paid and save for a trip to Germany—a dream he never fulfilled. He was a wonderful housemate. I smile when I remember hearing his car door close, then the back gate opening, then the slider, and the instruments and cases piling up next to the banister, then Michael's footsteps up the three stairs to the kitchen and the refrigerator door opening, then the cupboard, and then his footsteps back down to fill his glass with filtered water. "How'd it go?" I'd ask, knowing he'd just come from a performance or a rehearsal. "Good," was his usual response—a man of few words.

I'm reminded of how I would tiptoe in the mornings so as not to awaken him. His creative bursts were usually middle of the night occurrences, and his deepest sleep often coincided with my morning wake up routines. Flush toilet, let dog out, make coffee, empty dishwasher, somewhere in there take a shower, and hope I'm being quiet enough. Now I'm growing used to living without my favorite roommate, and yet I'll still catch myself tiptoeing.

I find playing his music is a way of connecting. I miss his late night practice sessions which filled the whole house with sounds. And, I miss the smell of garlic and onions and whatever concoctions he'd get going in the kitchen late at night when I was heading for bed. I miss the messes—messy and lots of music at all times of the day and night—the little piles of papers, music stands, a guitar propped against the sofa. Now there are no clothes piled up near the laundry, and no towels hanging from doorknobs. How I would love to see five towels draped over shower doors, and laundry piling up next to the washer, a few unwashed dishes in the sink. I would give anything to hear him practicing or watching him faithfully do his exercise routines.

For the first few weeks, I could not tolerate listening to the radio or TV, preferring silence in my car during drive time, silence in the house unless listening to Michael's music, and long stretches of not doing much. I've been taught to "notice what you are noticing." This seemingly simple instruction continues to help me on this journey with Michael. I listen to my heart in the moment, ask what I am to say or do, and act accordingly. I get to choose how I respond and how I rebuild. I continue to look for and discover the gifts and blessings.

I am daily getting to choose my way of being with the sadness that shows up. I pray to stay awake to whispers from Michael from beyond, and to remember to let my loved ones still here in this realm know how much I care about them. I study and teach and learn and love and give it my best. Life brings me an unexpected life-altering event, and all of my dreams and goals end up on the table for examination and review. Everything feels different.

I feel the sadness that comes from those shattered dreams, and the challenge of rebuilding them, with a gentle loving appreciation of how fragile life is, and how much our dreams need to include loving each other. Life is so precious. I saw a man scolding his teenage daughter yesterday for being late. He was thumping his wrist watch as he marched her toward his car. I thought if you only knew how lucky you are to be in her presence, that she is here with you, and you can give her a big hug!

Driving places—usually just me and my thoughts—in the quiet of my car, I'm aware of Michael singing to me. Better than the radio, it's like a private concert in my mind. I smile and say "hello," and tell him how much I love him. I try not to wish he were here, but I'd be lying to say I don't wish it every day. I want to talk with him in the flesh just once more. We never spoke about the possibility of him dying. Our talks were full of dreams for life. As his number one fan, I still catch myself scouting out venues for him. Every day with our loved ones is a gift—a precious gift.

Often, I'll well up, tears flooding my eyes and my heart with love, with memories, with wishes that I could have him here with me, in all of his radiant life and beauty. I'm so new and feeling very unskilled with the after-life connection. Sometimes I feel right there, and other times quite distant or blocked. I notice I cry less often, yet welcome the tears when they come. They are filled with a mother's love, blended with joy and sadness and gratitude--gratitude for my learning a new language of connection—moments when I feel his presence and hear his heart and feel his words of comfort. When I tune in, he is always there. I miss him, and yet he's with me. I am still working through this new territory of my heart.

I've heard grief waves are one of the signs that we are connecting. What about joy waves? I saw a beautiful hummingbird up close today at a home inspection. It hovered right outside the kitchen window long enough for me to say, "hello," and admire its green and red colors. Filled my heart with joy. So many sweet memories.

I turned on my fireplace for the first time this fall and remembered all the evenings Michael sat near its warmth to practice. I can see him sitting in his favorite chair with his beloved bandoneon and rehearsing for his next performance. The things we take for granted, as if they will never end. I'm learning about these in a most up close and personal way. How often I took for granted the simple hellos and nods of awareness, familiar patterns and subtle nuances—simple moments I now cherish as memories. What am I taking for granted now? I must pay attention and not miss the gifts.

Holidays are being reformatted. Thanksgiving first, then Christmas and New Year's, next our family birthdays, including his, and then Easter. I noticed right away the temptation to invite sadness to the family dining table, and I immediately canceled that invitation. So, while Michael's playful antics with his nephews are missed, and he's no longer doing the mid-night raid on leftovers, his joy is fully present in the laughter of my grandkids, his recorded music serenades us, his smile is reflected on all of our faces as we celebrate our love for each other and feast on delicious food.

Michael's words remind me to pay attention to the beauty in front of me and not miss it wishing things were different. So, while I acknowledge sadness, she's not invited to our table. Our seats are reserved for love and joy and gratitude and fun and wonderful memories and angels who are always with us. I am learning to appreciate and find the beauty in all of life, especially when it changes.

Perhaps the triggers will diminish. I never know what will bring up a wave of tears. One morning I was getting ready to cook an egg, and the pots and pans made me cry. I was reminded of teaching Michael to cook when he moved into his own apartment and I realized he was eating out all the time. We started with the basics, and he taught himself from there. He made such interesting concoctions beginning with garlic and onions and peppers, adding eggs, and whatever—usually in mid afternoon or midnight depending upon his entertainer circadian rhythms and when he was in creative mode.

Just going to the grocery store, knowing he shopped there too, was a trigger at first. Do people remember him? I'm sure they do, but probably don't know he's my son or that he passed. I almost lost it at the broccoli aisle, one of the vegetables I always made sure we had plenty of. I looked around and wondered how many others are dealing with loss and going through the motions of looking normal.

Looking at his photos on my phone can bring me to tears of missing him and trying to understand. Flashing on the accident and that whole period of 36 hours from when I last spoke with him to when I got the horrific news—it's not a place for me to go and feel nurtured. I do my best to not go there. Sometimes the thought "why didn't I know" triggers me. Couldn't I have stopped it?

Everyone tells me to trust that it was his time. All the books and mediums say similar things. I still want to turn the clock back, keep him home, stay by his side until I know he's okay. I weep with this pain of missing him and wishing I had known or asked or intuited or somehow tuned into this trouble ahead of time.

On September 11, 2013, I was remembering the many who lost their lives when the twin towers collapsed a dozen years earlier. In thinking about all of the families dealing with shock and grief, I see I relate to the pain of it from a much more personal place since getting that dreadful call telling me Michael was gone. Much like 9/11, life altered in a second. I had no landing place in my heart to even comprehend what I was being told. My sister taught me a phrase years ago that I feel helps me walk this journey: "Expand to include and have it contribute." I've been expanding, making space, feeling it all, and trusting that I am healing and growing through this experience.

I am noticing that since Michael's passing, when people ask how I am doing, I hear it from a place of knowing they are genuinely interested and care about me. It's different from the social exchanges to which we might reply, "Fine, and how are you?" and then keep on moving or talk about the weather. Instead, I stop to answer from my heart, and most of the time my answer is, "I'm doing great." And I mean it. Sometimes I'll answer, "Creating a new normal." I have found that response recognizes that my life has changed, and that I'm in a process for which I have no history. I do know I'm committed to having this experience contribute to me and to others in some beautiful way. I have recently been adding that I am learning new ways to communicate with Michael, and will ask if they have someone on the other side that they stay connected with. I love the moments of authentic sharing this creates. I am finding so many who love to tell me their stories of how they know their loved ones are near. This exchange blesses us both.

I'm drawn to any opportunity to connect heart to heart, to listen, to share my experience, to comfort, to be in the presence of the essence of life. I feel like a curious blend of open, vulnerable, strong, and tender—certain of my resilience and grateful for discovering a deep unshakeable core of knowing all is well.

About ten weeks after Michael's passing, I stopped to chat in the grocery store with a neighbor. I realized she hadn't heard about his death. I often tear up when the news is fresh for someone else. I shared how tender I feel watching parents with their children and how precious these years are. She hugged her pre-school son a little tighter as we headed off to continue shopping.

I've run into friends who weren't sure it was okay to talk about him or ask what happened. I can feel them dancing around, not mentioning Michael, so I do it for them. I reassure them that I welcome any chance to share and honor his life. I love talking about him. It makes me feel more connected. And, I'm finding that these conversations often go beneath the surface and create a heart connection, even for just a moment. Vulnerability and transparency—these are qualities I am learning about.

I am so touched even now by the many comments about how Michael showed up for life—so full of light and love and so gentle. I see his smile easily in my mind's eye because so many photos captured it even from the time he was tiny until he passed. My heart remembers him so clearly. Tears flood my eyes often and they are mostly from those sweet memories and my gratitude for the new ways I am learning to stay connected. I love sharing stories about him with anyone who knew him, and I am so much more aware of the love I feel for friends and family still here in the flesh.

While I'm not quite sure what my new normal looks like yet, I can feel it unfolding. I envision myself creating a way of being that feels whole and includes all of the joy I still feel when I think of him. He fills my hurt places with the love he is still sending my way. I know for sure that, "Life is precious...handle with love."

Brothers John, Troy and Michael just goofing off

Start with Saying "Thank You"

When I need to shift and lift my spirits

I know I can start with "Thank you"

Thank you, Dear Spirit,

For all the beauty,

All the love,

All the gifts

I've learned, even in the darkest time

Those most painful, heart wrenching, fear-filled times

That my peace comes when I start saying

Thank you

Not thank you for the pain, for the loss—

NO, not that

Just remembering in the midst of it to reach deep within

To the core of my being

Anchored in Truth and Love

Through the gateway of my heart,

Opening with a thank you

Gratitude and Thanksgiving

Giving thanks for the many blessings

Taking time to notice and to appreciate

Changes unexpected

Empty chairs and a broken branch

Missing his presence

Digging deeper to give thanks

To appreciate who is at my table

To love each day and realize it is a gift

To see beauty and joy in all of the sweet memories

To cherish it all and

Shine the light of love upon it

Not missing the beauty of this moment

Wishing it were different

Standing in Thanksgiving

Lifting my eyes to the heavens

Saying a prayer of gratitude

Knowing life changes

The unexpected and unwanted happen

I anoint myself with the healing oil of gratitude

And make every day

A day for giving thanks

Did I Pay Attention

Quiet for a while—everyone has gone

Our first holiday since his passing

I miss his playful antics—his laughter

His mid-night raids on the left-overs

The playful banter of cousins who have grown up together

So many Thanksgivings in this house around this table

Did I pay attention?

Did I notice or did I sleepwalk through much of it

Worrying about getting a feast on the table

When the real feast was right in front of my eyes

Bringing family together for the first time

After a change none of us expected or wanted

Still trying to make some sense of it

Still tender from the pain of it

Photos and CDs and DVDs

I would trade them all for having him back here with us

I am learning and growing

And choosing to find the blessings

I am a reluctant passenger on this grief train

Yet I'd rather embrace the journey—not resent it

Let it burn the dross from the gold

Leaving me refined by its intensity

Strengthened by the fire

Remembering to pay attention now to life

To each precious minute

No sleepwalking or worrying

And missing the moments that matter

When those moments soon become only

Tender, beautiful memories

Did I pay attention?

The Power of Focus

I get to choose

My life and my thoughts and my actions

No one can think my thoughts but me

I get to choose my focus

And my focus expands and intensifies my experience

I get to choose

No one can choose my focus but me

I choose love and I choose gratitude

And I choose deep listening to my soul and to your soul

And to my loved ones here in flesh and here in spirit

I get to choose

It's my life and my gift from my creator

I get to choose the power of my focus

And the direction it takes me

No one can choose my actions but me

I get to choose

Some Days are Easier than Others

Mostly my days seem normal

I'm present

I listen

I care

I do the doing that needs doing

And then a tender moment comes

I choke on the throat lump

I cannot speak my normal voice

Lips tremble

I am filled for a moment with sadness and tears

I'm present

I listen

I notice how much I care

I breathe into the pain

I take time to be my own comforter

To say it's okay to cry

Okay to miss his physical presence

Okay to grieve

Some days are easier than others

Grief as My Teacher

People handle grief in such different ways. I don't believe there is a right way or a wrong way to grieve. My mom says she can't listen to Michael's music or watch his videos because it makes her miss him more and she starts to cry. I think my daughter-in-law responds in much the same way. I find the more I listen to him, the closer I feel to him. Yes, the sadness comes but is accompanied by so much joy that it balances out. Do I miss Michael? Ever so much.

Grief has become an amazing teacher for me on life and living. Michael's passing has opened my channels of communication on all levels. My soul connection with him, my willingness to write publicly about my healing process, the poetry coming through—all of the blessings that I can see when I follow Michael's instructions to pay attention to the beauty right in front of me.

Sometimes it is so subtle and simple. For example, I'm sitting in the living room, and as I'm writing, I look up to see if any hummingbirds are feeding. They are precious to me, and it's a treat to see them zoom in on the feeder. As I look at the feeder, I notice my windows need to be washed. I see I can focus on the spots on the glass or look past them to the beauty of the park and the ever changing colors. My choice.

I also notice a tendency, if I don't stay alert, to drift back to old familiar patterns established before Michael's passing woke me up—patterns of drifting, of letting life go by unnoticed, of focusing on what's missing or on what I don't want, patterns that generate a vibration that is dull and flat. I didn't realize the contrast until after his passing. Michael's physical presence and creative expression sparked up my life while he was living here, and now he's juicing it up from the other side. He's calling upon me to write, to share, and come from my heart. I believe he is showing me what really matters.

Life presents me with questions, choices, and opportunities. How will I respond? When I sum it all up at the end, what has been my contribution, my legacy? I've used up resources, breathed air, engaged in conversations. My love for my sons and grandsons, my family and friends—all of the meals, gifts, time spent—did any of it matter?

So I ask myself, "What would make today a day that matters?" Who can I bless? Where can I pour out some joy or encouragement. Who can I appreciate? Who needs a listening ear? I'm the one who gets to choose my thoughts and actions and declare how I will be. Michael's passing has made me so aware of my heart space and spending time there, wanting to contribute, to leave a legacy. Did I love fully? Did I live fully? Did I leave the world a better place for my having been here? Michael certainly did. I know he could answer "yes" to all of those questions. He continues to inspire me.

I've found myself wondering, as I'm healing, if I'm moving back to living in my head space. It's familiar territory. I've grown very aware of the difference between head and heart. I notice how much I prefer staying in my heart as a come-from place. Michael told me in a meditation that the heart space is *"the sacred in life"*—it's *"being in touch with the love in life."* He flashed before me his formula (which my sister found in some of his notes and shared with me) *"Life minus fear equals love."* That's the sacred experience—a life full of love. I see the shift that is possible depending upon where I place my attention. What am I "C"ing—saCred or sCared? Love or fear? Fear lives in our minds—not in our hearts.

If I want to stay connected to my heart space, I must pay attention to the sacred and the beautiful, the love all around me, the joy I feel, and I must express gratitude for all of it. When I let fear in and get scared of losing something, my attention shifts, and I create the opposite of what I want.

I have also learned that pain and suffering are not the same. I've realized that feelings of joy and pain are "now-moment" experiences. I often feel them both at the same time. Peace of mind or suffering arise out of whatever story I tell myself and others about what happened. They linger and become states of being that are created by sustained and repeated thought patterns. I much prefer peace of mind to suffering. To me, this is a life-altering distinction. In my story that I tell myself, am I a powerless victim or an empowered creator of my life? I'm the author. I get to choose, and I get to do the revisions. Moment by moment I am strengthening my ability to choose peace of mind. Michael taught me this by example when he was here physically, and now guides me from within. *"Look for the joy Mom. Notice the beauty."* Quite the practice.

I am daily getting to choose my way of being with the sadness that shows up. I am listening to my heart when it nudges me. I pray to stay awake to whispers from Michael from beyond, and to let my loved ones still here in this realm know how much I care about them. I study and teach and learn and love and give it my best. I recognize the power of visioning and using my imagination to design a life I love living. I know it's powerful—and I feel the sadness that comes from shattered dreams as well. I am rebuilding, with a gentle loving appreciation of how fragile life is, and how much my dreams need to include loving one another.

Listening from my heart, listening to my heart, listening with my heart—all are practices I have been deepening since Michael's passing. Stillness, and now-ness, and presence amplify the sounds of wisdom from within, and I hear and feel deep channels opening—carrying me across the veil if only for a moment. When I take myself to the frequency of prayer, I know I am dialing in to a higher realm, and that's where the communication with Michael is possible. It's not in my head, but in my heart, that the vibration occurs, and the channel opens.

I've been considering how an infant learns to speak the language of its parents. We teach symbols. This object means this word, and this word goes with that thing. And I'm "mama" and this is "dada." And we delight in hearing them make the connections and begin engaging us with symbolic language. Now I'm the infant, and Michael is teaching me a new language. Quietly I listen and watch for signs and symbols so I can connect. I'm developing my skills of paying attention. I still awake each morning to Michael singing music in my inner ear. I watch for hummingbirds and numbers on the digital clock. I notice when he pops into my thoughts. Teacher is doing his best to get my attention and teach me the symbols.

My energies are drawn to books, and websites, and conferences on afterlife connections, and exploring those, learning all I can and sharing what I have found with others who are interested. How much does this help with the healing of grief? For me, it seems to be a major piece. Knowing I can maintain a connection and feel his presence lessens the experience of loss for me. I've noticed that if I start to worry about losing my connection to Michael, the next stop is a visit from doubt and fear. If I listen to those voices in my head, I can see the thought train they will take me on, and I don't want to go there. I've found my best remedy when this happens is to turn my attention back to the present moment and tap into gratitude. I hold onto a sweet memory, and call him to me, reminding myself of all of the ways he has shown me that he is still present. I find looking at his photo and telling him how much I love him will bring me back to joy. I know deep within my soul that Michael is happy, growing, and being his delightful energy for many on the other side.

This thing we call death, how does it really work for the living left behind?   Images and quotes and artifacts—none of it stays past a few generations unless your reach was wide and touched many lives—for good or ill. It becomes yesterday's news. Yet for me, this mother, Michael lives on in my heart—

forever—our love is here to stay. It's the love that I'm feeling, and the moments of love that we shared, that live on, and don't fade, and I get to take with me.

You, my dear Michael, have taught me this with your passing. I have a new relationship with listening to my inner world of which you are a big part. It takes a moment of slowing down and dropping in, of noticing, and then listening. It's my connection place from which my poetry and writing flows— that place within my heart where you also reside.

In my journey as a mom, in my growing up along with my three precious sons, I see the lessons I've been given in loving and letting go. I've learned to listen and not lecture, to watch and not hover, to celebrate wins and soothe disappointments. My sons taught me to be curious about the male side of the human race, to honor their space, to ask and not intrude, to appreciate and not baby them. My oldest two have given me the gift of being a grandma, have shown me how much I enjoy watching them take on parenting, how proud I am of the love they express with their own sons.

And Michael, my youngest, shows me the path of the gentle artist, the dedication to a love for creating music, for never giving up on his dream, and now, with his passing, he's teaching me the deepest language of the heart that bridges the dimensions of physical time and space. He's guiding me through grief and feelings of loss to embrace a new way of being connected—a letting go, and holding on, and staying open to joy and sorrow, and to trusting that all is truly well.

In listening to my own inner guide about the difference between "refined and defined," I can see an important distinction. The death of a child can *define* me, and I could become a woman who labels myself with that identity, or I can choose to see the many ways that the experience *refined* me, made me more aware and awake, added new dimensions of compassion, stripped away any layers of pretense, and opened my heart wider than ever before. If I choose to live my life trusting that I am being loved, and guided, and protected, then there has to be a blessing in all of this. I can choose grief as my teacher and insist upon my blessings.

Never Be the Same

Change happens

Sometimes fast, sometimes slow

So slow it sneaks up

And so fast the mind cannot grasp it

One a must-notice, cannot-miss change—

The other a slip-by-until-a-wake-up-moment change

Each moment, each day, one day to the next

Never the same change

And I say thanks for the variety and spice in life

This cannot-miss, heart-wrenching and shocking change

This rock-my-world change

This life-will-never-be-the-same change careens into my soul

Not a gentle, gradual getting-used-to change

One that buckles my knees

Rocks my world and

Shocks-my-system change

This no-warning change

Requires a new way of being

A retooling of my whole life

A life that will never be the same

Completions

Images of my roses

Buds to blossoms to rose hips ready to be clipped for new

growth

Chapters in a book

Leading to the final conclusion and closing

Celebrations and gatherings

Around a feast and then we are full and

There's a season to each new beginning

And its middle and it ending

So another beginning can bud and blossom and delight

Nature teaches me these cycles if I pay attention

Audiences applaud at the completion

And even with an encore we all know

It must end

I am paying attention

To the completions and the new beginnings

And I intend to savor all of the middle

The moments of Now

From beginning to end

Completions birthing my new beginnings

Dancing and Song

Dancing and song

Riding on vibrations of joy

Letting laughter lift our souls

To touch the angels.

Music opens my heart

And carries me into myself.

Not all music works it magic with me

Some sounds can grate and antagonize

So it's the tone and vibration I am feeling

Like all of my cells and atoms are dancing

I am transported to peace and joy

Grateful for the rhythm and pattern and instrument

For our voices,

For my voice...

For my Holy Om to and from the Infinite.

The Club

Welcome to The Club

New parents—an experience nothing can really prepare us for

Only having a child,

Becoming the mother-father

one-hundred-percent responsible person

Welcome to The Club, we say

That child, no matter how grown, always a part of us

Losing a child to death

Another experience nothing can prepare us for

Another type of Club

No one wants to join

And when you're in it

You know things only the other club members know

Once a parent, always a parent

Connected beyond time

Beyond genetics

Beyond dimensions

A bond deepened by death

I've learned this from being in The Club

Doing what he loved with those he loved—
Michael and Sammie in Stu's recording studio

Tuning in to Michael

My desire to connect and communicate with Michael grows stronger with each day. My mission is to dispel any doubt that this is possible for me. If others can do it, and I know this to be true, then I can do it as well. To say I've been consumed with studies of the afterlife would be an understatement. Within the first three months, I had read over 30 books on the subject and the research continues. Within six months, my Kindle library contained 46 books specific to this topic and is still growing. I've been googling scientific studies on communication with people who have passed. I find it very interesting how many ways are documented, and that the percentages are over 50 percent of people interviewed who say they are in direct communication with departed loved ones—a percentage that could be even higher if we were really paying attention.

The internet allows me to head down a discovery path that my heart is interested in exploring, take off on another path from there, which leads to yet another. One resource I discovered was AfterLifeTV.com, a site created by Bob Olson. He began exploring the subject 15 years ago when his father passed, and the interviews and information he has collected have become priceless to me. I've given myself permission to follow the nudges of my heart when it comes to learning about the afterlife. What a journey I find myself on—I feel like I need to drop breadcrumbs so I can retrace my steps.

Most lead me to the same conclusion which Michael Newton states in *Destiny of Souls,* "Survivors must learn to function again without the physical presence of the person they loved by trusting the departed soul is still with them. Acceptance of loss comes one day at a time. Healing is a progression of mental steps that begins with having faith you are not truly alone."

"A progression of mental steps which begins with having faith"—I find this comforting. My steps to healing are noticing the many ways I feel Michael's presence, tuning in, hearing his voice singing to me in my inner ear when I awake each morning, paying attention to synchronicities, and having a powerful intention to stay connected. These mental steps are building my faith and strengthening my new communication channels.

I have learned to listen when I ask him a question, to write down what I hear, and to trust. I pulled the following exchanges from my journal where I've caught the many ways Michael has made his presence known both to me and to close friends and family. I hear his voice singing to me and, a couple of times, clearly speaking comforting words. He answers me in meditation and in my inspired journal writing. I've recognized unexplainable coincidences, especially when we were doing all we could to bring him home to us the day of the accident. Friends who can see energies have described his presence with me and given me messages. And then there are the delightful hummingbird sightings.

A dear friend recently told me of vivid dreams she has of her dad on the other side. I love hearing these stories. I feel so much joy knowing that we are never really separated from those we love. I envision Michael on tour, singing with the angels, making people happy with his music and his loving, mischievous personality.

Having read multiple books on the subject, I feel much more certain of his presence as real and not just my imagination. I love when I get clear signs, and yet I am reminded that I'll see it when I believe it—not the other way around. I would love a vivid dream or an appearance. Perhaps those are also a matter of believing that's possible for me. I have no skepticism that it's possible for others. I believe souls communicate all the time. I just want to make sure I don't miss any of Michael's attempts to reach me.

Miracles and gratitudes have my attention. I read *"Meant to Be,"* a book loaned to me by a dear friend, whose miracle story with her husband after his passing is included in the book and was part of a TV special on angels. As I was reading each story, I found myself so moved by the unseen force orchestrating behind the scenes—a mystery I cannot explain even though I have my personal beliefs which sustain me. I have been writing down my own list of miracles that I'm aware of and grateful for. Kind of like whale watching—I really have to pay attention or I'll miss them. First there's just a puff of a spout, then maybe a roll of the back, and then the flute as they dive. Little signs are so easy to miss in the vastness of the ocean, unless I'm really paying attention.

I've been reading about after life contacts from several sources—some very scientifically documented and categorized, others more anecdotal. I feel these stories really inspire hope in those of us left behind when a loved one passes. I know I began to heal, and my grief began to ease, from the very first indication that Michael was just on the other side, and doing his best to let me and others know that he's present and filled with joy. I am writing down all of the stories I have. I love hearing from his friends of the many ways he's staying connected to them—dreams, hummingbirds, dolphins, soft rain out of nowhere, whispers, and always a song. Friends have shared with me similar dreams of him hanging out with them—very lucid, clear conversations. I would love a dream. So far that hasn't happened that I can remember, and this seems to be one of the key elements of being visited in a dream by a loved one— they are vivid and easily remembered.

I can still vividly recall when he came to me July 17, 1976, in my dreams, nine-months to the day before he was born. He was about two years old, and running to keep up with his two big brothers. He stopped at my side long enough to gain permission from me to join our family. I can still see that blond two-year old gazing into my eyes, and I feel my big "yes." I awoke the next morning knowing I had conceived, and predicted he would arrive on April 17, 1977. My belief that I needed a daughter was set aside, as I accepted his sweet telepathic request. We would joke with each other, as he grew up, that his feminine side was well-developed, so I got close to having a daughter anyway.

I'm grateful for the ways I feel Michael has reached through the veil. My first reading with a medium confirmed how much we all love and miss him. Michael used the image of a rainbow to express how we are all still connected, and there is no end to it. He said his accident was supposed to happen, and the chaos was needed, or he would have figured a way to get out of it. I'm not sure that's comforting to me. I would have preferred he stayed here. My overall experience from the reading was a peaceful recognition that the love I feel for Michael is matched by him, and our souls are working together somehow. The medium picked up that the energies of this world were very hard for Michael to be in. He is so sensitive and compassionate. He felt no pain in passing over, and his guides were with him at all times.

Playing his music helps me tune into his voice in my ear. I hear his songs in my left ear, and when I feel he is speaking to me, it's on my right, almost over my shoulder. Whenever I hear *"Our love is here to stay,"* I know this to be true—the love I feel for all of my sons is so visceral. I remember holding each one as a baby and thinking how lucky I was.

I recall watching a Hallmark movie, and a background song for a romantic scene began playing—an Italian love song Michael almost always included in his shows. I smiled, and said "hello" to him through my gentle tears, and then looked at the time: 11:11. I am now so drawn to nines and elevens, and see them way more than I ever did when I wasn't tuned in to them. I think that's part of the lesson—I can't notice something I'm not looking for.

The lyrics to *"Luck be a Lady Tonight"* came with an image of him entertaining, doing his cabaret show, still having a wonderful time, doing what he loves to do. I'm beginning to call this frequency he uses my "love channel." I am noticing a similar frequency, which feels like a "wisdom channel," that I can tune into more easily when I'm quiet. There's also what Mary Morrissey refers to as "CNN"—"constantly negative news" channel—which I do my best to tune out. Since our minds think in images, I find this channel metaphor helpful, especially as I am learning to tune into new ones from a higher dimension. Sometimes it's my gentle tears that let me know I've made the connection.

I firmly believe our loved ones are learning to break through the dense barriers to reach us, and praying we'll pay attention. We are working out our own language of Spirit, and when we make a connection, we must celebrate. When Michael was an infant, I had to learn to communicate with him. It's kind of like that now—some new channels and symbols to learn, and I am now the infant.

"If we can feed into a highly charged state of emotion during our grief, we can both heal and learn about our inner selves," says Michael Newton in *Destiny of Souls*. When I read this line, I realized how true it is for me. Somehow I knew my way through this was to fully experience the grief and demand that it bless me. At Stu's home one night, while helping with some cover art, sharing homemade soup, looking at photos of Michael, listening to his music, knowing how many lives he is still blessing, I felt the healing, and the beauty, and the perfection of it all. I am learning and expanding, and the broken places are filling with light. Most of my tears come from joy these days.

When reading *"Vibrating To Spirit"* by Kathleen Tucci, I confirmed my intuitive knowing that my ability to deal with and heal the pain of the physical void is linked to my ability to develop a new spiritual relationship with Michael. I can do this by paying close attention to signs and symbols, listening for his voice, building new channels for us to share beyond the physical dimension. This morning I could hear him singing *"Listen to your angels"* so sweetly in my ear. This walk of faith and trust keeps my heart open and feeds me. I miss him, even as I learn to recognize all the ways he is still here with me.

I have a burning desire to know all I can about the subject of afterlife communication in an experiential way, as well as the intellectual. I intend to pursue every possible way to stay connected to and communicate with Michael. I know his physical body no longer exists here in my space-time reality. How are our two realms interconnected? How does this connection to the other side work?

I'm told Michael is always with me. I have direct experience of hearing him loudly and clearly from behind my right side on two occasions. Within moments of my learning of his death I heard him say, *"I'm so sorry Mom. I'm so sorry."* And then, on Day 21, on board the cruise line, he reminded me to stay present to the beauty in front of me. I've spoken with him in my journal, and I've heard him singing to me from within on my left side every morning.

Michael can be in multiple places at once—this I do know. I get to be confined by time and space in my physical body, yet my imagination let's me go anywhere. I believe Michael now has freedom to express all of his talents, and all of his healing and nurturing qualities as well. I can see him clowning for the kids over there like he did with his nephews here, and doing his comedy routines as Kurt saw him doing in a vivid dream.

I have pulled into this chapter a collection of communications with Michael from my journal. Other than trying to introduce them so they make sense, they are unedited. Just straight out of the pages of my journal, but in italics to set them apart. You will see they are repeated in the Raw Footage section at the back of the book.

One of the first communications came after I specifically asked him, "How do I communicate with you, my dear sweet son? What is the channel?" *"Listen in your heart Mom. I am right here. It's okay to cry. It's okay to laugh as well. You are still the best mom. I love you."*

Watching a sunrise, sobbing, on board the cruise ship, I heard Michael's voice over my right shoulder as if he was standing right there. *"Mom! Pay attention to all the beauty in front of you. Don't miss it by being sad and wishing things were different. I'm right here."* He was a wise man. I immediately took in the amazing light of the sunrise over the ocean and was soothed.

At a regular book group gathering of close friends from my church, Michael chose to speak to Lisa who is very sensitive to energies from the other side. She had never met him. As we were taking turns catching up with each other's lives, Michael continued to speak to her, and finally she had no choice but to speak up through her own tears. She said he was insistent, and wanted her to tell us how hard he's been working to let us know he's present—all of the signs and coincidences. He also showed her how full of fun and life and magic he is—that he is enjoying the experience of not being tied to this three-dimensional world, where he struggled with the day to day. He truly did need to go—to be set free. Now he can be with any of us whenever we think of him and call him to us.

Speaking through others was wonderful, and yet I wanted direct communication with Michael—to know he is here and present from my own recognition, as well as from other sensitives being able to tell me about it. I began asking and engaging him. What is my channel? I have heard you, Michael, the day we learned of the accident. I heard you clearly over my right shoulder, *"I am so sorry Mom. I am so sorry."*

I asked questions with the pendulum when you were here with your body. I felt like I was getting answers from you. All of the miracles that needed to happen to bring you home. I feel you had a hand in all of it, as if you were orchestrating it from the other side, saying: *"Bring me home, Mom, bring me home."* I need to stay connected, and learn to recognize signs in this new place that I find myself in. Help me sweetheart. Help me. I love you. I am listening. I am here and open.

Thank you my dear sweet Michael for connecting with me so I could learn more. I love you so much!! What do you want me to do? *"Website; Write Books; Kurt—music; Stu—albums; Grams—comfort; John and Troy—connect; Sammie—love, love, love and enjoy and encourage and be there for her like you always were for me; Dad—forgive. Yourself—know you were the best, most loving mom I could have ever dreamed up. I did dream you up. Know we were a team and still are. I'm right here with you Mom. Never forget that. Listen and watch for me. You've been doing great, so keep on listening to your heart. Do not worry about anything. All is provided for. All is well. Give that big gift of your love to all who need it. Let it shine, let it heal, let it teach. I love you so much, always and forever and we will meet again. I promise. And for now, I'm right here loving and supporting you!"*

Michael, I love you. I believe you are in a wonderful love-filled space, and you can feel all of our love coming to you, enfolding you, from this side. Maybe it pales to the love embracing you on that side. Is there anything you want to say to me as I write?

"Have fun with Sammie for me tomorrow. She can use some of your wisdom. Go to sleep Mom. I'll see you in your dreams. I love you. You're the best mom. Take care of yourself. Trust that I'm okay, and pay attention to my songs I sing to you. I'm forever with you. Forever and ever. I'll love you forever. Cheer up! All is as is should be. All is well."

Woke up at 5:55 a.m. with Michael's angel song in my ears. I love that connection. Reading more about Gary Schwartz and his after life experiments. I have no problem believing all of this is true. Even more strongly now, because of Michael's passing, I have this strong desire to develop my own abilities of communication with the other side. It seems ironic to me that I want to ask him questions now. I was very mindful of his privacy while he was living here with me in the flesh. I believe he's still here, and also able to be anywhere else he chooses to be as well. So, here's my experiment. I'm tuning into Michael and asking some questions. I'll write what comes through.

Surroundings? *"Mostly right here with you and Chewie. The colors are more intense, and I have no need to sleep or eat. Just like I used to, I come and go, but I can be here immediately if you call me. I will always be able to hear you."*

Activities? *"Mom, the music is incredibly beautiful. All of the masters are here. I can hear and feel and even taste the music. Chopin, Strauss, Tchaikovsky, Beethoven, Bach, Jerry Garcia, Elvis, Jimmy Hendrix, Pavarotti, Puccini. I can play any instrument I want to. I love my bandoneon most of all. Thank you for always encouraging me."*

People? *"Yes, Aunt Betty is here, and so is Uncle Ed. Grandma and Grandpa Ortego, and Charlotte's little boy. I spend most of my time with family, and you and Kurt and Stu and Sammie and Grandma, John and Michelle. I'm watching out for Troy and Riley. I get to be the big brother in some funny way now. I'll be there tonight with the family at John's to celebrate his birthday early. Dad isn't handling this as well as you are.*

Have to go now. Off to a concert. Love you Mom."

Asked Michael what he can tell me about the best way for us to communicate. I sensed I had best grab my pen and journal. He's singing, *"Free from doubt and free from longing, come home to me, set me free..."*

"Hi Mom. You've noticed the way I use lyrics from songs I've recorded to send you comfort and love. I am always here and other places at the same time. Your thoughts include me and connect me. We are all connected through our love for each other. Our family knows how to love and be loving with each other. It's easy for me to connect in when there is so much

love. Use joy and laughter to open the channels of communication with the angelic realm. It is the surest channel. Gratitude and joy carry the same vibration.

Did you notice how often the Dalai Lama laughed in the film you watched? I was there with you. Yes, I loved the film and the director. I am teaching and learning and growing and feel none of the restraints from being incarnated. I know music in a whole new way, and see how it can heal, and align the very cells of the human body so they are back to their perfect pattern. Continue to work on your book about your process. It will inspire and help millions. We are a great team. I chose you as my mom and we grew together.

I am always with you. I'll meet you at the end of the rainbow. That is for now and future and always—the rainbow—joy, hope, light in all its dimensions, primary colors, rain clouds storming. This is a bridge of light to follow, and I am always there to meet you in this present time. I promise. Take my hand. I'm guiding you now. I love you forever. You learned unconditional love. You gave it to me. I give it back to you, and it grows for all of us to see and feel. Your way of coaching leads people to their own truth, and holds them in love's truth as they open. You are learning to trust even more the Divine side of your nature to lead you and provide for you. Each day is a gift, and you get to give your gift of unconditional love to the world. It makes a difference. I love you. Michael. I love you."

I wrote all of this down, and he continued to teach. I had interpreted, *"I'll meet you at the end of the rainbow, I promise you this,"* as a future promise for when I pass. He corrected me by saying, that the promise isn't for the future, but for

154

now. I loved the imagery of a "bridge of light to follow," right now in the present moment. These were powerful words for me to hear and take in. I'm in bliss and awe as I share this. It seems to be a message not just for me.

Michael talk to me about what you are learning. *"The thoughts of fear and doubt that came to you this morning— when those are present, fear and doubt, your connection to higher frequencies is kinked or filled with static. I experienced fear, and then when I ascended, it was instantly gone. Please know that I experienced no pain. I gave you the image of wings unfurling. It's the best description I can give. I am learning how to connect with you just as you are to me. We are on similar study programs. You are working for both of us on the lower plane. Fear isn't the big one for you. Doubt is where you've been stopped before, but not anymore. I'm here and we will conquer this together. Limit the TV. Increase the meditation. Get the CDs that work with brain waves. They will help. Keep studying and keep writing. Yes, I love to say hello through the images and energy of hummingbird. As you are teaching others about spiritual principles, I am helping. I love you Mom. I was ready for this new assignment. We were both ready. Listen to your angels. I am one of them."*

Several new poems have come through this week, and I'm feeling Michael nudging me along. *"Listen to your angels Mom. We are whispering to you."*

Hi my sweet son. I am very present to how much love we share, and how blessed I am that you are in my life. I have been cracked open from this experience of your death—this change of venue—this unexpected twist. I have made peace with our new circumstances. I do most of the talking. I listen for your voice on the inner wisdom channel, and your songs keep me company. I would love a conversation. We've had many over our time together before you passed. I did my best to listen for your dreams and encourage you. I still find myself seeing opportunities where you would shine as a performer. I would tolerate no criticism of you or your path. I was your protector—and now I feel you are protecting and loving me.

"I'm right here Mom. Right here. Always just a thought away. I love you. You will see the hand of God in all of this, I promise. And, I'll meet you at the end of the rainbow—full spectrum love. Always here, now. Kisses. Kisses."

I have faith, and I believe this to be true. I know his physical body no longer exists here in my space-time reality. And I wonder, "How are our two realms interconnected?"

Michael, your presence in my life from the beginning has been a blessing and a teaching. You didn't fit into any mold and you taught me so much about listening. Even now I'm learning to listen with new ears and see with new eyes. I want to explore the after-Earth, after-life-as-I-know-it realm. I want to sort out the facts from fiction, yet what is the difference really? Fiction often becomes fact when new information is revealed. The thought that we could fly used to be fiction—now we can. What if I could just as easily speak with you now as before? Is that possible? If it is, I dedicate my life to that exploration.

Am I picking up on one of our channels? I can hear a prompting from within. I hear the hippopotamus song and realize how you lit up the room again last night at the Christmas party. Everyone loves and remembers you. I love you—my dear sweet Michael—my angel of light and love—my teacher for what lies beyond. Help me give my gift.

"Listen to your angels, they know why you're here and what you've come to bring. I'm one of them, Mom, my dear sweet mom."

"Wow, wow, wow!" said Steve Jobs when leaving his body. "It's all a hoax!" said Roger Ebert, in his last breath of this life. Here's my question for you Michael. In my reading with JG, he said you appeared to him as a being who is teaching children, and there are rainbow lights all around you. In my reading with Saireh, she saw you as a WWII chaplain who was killed, reincarnated here with me, and now on the other side you are helping victims of current wars cross over. What am I to believe?

"Mom, it's all possible at the same time—not limited, linear, singular reality. I know you miss me. I know this was a big impact experience, and you signed on for it. You want to help people at the deepest, most profound level, and to do so from your own heart-felt experience. You and I, we are complete and one and always connected. I am here to help you help others. We are a team. The groundwork is being laid, and you just need to listen to your inner voice for what's next."

Woke up at 7:11 hearing *"Who can I turn to if you turn away?"* It's one of the more difficult songs for me to listen to. It brings up all of the "what ifs" and "how comes" that have no answers in this dimension, and change nothing in the overall scheme of things. I know Michael doesn't want me to go there. It distracts me from what I am creating—a now-new way of being in communication across the veil. That's where I need to start.

Last night I was speaking with Michael. Even now, I stopped writing to tune in. He's saying *"my romance doesn't need a thing but you,"* and it feels like he's leading me with his voice down a path, showing me all of the beautiful places and faces that have ever been created—both urban and pastoral, old and new—with rainbow skies. He's telling me, *"I can see everything beautiful that was ever created in all of its glory— music, art, buildings, creatures."* He's showing me the domain of dinosaurs. *"Mom, it's like a living beautiful museum—a mosaic of all the good we have created, and that God has created, and we are all part of it."* I could feel my vibration lifting, as I followed his teaching. *"It's like a living book of life, and any page you pick has a story to tell and a gift to give."*

As I was speaking to him last night, I wanted to know that he hears me, that he is really present in my life. So I got out my pendulum, and received a strong "yes" that he hears me. My intuition says "yes," and my heart feels the deep love we share. I love you Michael, now and always and forever, into infinity and beyond.

One morning, I went into our back meditation room to sit in the sanctuary space and connect to Michael from there. I asked him to show me one of his favorite places where he is, and he took me to the set of "It's a Wonderful Life" with Jimmy Stewart. He says he has the choice of seeing the movie being made, or watching the debut of the film with Jimmy himself. There is a wonderful joyfulness to his energy. He is full of life, and doesn't ever need to sleep. He says we need sleep over here so we can reconnect with that side and be refreshed while we are sleeping.

He is showing me his dance moves—Fred Astaire style. He's understudying with the best, and loves that he no longer needs to be concerned about making money—only with making music, and learning all he can about music, art and entertainment in their best circumstances. Now he's showing me his trick that he did on stage of jumping over his own foot.

On another morning, I woke up at 7:20 hearing, *"On this night of a thousand stars, let me take you to heaven's door."* Feels like Michael has been taking me on mini tours when I let my heart wander with his. So, I'm going to be still, and see where we go this morning.

Went on a beautiful ride on an avatar-like blue-feathered bird, holding tight to Michael, feeling the rush of wind in my face, then losing it all to left brain, and beginning again. Losing to distractions, and beginning again. Very patient is my guide.

My dear Michael, I miss you every day. I tear up often, flooding my eyes and my heart with love and memories, with wishes that I could have you here with me in the flesh. I'm so new, and feeling very unskilled with the after-life connection. Sometimes I feel right there, and at other times quite distant or blocked. I love the silent, still moments. How do I tap in, no matter who or what is filling my external space?

"Hi Mom. Be still and listen for me. I'm right here, right now." He's showing me an image of himself in the brown chair with his bandoneon and music stand. He's sitting erect and beginning to practice.

"Mom, I can pour myself into anything that brings me joy, and I cannot begin to explain how easy it is to be anywhere, everywhere, all at once, without limitation. I love you. Write your book—our book!"

"Mom, before I was born, I came in your dream. It's all a dream, and we awaken into such love and beauty when we drop the body. I'm here, there, everywhere. Teach yourself and others how to stay connected. Learn, and teach, and be the light you came to be. I'm your test pilot. We'll fly together. Hold the image. Edison was working on his next invention, a device to be able to speak to departed loved ones. Who else is on this path? Find them. Study them."

One evening I was watching Dr. Brian Weiss on Oprah, and hearing the story of woman and her sons each being contacted by her deceased husband, their dad, and each hearing a whisper in their right ear. He said the same thing to every one of them, "It's more beautiful than you could imagine. I'm safe. I love you. I'm always with you." Very similar to what Michael has shared with me. Weiss says that somehow when we connect, and are filled with the joy of that connection, we can find ourselves feeling even closer than we were in the flesh. I've experienced that.

Another time, checking in with Michael. *"Mom, you've always wanted to touch people at the deepest level. This is your path to doing that. I'm right here with you, supporting you all the way. Tell Sammie about it. Stay in touch with her."*

I asked him if he had just shown me a piece of life's puzzle. I saw that I'm here, but my soul is also there with him, as are all of our souls, and we are connected and communicating, like in the movies Avatar or The Matrix, when we're in two places. I'm seeing a cord connecting us from spiritual being to human experience. You, Michael, cut your cord for this chapter, and I'm still here, but I am also there with you. We are never alone. God is with us. I recognized that he was giving me the chant he recorded for the SLC choir.

I asked Michael again about suicide, and I got another strong "no." I also consistently get that same answer from the readings I've had as well. Michael was running, and frightened, and in a chaotic state of mind. He also acknowledges that it was his time. This is the part I have a tough time with. Seems like he still had so much living to do, and so many gifts yet to give.

I have experienced Michael stroking my arm, using my own hand to do it. I vividly feel his presence and his tenderness. I love hearing his songs several times during the day, and catching him digitally saying "hello" with 9s and 11s.

In my heart meditation one morning I felt a presence and a strong connection to Michael. I asked him how I can recognize his energy and essence without his physical body. He explained that the body is like a familiar outfit—something to be worn—but it's the wearer of the outfit who matters. I can reach him on my heart channel. I told him I want to learn and teach this. He just showed me masses of people in comas, and those on the other side are trying to get through to them, and only a few are awake enough to pick up their signals.

"Keep trusting yourself and our connection Mom. I am here, and this is our work to be done together. Keep writing the book. It is the first of many. Listen to your angels Mom. I'm

one of them. Always was, and I tried to stay as long as I could before going back home. You are also here with me. Someday you'll understand. Right now, you just need to trust, and listen, and write. I love you Mom. We're a team. Always have been. You can let go of any worry about your real estate business. It is solid and will flow to you. Just stay in grace and receptivity. Let go of worry. Make the phone calls and visits you get nudged to make. You have a whole team over here supporting you."

Another message captured in my journal: "Hi Mom. You're doing great. I catch you when I can. Good job working with Scott on Saturday. Help him keep his dreams alive. You and I have the same tender heart. It's what makes you a good mom and grandmother. Look at all the people you help.

I couldn't really grow up in the traditional sense over there, and here I am able to just be me, and it's perfect. No stress. Earth school is filled with the dark and the light—duality— good and evil—it's all shadows, and we learn to love, and add our song to a concert that never ends—and when we drop our bodies—our love stays. I love you."

What was our contract? What did you come to teach me? "Unconditional love. You taught it to me, and I experienced it through you, and passed it on to others. I've taken it with me, and use it in my work over here. You agreed to let me go early, and promised to use the pain of my death to grow your heart, and deepen your practice, and teach others to heal by learning how to stay connected to their departed loved ones."

One morning I asked him to show me some of his world like he did before. Here's what I received. "I'm showing you dolphins *and whales up close, and they are able to share communication with all of us. Look at the beauty of the hummingbird as it rests on my hand. There is no fear here. The beauty you love on Earth is magnified and always just a thought away. Lights and music and all the animals and architecture and beauty of the world from every century and civilization, many no longer even a remnant on Earth, are all here in all their splendor. I love you Mom. Listen for me as I sing to you and watch for me as I wink at you in numbers."*

Just completed a 20 minute meditation, and Michael kept popping in. It was quite pleasant. He thanked me for bringing his body home. He showed me that he was here with us the whole time. He was sitting in the room with his body, and then he would sit with Kurt and me to help with the photos for his service, and then he would hang in the kitchen. He was very happy that I managed to get him home. I told him it was one of the hardest things I've ever had to do. He flashed me photos of himself as a baby. I felt him in church with me this morning, and here with me in this room meditating along side of me.

I'll often get messages as I write. *"Focus on what you want. That's the antidote for most, if not all, of what ails us. Keep journaling. This is one of your best ways to hear me. Listen for the music—that is always me, and I love connecting in that way. Numbers 9 and 11 are easy winks from me to you. Images of me—when you sense me sitting next to you or draping my arm around you—that's me. Tune in and trust. Fear and doubt cause so much static that signals don't get through as easily. Heart meditations clear the space. Daily take time to go into heart silence and listen. I'm there, and so*

are many guides and angels loving and supporting you. Keep
moving forward on the book and the gatherings. I love you.
Your wealth is in the loving relationships you have created.
Nurture them. Focus on the good, and the sweet, and all the
ways you can serve the light. I practiced my music daily when I
was with you, because it was my passion. You must practice
daily connections. Writing and teaching are your passions.
Practice. Big hug."

So those are the messages I've captured in my journal. I
consistently hear that he loves being able to be anywhere,
everywhere all at once—he is no longer limited. This is
consistent with what I have heard and read about the afterlife.

You Woke Me Up

Your passing from this life

Woke me up

I discovered untapped strength

I found courage

I fell into vulnerability and arose softened

Your death stretched my boundaries

Of known and unknown.

You speak in new channels

I listen from new ears

I see with new eyes

I speak from raw now-ness

You unleashed my pen.

You've taken me to new joy

And to the depths of sorrow

You showed me pain and soothed me.

I'm learning acceptance and serenity as a practice

Suffering is only optional, not mandatory

You woke me up to me

I thought I knew.

Now, knowing turns to mystery

You woke me—I love you.

Peace in My Heart

Oceans and rainbows, starlight and moonlight

Meadows and fields of green

Valleys and mountains, rivers and streams

Shelter from the storm

Blessing and protecting

Guiding and teaching

Keep us safe and keep us warm

Prayers in song and music

Love songs and ballads

Lighting our way through the darkness

Giving us hope for a better way and a better day

Symbols of peace and love fill our songs and soothe my heart

Thank you for the music created through us

The beauty that unites us in song

And the peace it brings to my heart

Anywhere Everywhere

Anywhere everywhere all at once

Imagine

Omni-tasking awareness

Here there now here nowhere

Boggles mortal mind

My attention so specific

My children, three sons

Shot forth from my heart

Free yet never separated

Knitted within my womb

From my flesh

I belong to my mother grandmother lineage

Knitted in their wombs

The seed in the seed in the seed

And the blueprint a heavenly design

An idea from Divine creation

Flesh just the canvas upon which Spirit paints

Rainbow essence

Stardust

And my son, my precious son

A gift from anywhere everywhere all at once

Now here

Living with Resh

Lyrics on envelopes and scraps of loose paper

Tiny writing in pencil that only he could decipher

Towels everywhere—always a fresh one every day

Clothes everywhere—whatever was in the clean pile

Or didn't smell too bad

Unless on stage – then very put together, prepared, polished

Music mastery—practice until it becomes body cellular

memory

Repeat, repeat, repeat, repeat again

Wade into his room through microphone cords, speakers,

Stacks of music, CDs everywhere

He came to me in a dream—

Trying to keep up with his older brothers

Named by them after Life Cereal commercial

Our Peter Pan—flying on to his next adventure

Blessing us all by his presence

Showing up in the cooling, calming breezes

And hummingbirds of joy...

Missing You and Finding Me

Missing you and feeling for your presence

Moments in the silence,

Turning within

Deep listening

Waiting for the awareness

Images and memories and lyrics repeating in my heart

Tears of sadness and gratitude

Sometimes new vistas flood my inner world

You taking my hand

Leading me through a garden

Flying me over rainbow skies

And fields of greens and blues

My world altered with your passing

I am missing you and finding me

Feeling your presence

Wishing for more

Looking Back—Looking Forward—
Looking Within

What is the measure of a life well lived?

If today was my last one

Would I feel complete?

My sons know I love them

These amazing men who chose me as their mom,

I see the way they love their own sons and I say thank you

My mom and sister and niece and nephew know I love them

My dad knows and my Louisiana family knows

My friends and clients know I care

To leave the world a little better because I was here,

I hold that as an intention

Each day is a gift

May I remember that and treat it as such

Is love the legacy we leave?

Is that the measure?

To live and love fully?

If today was my last one

Would I feel complete?

Endings and Beginnings

Endings and Beginnings

Completed the last journal

Captured the precious journey of the first nineteen weeks

Walking the new path with Michael

Learning a new language

Paying attention to nuances

Watching for signs

Noticing how present I am to the love of a mother for her son

Even when he has passed from my sight

I hear musicians being interviewed and I think of him

And weep for our loss

I hear a tenor sing an Italian aria

And my eyes fill up

I see a young man crossing the road

And I catch my breath

I find cards and notes he wrote

And I miss him

Learning and loving and ending and beginning

Making Sense of It All

Remembering the first time I looked into his newborn eyes

So peaceful, so awake, so aware

Taking it all in

I called him my Buddha baby

Making sense of it all—this human experience

This world of contrasts and opposites

and things that go bump in the night

Nurturing and protecting and encouraging

and teaching him as his mom

Appreciating and marveling and basking in the joy of his being

As his friend and admirer and number one fan

Grateful for the moments we shared in the time that we had

As we both did our best to make sense of it all

Parent and child, mother and son, friends and roommates

And now, as I celebrate this first birthday

with him no longer here in the flesh

No longer able to look into his eyes or hold him in my arms

I do my best to make sense of it all

To trust and to know and to sense the Divine in it all

To stay peaceful, awake, aware and take it all in

This human experience we call life

Knowing Who and Whose we really are

And that someday I, too, will return home

And then, perhaps, it will all make sense

Michael Stories—

Celebrating a Life Well Lived

We gathered at our little church on July 30th to celebrate Michael's life, to honor him, remember him, tell stories about him, and to wish him well on his new journey. The sanctuary could not begin to hold all of the people that showed up, so over half had to stand outside and listen to the service over the speakers set up for that purpose. I estimate over 400 people came from all of the circles Michael's life had touched.

We laughed, and we cried. We prayed, and we listened, and we held each other. I was surrounded by so much love and tender caring. Sitting between my two sons, Troy and John, breathing in the beauty of the flowers and photos, and seeing Michael's beloved bandoneon on the altar, hearing his singing in the background, I accessed a strength within myself that came from knowing that the bonds of love can never be broken. Sadness and joy, pain and peace, hugging and being hugged—I let it all in.

Michael sang at his own memorial. Stu directed the sound, and as people were gathering, he played the Broadway standards that he and Michael had recorded together. During the service there were more songs performed by Michael, one of which was *"You'll Never Walk Alone."* Kurt wove together slideshow of photos with five songs from Michael's recordings, the final one being *"When Angels Whisper."* This was a collaborative where Stu wrote the tune, and Michael wrote the lyrics afterwards, not knowing that the tune was inspired by the passing of Stu's niece.

What follows is a blend of stories about Michael collected from family, friends, postings on Facebook, letters, and from some of those who spoke at his service. I am so blessed to be able to share from such a rich treasury.

Big brother Troy is ten years older, and John is six and one-half years older than Michael. Having been the baby brother for so many years, John was especially excited about becoming a big brother himself and having a baby brother to watch over. From the moment Michael arrived, whenever John would hear him crying or even starting to fuss, he would immediately run to find me. This was before the days of baby monitors, which allow you to listen in from a distance. John was my monitor, and a very dedicated one.

I remember the time he didn't run to find me first though, and took things into his own hands. I don't know how John even got Michael out of the crib, but he managed to do so. Michael was probably three or four months old, and I thought he was sleeping. We were visiting with friends on the outside patio deck of our home, late afternoon, windows open, and I didn't hear Michael wake up from his nap. Next thing I know, I see

John coming through the door, holding onto Michael like a rag doll, very concerned that he had been crying, and no one was paying attention. No harm done to Michael, and a lesson learned. I look at family photos, and if John was in them, you can bet Michael was stuck to him like Velcro. They were quite the team.

Michael and brother John

John now has three sons of his own, my beloved grandsons, and I adore watching him pour his love onto them. Here is a letter from John to Michael, written within hours of learning of his death. He read it at Michael's service, and gave me permission to share it in this book.

"My Little Brother. I'm devastated you're gone. When you were born I dialed the phone to each of my friends' homes to announce your arrival. I was so proud. Not long after, I taught you to say bad words on cue just to entertain them. When you told me at age four of something you'd done that I could not understand and did not approve of, I tried to convince you that you were both retarded and adopted. I hurt you and probably scarred you with this. From a young age you loved to sing, and I would tell you "stop, you're annoying". But we grew up together, and played, and loved each other as brothers are

supposed to. Some of my best memories are from days when we would challenge each other's skills at skateboarding or guitar playing—in both activities you quickly surpassed me. We'd listen to our shared favorite bands, and see them in concert together. Everywhere we went people commented on how much we looked alike. The girls always found you funny and cute, and I was proud to show you off to them.

We watched our parents split apart, and I know this was especially hard for you. Regrettably, in adulthood, you and I also did grow apart some. I always wanted more for you, Mike. I wanted you to conform to the world and give up your dreams of becoming a professional musician—or at least make them secondary to a more stable and promising career. I'd tell people "Yeah, I guess he's a very good, professionally trained singer, but I mostly just still hear my annoying little brother."

You were painstakingly devoted to your craft. You were amazingly hardworking and dedicated to mastering your musical instruments, and writing songs and music. You were a renaissance man. You blazed your own artistic trail. You never attained the recognition and appreciation you deserved. I was probably, aside from yourself, your worst critic. I'm sorry I was so rough on you. I guess on the one hand I wanted you to find something else to hang your hat on, while on the other hand, if you were going to be a musician, then I wished you'd create music with more practical popular appeal.

I was not aware of the torment you were suffering. I would have been more empathetic. If you would have at any time asked me for help, I hope you know, I would have dropped whatever I was doing and rushed to help you. But it kills me you're gone now, and I'm too late. I'm not sure I could have *done anything more to shield and protect you from this sudden and tragic event. But, I am certain I could have been more kind and loving.*

You treaded so softly through your life. You never spoke an unkind word about anyone. You lived to make people laugh, to perform on stage, to entertain and inspire with your special gifts. You knew and understood your way. You lived true to yourself and true to your path. You honored your family and parents. You never, to my knowledge, intentionally harmed a living thing.

You leave us having been very honorable and completely loving. I understand the tremendous pain we feel with your passing is going to heal with time. But, may your memory never fade. You will be remembered in the hearts of your loved ones for the rest of our lives as the wonderful soul you are. You're free now of your earthly body—free of pain, free of fear, free of sorrow. Free to sing with angels, and play your music to a celestial choir. I hope I can catch a glimpse of your performance in a dream. And, I know if you can, you'll be looking after and protecting us. We're just surely going to miss you something awful, Little Brother. I wish I had told you this more often Mike... I love you."

Michael and brother Troy

His older brother, Troy, had the following to say at Michael's service.

"I just have a couple of stories about my brother. For me, he's Mikey. Mom was struggling, trying to figure out a name, and John and I used to have a ritual in the morning with the cereal. One of us would get the cereal out, and then the bowls, and then we'd see who was going to put it away. 'Well, I got it out, you put it away. No, you got it out, you put it away.' So, one morning we're eating cereal, and Mom's going, 'I don't know what we're going to name him,' and there was that commercial with this little terror of a kid, little rascal who didn't like anything. So anyway, 'Mikey, he likes it.' And Mike liked everything and everyone. He was an angel from day one. I don't think I ever heard him mutter an angry or a mean word about anyone. He's a beautiful example of how to walk this planet. Thank you for that brother.

He was also affectionately known as The Prince. And, we recall one time when he was probably eight years old, and we were probably still tying his shoes, and putting his socks on for him, and we were sitting around dinner chatting, and Michael just looks up and says, 'Excuse me, I'm out of milk.' We all got up, because the kid needs milk. And it just went on from there. It became a joke. I remember so many times at Thanksgiving coming home, and Mom's cooking these fabulous meals, and Mike has this way of just showing up when dinner's ready. And then, you know, there's a lot of production and washing dishes after. And, I'd instigate it by calling out, 'Mike, time to wash some dishes.' Stunned and surprised at such a suggestion, he would smile and ignore me, and continue to play music for us, and I would wash the dishes.

And life goes by, and you get busy, and you think you're going to get together, and I certainly wish I could turn back the clock, but I know he's an angel with angels, and I'm so grateful for him, and to have been able to be called his brother. And I'm so grateful we have the strength in our family to heal this. Thank you brother, I love you."

Michael, John, and Troy—three amigo brothers

I believe that the most important thing for children to know is that they are loved no matter what, and that they have unique gifts to share. This was a guiding principle for me as a parent. Michael knew he was loved, even though he didn't quite fit into the mold, so to speak, from the beginning. He was our prince, our youngest, our baby, and the one that tended towards worrying about things that most kids aren't even noticing.

He woke me up one night at age 12, in the middle of the night, to tell me that he had sneaked out to meet someone at the park and try smoking, and that he had lied to me. I had seen his alarm set for midnight, and questioned him about it, since he needed to get up around 5 a.m. for his paper route. He told me it was so he could make a request on the radio. This wasn't true, and the fact that he had to awaken me, because his conscience couldn't handle lying, was forever imprinted upon me. He couldn't stand deceit in any form.

Fear could certainly get a grip on him—fear that something had happened to me, or his dad, or his grandmother. When he was little, he worried about leeches in the river. Then he was concerned about heart attacks. When he was still in preschool, if he took a nap, and awoke no one in the house, even though we were right outside in the yard, he would be alarmed and in tears. As he got older, he worried about the planet. He felt concerned that humanity was wasting energy, and we were destroying our home. He feared that we would never learn to stop creating wars. He wrote songs about some of his fears. I'm not sure he ever felt completely secure except in our home, the only home he ever knew, having moved in when he was only ten months old.

Most kids cannot wait until they are old enough to leave home. Not Michael. He did not like the idea of leaving home. I remember when his brothers had both moved out. He was only 10, and he noticed that they would come home with bags full of dirty laundry, and head straight for the refrigerator, because they were starving. He asked me if he was going to have to leave when he was 18. I could tell he didn't want "yes" to be my answer.

However, when it came to making people laugh and entertaining, fear had to take a back seat. When he was on stage, he was fear's master. He had his first taste of watching live theater when his brother John was in a sixth grade play. We were sitting up close, and Michael was in my lap so he could see over the heads in front. His five-year-old imagination was captivated, fixed on watching not only his brother, but friends of his brothers that he knew really well.

He turned to me in the middle of the performance and declared, *"I'm going to turn into that when I grow up."* And he did. Watching Michael perform would light me up with a glow from within that is hard for me to describe. People would comment to me that they could just see how much I loved him by watching my face beam with joy. And it was so true. I loved every moment. He was so generous with his time, and played for many a gathering of my friends at home, or at fundraisers that I would volunteer him for.

My sister, Alorah Christina, wrote these words in her blog which I find inspiring and comforting. *"Naresh was 36—an opera singer, a tango musician and dancer, an actor, model and magical man. He was never of this earth—he was always uplifted, he was always light-filled, he was always singing or playing his music. As I drove up from Los Angeles to be here with my sister, I kept feeling inside—"He stayed with us as long as he could." My instincts kept saying that his exit was right. That he was one of those icons who was meant to die young. To never age. To never lose lustre. To never endure the death of life's dreams. As we have processed the death of this dear one, we have all been inspired by the grace it contained. The grace of getting to handle his death through the natural death care project, to not have to turn his body over to some impersonal mortuary, to not have to pay exorbitant fees, to be able to hold him, and love him, and let him go slowly. The impossible perfection of how it unfolded has given each of us trust in the process itself. Forever desiring that it never had happened, we can each also feel its perfect design."*

Michael's gifts were special. He was sensitive, and usually had a smile on his face. He was a good and loyal friend. I love the stories that I continue to hear about how much Michael impacted people's lives. Here are a few.

I received a letter from one of the residents of the Covenant Village of Turlock, a retirement village that Michael performed at several times. This is what Ken wrote upon learning of Michael's passing. *"May I thank you for sharing your wonderful son with us, the residents at Covenant Village. At his last performance with us (with his Venetian straw hat), he sang, at my request, his 'This is the Moment.' I was so moved that I left the auditorium without being able to find words of appreciation for so much beauty. This belated, and bit of inadequateness, is my attempt to thank him for bringing such brightness into so many of our lives...Weren't we fortunate?"*

Fortunate indeed. I so agree. Michael toured the west coast with a friend one year, and by himself the next, taking his music to over 50 retirement villages up and down the coast from Los Angeles to Seattle to Sequim, Washington, and back. He would spend the night on site, eat with the residents, and entertain them with his light opera, songs from the Big Band era, and those from his musical theatre performances. One of his trade mark songs was *'This is the Moment'* from his lead role in Jekyll and Hyde. He spoke many times to me of the joy he felt when he sang at retirement villages. I found a map of the places he visited on those two tours. He came back with a full heart, and an empty wallet.

I found Michael's application to America's Got Talent. He didn't make it to the finals, and took some time recovering from the disappointment. But, he rallied. In the application, when asked what made him start doing his act, and what drives him to keep pursuing it, his answer was, *"I love music, love the bandoneon, and from a very early age—probably five years old, have enjoyed entertaining. The music, the instrument, the use of my voice—all feel very healing to me. Last fall, and again this winter, I toured many of the retirement villages up and down California. The enthusiastic response I receive from these seniors who grew up with this music is beyond words. I've watched people come to life and replay memories that made them laugh and sing and dance when they could—even if it was in their wheelchairs. The joyful response from the audience brings me great joy in return. I've performed for weddings, birthdays, anniversaries, fund raising events, and always the gift I give comes back to me multiplied.*

When I was going through the many boxes of papers and music he left behind, I found a letter he wrote about himself to raise funds and explain why he dreamed of going to Germany. (He didn't squeeze the trip in before he passed. It was still on his dream list.) Here is what he wrote in an attempt to crowd-source some funds.

Germany or Bust? Help make a singer's dream come true.
Singing didn't come naturally for me. I was nearly tone deaf when I started in high school. My audio comprehension skills were also far below average, which put me at a slight

disadvantage in school. I was always the last one to get what was going on, and the last to finish my tests. How then, you might ask, did I become a musician? Music just wouldn't leave me alone. At six years old, while my older brothers were playing football on the field, I was sitting with the marching band making friends with the French horn player. When I got my first guitar at age 13, I would fall asleep with it and wake up with it next to me. I never missed a guitar lesson, and no one ever had to remind me to practice—more often I had to quit so my family could get some sleep. They converted the garage into a studio for my first band—The Blue Spoon. I began taking voice lessons, working with two great teachers over the last 20 years. I took every music course offered at my local community college, sang with amazing choral groups, and then turned to opera and classical training. I love music. I love writing it, performing it, practicing it, learning how to improve my craft day by day. It still won't leave me alone.

What is it about music? *It's transcendental. Everything is energy, and when you conduct and direct that energy towards a beautiful feeling, that is music! It can inspire, it can heal, it captures the emotions, everything improves when music is added.*

Of course, musical performance as a career has a reputation as probably one of the hardest things one can set out to do. Only a small percentage of people ever actually succeed at making a career in singing. There are so many reasons not to! I've heard them all, known the odds, and yet I'm still passionate about going for it—perhaps haunted by the ghost of perseverance. It seemingly requires a certain kind of madness to keep at it.

The bandoneon, which is that squeezebox I play, used primarily for tango, is a church and sanctuary in a box. The sound is such that it could easily be the portable outside church organ for a marriage or funeral. It was invented for the purpose of bringing the sacred church music out in the world, but it failed to take off in Germany right before the world wars, and the strange accordions somehow all ended up in Buenos Aires, Argentina, being used for the tango. My path to this instrument actually came through Germany. My Uncle Michael Naumer's father brought a beautiful concertina (which looks much like the bandoneon) with him when he came to the United States from Germany as a young boy. My cousin, Kurt Naumer, gifted it to me, and I taught myself to play it. Then tango entered the scene and with it, my love of the bandoneon.

Why Germany? Could it be the voice of the instrument calling me to take it home? Perhaps. There appear to be many people in Germany, and the rest of Europe, who appreciate and support really great music! My research indicates Germany offers more opportunities for a classical singer than does the United States. Many opera singers have started their careers in Germany, where the government actually subsidizes the theaters and requires that all opera singers are contracted to work for at least a year when hired. This applies whether singing as a soloist or in the opera chorus.

In addition to opera, there is much more work and support for tango musicians as well. So either way, I believe I will have more opportunity over there to truly live my dream of a successful singing career.

Why sing? Applause, Applause, Bravo? *In spite of all the sour notes along the way, the performances that went sideways, the sound systems that didn't work, the empty rooms, unimpressed critics, lack of payment, there are still too many beautiful reasons to keep doing it. I am talking about something spiritual. The gift of song and poetry is intangible, perhaps even priceless.*

Finding the joy of singing and sharing that with people who could use some more light in their life is what it's all about. It certainly isn't about looking cool on stage or feeling glamorous—takes just one wrong note to remind me of that. It's not even about the money, that's just the means to keep giving the gift I've been given. It's about bringing and sharing the light, transforming the demons into angels, or shining into darkness. Singing to people personally, in a small intimate setting, is for me one of the highest expressions of love. Despite the struggles, life has blessed me with a way to give back to the community. I create opportunities to give the gift of song, even on the street, which I do from time to time. I also find a deep joy and satisfaction in helping people with Alzheimer's, dementia, and Parkinson's through my singing. Studies have verified the magical effect music seems to have on the brain.

A new chapter. *It would be fantastic to be able to afford a nice place for once. I've lived in some pretty interesting places so far in my life. One of my favorites was a tent at Mount Madonna, in the mountains south of Santa Cruz, California. It was there, as part of a spiritual community, that I meditated daily for hours, and helped with everything from cleaning toilets to cooking the food. I washed my hands of course. I* wrote some interesting songs at the time. I took a vow of silence for several months and was given the name Naresh by the spiritual leader Babaji, a silent monk who has not spoken since 1952 and communicates by writing on a small chalkboard.

When I first moved out to live on my own, I found a cheap studio without a shower or hot water, set up for painters and loud punk bands to practice. It was all I could afford, and I squatted there until eventually the fire marshal shut the place down for not being up to code.

The real reason—too many hip-hop shows down in the basement of the Sacramento catacombs. The next place I rented put me into serious credit card debt, but it was a taste of the good life for three months. The place after that seemed nice because I could record there and at the time I didn't mind so much that the room I was sleeping in had unsealed sheets of fiberglass everywhere. It was later that I realized, after I got sick with pneumonia, that breathing in fiber glass night after night isn't the best thing for a singer. I moved home to save funds for Germany. Now the time has come—I have purchased a one way ticket. I need just enough seed money to get a good start.

What does SUCCESS look like? I'm not attached to the outcome. I have a dream of singing, and in the end, the road still points to Germany. My intuition and everything I read tells me something will happen over there if I only audition. The point is, if I am supported in launching my career in Europe, there would be so many more gifts to give; more shows, more beauty, etc. It's all about doing the same things I've been doing but finding the support to keep doing them.

Auditioning and being selected for venues in Germany, Switzerland and Austria would be a dream come true— allowing me to live truly independently. I imagine getting that first contract and then the next and the next. I envision renting an apartment and tango dancing with friends after performing in an opera or operetta.

There are hundreds of theaters and opera houses close together, and I can get to all of them fairly quickly by train. So success, for me, would look like a year contract of singing in an opera chorus, or as a soloist for a year, while I hone my tango chops on the bandoneon, singing at retirement homes and sharing the love and light. A beautiful life awaits the classical singer in Europe. I can feel it in my soul, and I would really appreciate the chance to make it mine!

Thank you so much if you can help this dream come true! Whatever you can give to help me make this happen is immensely appreciated!

God bless you!   Resh

Michael's childhood friend Terra wrote this to me. *"For me it seems odd to call him Resh or Naresh, because to me he will always be Mike, as that is how I knew him. When I was six, my parents moved to the Arden Park area. It was a very big change for me, and I didn't do well with change. It didn't help that it was the middle of the school year. I was painfully shy with people I didn't know, so it didn't make the situation any easier.*

Mike and I were in the same class. I was working on a puzzle—a puzzle he knew how to do, and I didn't. He watched me work on it, and try to figure it out, but I must have been moving too slowly for him, because he very abruptly walked over to me, physically moved me out of the way, and finished the puzzle. When he was done, he very frankly said to me, "See that is how you do it. Hi, I'm Mike Ortego." I was so shocked. I wasn't sure what to say, so, "Terra" is all that came out my mouth.

We were friends from that moment forward. Because of my friendship with him, I made many other friends at school. Every girl thought he was dreamy, and every boy wanted to be his friend. I just thought of him as Mike, my best friend. I never heard him talk bad about anyone, and when I would talk to him about someone making me feel bad, he'd always say, "Why do you care?" It always made me think, "You're right. Why do I care what they think?" That little saying helped me through all the moments a girl deals with with other girls, and I learned to not care. He was a gift for sure. He was special. Even at six years of age, he was wise and kind. It was so wonderful to see that life, and all its ups and downs, didn't change him—didn't make him hard and insensitive. He really stayed true to that little boy I had met when I was just six.

I remember Mike in his polo shirts, his perfect hair, his jeans and loafers. He could have been in ads, he was so put together. This made the 6th Grade Talent Show so shocking to all his friends, when he stepped out as Axel Rose on stage, and started to perform Welcome to the Jungle *from Guns N Roses. I knew in that moment Mike had made a decision to shed the pretty boy conformist image of himself. I just had no idea how far he would take it.*

After elementary school, my parents had divorced, and I ended up not going to Arden Middle, so Mike and I lost touch. I thought of him over the years, and in high school we reconnected. To my utter shock, Mike didn't look like Mike anymore, and he wasn't really friends with most of the kids we had grown up with. Mike had long hair, and was very into his music. I can remember staying up all night talking to him in his room about his choice to change. Once again, Mike didn't care what anyone else thought, including his family. This was him, and everyone would just have to accept it.

He was brave and true to himself in every way, and he taught those around him to do the same. I knew a shyer side of Mike that a lot of people, other than his family, didn't get to see. This shyer one was the one in his room, in his own head, working it out. He wasn't comfortable being thought of as a "Hot Dude," and he was terrible at public speaking. He would always get a big smile and giggle a bit while he spoke, stumbling if he was put on the spot. The performer was confident, but the boy in his room wasn't quite as put together.

He never was sure what to do with compliments. He would always turn red, and his head would drop, then his eyes would peek up at you, and he'd smile that million dollar smile, and I would see that six-year-old every time. It's not often in your life that you get to know someone, and get to be a part of their life for such a long time.

For me, he will always just be Mike, the six-year-old boy who rescued me from social oblivion, who called me out on my wild tales, and who treated me as a friend should—the one who I would sit with in his room. We would talk about our families, our concerns, our fears, and our joys, even as little kids. I have so many memories of Mike. I saw him every day for six years, and then on and off for twenty-four years. There were birthday parties, school functions, play ground antics, swimming, skateboarding, hanging at the park, walking home from school, hanging out at friends' houses, and each other's houses, and the list goes on and on.

But in it all, there was silliness and laughter always. I got to watch him grow, and shed one skin, and find his own skin, and I feel so blessed that I get to be one of the few that was a part of the journey from the very beginning. He really was something special, and I will miss him. He was a kindred friend for sure, and our spirits were forever intertwined at six.

I love that story because it reveals Michael's wisdom and compassion which began at a very early age. He sometimes struggled with being different. I remember asking Michael a few months into the seventh grade why some of his grammar school friends weren't hanging around our house as much. He proceeded to tell me that they were with the "smart" kids, and he was with the "dumb" ones. Shocked, I remember explaining to him that if the tests at school measured musical and artistic talent, he would be placed on the "smart track." He had already begun playing his beloved guitar, and no one ever had to tell him to practice. More likely we would need to remove the guitar from his arms after he had fallen asleep with it. In this instance, I was doing my best at self-esteem damage control. Right-brain brilliance can be over-looked in a system focused on science, math, and left brain measurements. I realize how truly brilliant and masterful he was and is. Michael memorized thousands of songs, many in foreign languages. He not only learned the words and musical scores, but then taught himself to play even the most complicated operas on the bandoneon. My good fortune was to be able to pour love on this child from the day he was born and watch him bloom. What a treasure.

His long time friend Sean shared a story with me as we sat on the front porch swing where Michael used to play his music. Sean is an amazing artist himself, as well as a musician. I remember the many hours they would spend together in high school. I wish I still had some of the videos and home movie productions they dreamed up together. We talked about how Michael has touched so many lives and always lived with such honesty and authenticity. Sean said he had some tough times in his teen years and felt like he just didn't fit in. He used the term "bent" to describe how he felt, and then told me how Michael's total acceptance helped him accept himself. "Bent" was no longer a problem, but instead became a beautiful asset to be treasured. Sean worded it much more poetically, but I could feel the positive impact that Michael's friendship had upon his life. While we were sharing, two hummingbirds swooped down and hovered for a moment. We both smiled.

I heard similar stories as people began calling and coming by to tell me about their relationship with Michael, or I would read posts on Facebook.

Selena, a friend from grammar school wrote: *"Why you, Resh Michael....why you? You were the kindest soul...your friendship started in 6th grade for me at a new school where almost everyone was mean. You were my first buddy. You were real. I remember times since we lived three streets from each other that I'd be sad, knocking at your door and you* weren't home....but your parents would say...you wanna come sit in his room and listen to his music? Even as young as 10 years old you were such an earthly gift. I am so saddened that your time on earth is gone, but I know someday I'll see you again. I hope your settling in where your spirit has gone...."

Alice wrote: "Not only was Resh Michael incredibly sweet, he was also very, very fun. I didn't know him past high school for very long, but when we were teenagers, Resh was always down for hi-jinks. I have one especially fond memory of him striking hilarious poses while my sisters and I sporadically shone a flash light on him as we were all hanging out in a pitch black room. Each time the light shone on Resh, he was doing something more and more crazy. I couldn't stop laughing that night. You will be missed Resh Michael!!"

A friend of his named Dean, whom I have yet to meet, posted the following on Michael's Facebook. "Friends of Naresh Michael Ortego Resh Michael. It is my displeasure to inform you that he died a couple of weeks ago in a car accident. Damn cars. I remember being at his aunt's house where he was living, couple times, and walking with him in the trails behind the house, and us putting our arms around each other, and him saying to me about how it's unfortunate that us with our arms around each other might feel a bit uncomfortable to our American sensibilities at the moment (we remained arm locked and kept walking and talking), and that it's in Italia! that men are men, and not afraid to lock arms around each other and walk around the streets. He touched you. He made it okay to touch. He penetrated, he did. What a deep man. His self-expression was honest and inspirational and FUN. Someone else on his Facebook pointed out how fun he was.

First to go to the Fun. Fun immediately. So inspirational. Keep it fun people. Life is short. I love you Naresh (or Michael...I want to call you Michael but dammit, our first meeting at an Old Ironsides open mic, all those years ago involved you telling me you were Naresh. So, it remained first impression imprinted...Nar Nar. I love you."

James, a dear friend and drummer in one of his bands wrote: *"With a heavy heart and great sadness, I say Rest In Peace to the beloved and gifted Michael Ortego, known in the music and theatre world as Resh Michael. He was one of the kindest and warmest people I knew. He had a heart that was truly open to people as well as to the call of his inner genius, which he shared with the world and with those lucky enough to watch him. His voice was of a caliber that many of us had never heard, and it lifted us up. I've been crying at the thought of the songs he will no longer sing, but I rejoice in the memories of grace and beauty which he shared with me and countless others. I'll miss you, brother."*

And from another musician friend named Christopher whom I've never met. *"I met Naresh in and about the Sacramento open mic scene about ten years or so ago at the Fox and Goose. He was an individual you wanted to rub elbows with, but not follow as an act. The last time I talked with him was at a Christmas party two years ago, and he introduced himself as "Mike." I knew that I had known this dude from somewhere, and it did not take us long to figure out our musical connection. I think when he said, "Hi, I'm Mike," he knew his cover was blown. This dude used to get up in front of a handful of songwriters, plug in an accordion, and rock the **** out of it without worrying about what people thought of* *him. His smile had natural gravity. He could not hide his natural affinity for performing and for performing artists. May you rest where you like Naresh. I am certain that we will meet again. Thank you for always being yourself. Bye bye for now.*

Daniel Zuckerman, his friend and violinist, shares about Michael and practicing. *"Resh would show up for practice like he had just fallen out of bed, unshaven, dozing through rehearsal, and then suddenly he would just pop in to a different gear. It's so strange that cars were around at the end here, because he was just like a race car that could go from zero to 60 with the snap of a finger. Sometimes we would tell him, 'You don't have to sing full out. It's just a rehearsal.' But his response, 'No, that's fine,' or at a dress rehearsal, and he'd be going full bore, and we'd tell him to save it. And there were just times when he did not know how to 'save it.'*

Hi musical friend Winko tells the following story. *"I was in a trio with Michael and Daniel, and we would play various clubs and special events. I started my career as a one-man band probably about the time Michael was born. He came to me about five years ago, searching for 'the way,' and ended up showing me 'the path.' There's an old Zen saying that when the student is ready the teacher will appear. And the best student ends up teaching the teacher. And another saying is, 'No prophet is accepted in his own home town or by his own family, because they all think he's crazy.' And so if anybody tested, or doubted him, or tried to sway him to be doing something else, don't despair that you didn't believe in him, because that is the true test of a prophet that makes him worthy of the title, and that was your job to test him. And success is nothing more, nothing less than your best effort.*

Money, fame, all of that stuff is a by-product of your best effort. And that's what I learned from Resh the Prophet."

From one of his best friends, Ben. *"What do we say between the songs? We were so bad at it. I remember a Blue Spoons gig in 1996 where we were tuning our instruments and it turned into a jam session. And after it was over, Michael exclaimed, 'That was the key of G.' I'm very blessed to have shared music with Michael for over 20 years. I miss him a lot. From Colossians 3-4: Put on therefore as the elect of God wholly and beloved bowels of mercy, kindness, humbleness of mind, meekness and long suffering. I wrote this about two or three in the morning, which is when Mike is most active in writing.*

One night, Mike, me and Darren, Matt and Ian, we jammed at Mike's until the sun went down, and the neighbors yelled at us. Exactly 10 o'clock, the neighbors yelled at us. Every night. We practiced a lot. Five nights a week sometimes. This one evening, after we rehearsed, we went to a party. I don't remember the party, but I remember coming back to the Ortego house, where we had nailed carpet to every square inch of the garage, and even wrote a song about it. And we snuck back into the house, very, very quietly, just turned our amplifiers up ever so slightly, and Darren sat at his drums, pulled his brushes out instead of drum sticks. We were in mid-down stroke of the first note, and Robyn opened the door of the garage and said, 'You've got to be kidding me.' We all just looked at each other, and she was right, time to go to bed.

I believe Michael, my dearest, sweetest friend, was chosen by the almighty hand from above to give to his family, his friends, and anyone who knew him even for five minutes, a gentleness, a patient friendship, heartfelt compassion, and kindness that is rare and meek. Michael was the most humble of friends, and his true love shown in the way he conducted his life long after, to give the gift of music to those who would simply listen. There is not a single musician in the entire city of Sacramento that I know who has achieved more on their own by way of pen and guitar, or that box I could never pronounce the name of.

Last time I saw Michael was at Darren's house. He sat next to the fire in the back yard, and he sang songs to us for at least a couple of hours. And he told me, it's the word 'band,' and then you have to sound like an Italian saying 'onion.' So it's 'band-own-e-yon,' or something like that. He left me a gift of music that I will truly be grateful of for the rest of my life, and I will make it my duty to pass along the stories of his incredible friendship. He made it his duty to suffer and compose, to rehearse, to perform, and to be the best musician he could be. And his long suffering, and love of music, did not go unnoticed. He left for us an incredible catalogue of works."

From a woman named Atousa, who took the time to write to me about Michael, when she learned of his passing. She captures the way Michael was able to listen. His gift of being present is hard to describe. Here's what she wrote. *Hi Robyn. I first met your son at an ARC theater play.... what a voice, and handsome too! I was dabbling in some stand-up comedy, and during an open mike show, he happened to be there. After I was done, he took the time to come over, to talk with me, and encourage me to move forward with theater and comedy. Soon after, I married a man, to whom I am not married anymore. He hated theater. He hated my involvement with it.*

199

So I abandoned it. During my short marriage, I reached out to Michael, and he was so beautiful and humble and encouraged me to go and explore theater again. You know, people don't look at you any more—and though I didn't have much of a friendship with him, when he looked at me, he really looked, and I could see that he really saw me—all of me. So for these small beautiful moments that he gave me, thank you for bringing him into the world, and allowing me to be able to feel those moments, that I very rarely experience. I am 4 months pregnant with a son now, and your courage just brightens my whole soul.

From his dear friend Jamie who didn't hear about his death until almost a month later and couldn't figure out why he wasn't returning her calls or emails or texts. She writes: *"One of my favorite memories of Michael was the day we rode to the river. The sun was setting, and we got off of our bikes to watch the sunset from the water. I had been going through a messy separation, and Michael totally cheered me up. In that moment, watching the sunset with Michael, I remember thinking, 'this is as good as it gets.'*

Last night I was almost asleep, and I was subconsciously thinking about the accident, and started to feel really sad. I so clearly could hear Michael saying, "Don't go there, it will only bring sadness. Think of our happy times." It was surreal, and what I've been hoping for—I HEARD him. The weight of the situation was so intense that I couldn't bury it. I decided to open up, and let it out. So I closed my eyes, and let go of my earthly restrictions. I saw Michael. He reached out his hand to me. He was smiling so big, and his happiness was so radiant that I actually felt it. He said he was having a glorious time and seemed so very free. The tears rushed down my face, and I told him again that I missed him. Michael has been my teacher. I still miss him terribly and always will.

Excuse my pouring out my heart, but Michael's memory deserves my honesty and vulnerability. I was talking with my mom this evening about Michael—allowing the hurt to resurface, accepting it...sort of. Later I was in the laundry room, and I voiced my frequently muted thoughts, "Michael. I just miss you." In that moment I thought how I'd love to "notice" him. In the same moment, I decided to look at the clock—hmm... 11:45—your Facebook post crossed my mind—11's and 9's. "Hi Michael," I grinned. He always had that effect on me.

Sometimes I have trouble explaining Michael to others. Different doesn't quite do him justice. Nor does weird, although I love weird. Maybe other-worldly. But tonight it came to me—a simple saying but perfectly fitting—Michael was and is a breath of fresh air—pure hearted.

He had that actor's good looks. I forgot sometimes, then I'd really look at him. Even other men noticed. I always felt very, very lucky to have his friendship. Lucky just to have known him. I see his face in yours—and in sunsets, and all things that are beautiful. I think of him every day, usually many times. I'm thankful for knowing him. He's taught me a lot in life and passing.

From his friend Athena, whom he helped with her bid to become a cooking celebrity. He videoed her cooking, and spent hours editing the material for her. She says: *"The night I found out he passed I had a dream about Michael...and my Mom who has passed was there too. I was in a coffee shop, and he grabbed both my hands,*

201

and said, "I'm right here...come sit with me." We sat on the couch, and he gave me a big hug, and told me with his soft voice and giggle, "Don't worry it will be ok...I'm still here"...after that I saw my Mom and she says to me,"I'm here to fix everything and sort it all out...it's ok...."

Stu worked with Michael as a friend and musical collaborator. He spent hours and hours creating Michael's Legacy Collection CD set that they had been working on for months prior to his passing. Stu says losing Michael was one of the hardest losses he's had to bear. They spent hours together in his studio, and became the best of friends. Without Stu's help, much of the music Michael was in the middle of creating would have been lost. When I visited Stu's studio for the first time, I could see why Michael loved spending time there. They would get together late at night and spend time creating musical tracks. Michael was a perfectionist. When Stu showed me the amazing complexity of how tracks are laid down, I gained even more appreciation for the talent of this man I got to call my son, and the special relationship the two of them shared. We watched video footage of Michael's unfinished cabaret show, with Sammie and Scott playing their parts to Giovanni, his central character. What a comedian! He had removed parts of the video to shorten it for sending to cruise ship booking agents. Even with the cuts, we could catch the one-liners he was dropping, as he tried to woo the waitress (Sammie). I have the entire cabaret show script as he had written it out. I remember listening, as they would rehearse in our living room.

Whenever am tempted by thoughts of blame, which I know better than to listen to, I find it helpful to remember the example Michael set of acceptance. I found this quote from him on a yellow pad in his tiny writing, *"When you really love someone, it's unconditional. There's no such thing as flaws. We're all working on ourselves...and everyday's a new chance to grow from mistakes with compassion."*

And here's another paragraph he had written about his love of Tango, and the people in that community. I read it at their gathering in his honor. *"I'm a very private person. I keep a very low profile; even my music has still remained unpublicized for the most part for the time being. This morning I woke up asking again, "What is it that I want, or what do I not want?" Thinking that if I knew exactly, life would be easier. They say it's especially important for an Aries to know what he wants, which I am, born April 17, 1977. I know that I want to surround myself with positive, healing people who really care about humanity and the planet. I want to feel hopeful for the future somehow, somewhere, with people who are creating this together. I believe there are many paths to unity. How does my background as a sensitive massage practitioner and musician come into play on a bigger level? For now the natural evolution of tango has been connecting me with different communities who all share a sense of refined taste in everything from wines to graciousness.*

Important to remember we are not stagnant fixed identities, but a precious being in process that remains growing, like a beautiful unfolding melody or whatever magical metaphor reminds one of who we might really be. I choose again to identify with greater divine presence in all of us, and I share this with you from my heart. Your heart is my heart. Best love, Michael Ortego aka Resh."

Michael and his mom

The Final Curtain Call

Thirty six years—such a short life. Yet Michael didn't waste time. No TV for him. Nothing held more interest for him than his own practicing or writing or reading or meditating. He was preparing for so much, and so full of ideas and enthusiasm. As you can see, people loved him. And I love the many stories told about him—sweet loving stories, funny stories, stories of how he cared about others, how he listened and tried to help, how he tried to make sense of this world. At his celebration of life service, I heard new stories and some favorite familiar ones. The story that is most difficult to tell is the one that follows.

I had to piece this story together from reports, and intuition, and mediums, and conversations with Michael on the other side. It is the story about the last few hours of his life—the hours, that if I am not mindful, will spin me into anger and regret and blame and deep, deep sorrow. It's about the circumstances leading up to the end of his life as we knew it. I am reminded that what truly matters is how he led his life, not how it ended.

In the Unity church that I attend, we state at the beginning of every service that "You are here not by accident, but by Divine appointment. We are glad you kept your appointment to be here with us today." It begs the question, "Are there accidents? Do we have Divine appointments to keep?" When I am faced with the "accident" that claimed Michael's life, I have to ask myself, "Was this a Divine appointment?" The answer I choose to gather evidence for makes all the difference to me, and to my peace of mind. I also appreciate the distinction between evidence and proof that I learned from Bob Olson, in his new book entitled *Answers About The Afterlife*. He states that evidence is not the same as proof. You can present the same evidence to multiple people or juries, and their interpretation of what the evidence proves will vary depending upon their belief systems and point of view.

Here is the evidence that I was able to piece together. Michael had not slept for over five days, most likely closer to seven. He had been staying in Santa Rosa with his cousin Kurt for ten days, when I got a call from him on Friday night, as he was driving home. He was having some frightening beliefs that people were following him, and that I was in danger. He spoke to me on the phone from his car, and was concerned about coming home in case they were watching him. I knew this wasn't a normal state of mind for Michael, and I stayed on the phone with him until he made it into our driveway around 11:30 p.m. He hadn't slept in a couple of nights. We sat and talked for an hour or so, and he went to his room to try and get to sleep. I heard him in the night, and learned the next morning that sleep had evaded him once more.

On Saturday, he drove to get a massage from his friend Al, thinking that would help with the insomnia. On his way back, he sideswiped another vehicle. No one was hurt, but when he got home, he told me he was not safe to be driving. I thought maybe getting his room cleaned up and organized might help him sleep, and he agreed, so he accepted my invitation to help sort through the mess that had overtaken his bedroom. Saturday, Sunday and Monday were spent cleaning, and tossing, and making headway. He would meditate to see if he could get centered and successfully fall asleep. He reported that he would get to the very edge of dozing off, and then come back. I could see how tormented he was. I drove him for another massage on Monday evening, and then his friend was to drive him to his step-mother's office in Cameron Park for an acupuncture treatment on Tuesday. That was the plan. He called me Tuesday night to say he was staying a couple of days at his dad's in Pollock Pines so he could have another treatment. It's the last time I spoke with him.

I have since done some research on what can happen with long term sleep deprivation, and it's not pretty. The symptoms include severe paranoia, hallucinations, fear of being pursued by stalkers, a black pit of exhaustion, nightmares, and vulnerability to impulsive suicide to escape the pain. These are all linked to REM sleep malfunction. I had no idea what he was dealing with when I kissed him goodbye on Monday evening.

In addition to lack of sleep, he had been reading books and doing research on the internet about extra-terrestrials called tall whites and tall grays. I remember him telling me about a book on the subject that he said was non-fiction. He gave it to his grandmother to read. She felt sure it was fiction, but Michael believed the stories and events to be true. Combine this study with lack of sleep, and you can see the toxic cocktail of fear being brewed. Apparently, Michael believed he had been targeted by these ETs, and didn't know how to escape. He thought they had implanted worms into his arm and his ear. He had attempted to cut the worms from his arm, and then woke his dad to ask him to take him for help in getting the bugs out of his ear.

On the way to the ER, Michael changed his mind about going, but his dad didn't stop and turn around. I'm sure he felt it was best to get him some help. When his dad slowed down to take the exit to the hospital from the freeway, Michael jumped from the moving vehicle and ran. His dad could not get him to return to the car, and eventually left him to get assistance. Michael must have believed that aliens were chasing him, and he couldn't trust anyone. Whether he intentionally ran into traffic, or was chased into it by imaginary aliens, the result was fatal.

So, I'm back to my initial question—do we have divine appointments to keep? Did all of this chaotic build up have to line up the way it did so that Michael could "go home" to the spiritual world? When I asked him directly in a meditation, "Michael, why did you leave the way you did?" Here is what he answered, "*It was an opening in time and I had an appointment to keep. If I had stayed home here, I couldn't have gone. I actually needed Dad to not listen and to leave me so I could take the exit. Try to let him off the hook. I know you carry anger towards him.*" He needed his dad to not listen, and to leave him, not something I could have ever done. I would have stayed by his side no matter what and talked him through it. This is not to say his dad loved him any less, just that my nurturing, protective, mom energy would have me sit next to him until the sun came up if need be.

I've heard from others that his dad believes Michael came to their home intending to take his life. I've struggled with his story, and the anger it stirs up in me. I know my son, and this was not an intentional act. When I look from a higher perspective, which is where I turn to for guidance, we were both correct. I could see that if this was a divine appointment, then Michael's soul was calling his spirit home, and in that story, the plan was followed.

The Michael who lived with me, who loved to entertain, who loved people, and cared deeply for his friends and family, the Michael who was making plans to work on a cruise ship, and was writing a new cabaret show for Las Vegas, who was planning to record more CDs with Stu, planning to spend more time recording with his cousin Kurt, and possibly move in with him, the Michael who loved me, and his grandmother, his brothers, and nephews, and cousins and aunt, the one who was in a loving relationship with Sammie, that sweet spirit had no intention of taking his life. He was trying to get a handle on insomnia. I'm sure his human personality was as shocked as the rest of us by his sudden departure.

Divine appointment—no accidents—divine timing—either I have faith and believe in this or not. My peace of mind comes from stacking my evidence on the side of divine planning. Michael came to me in spirit before he was born. Somewhere I must have made an agreement to let him go home early, and to allow his departure to become a blessing to myself and others.

Olson's book reconfirms what my intuition was telling me all along—we come here as spiritual beings to have a human experience. It's all about the experience. We have done some pre-planning which we don't remember, we have guides and guardian angels, who never leave our side, and we have soul contracts, and free will about how we will execute those plans while here in human form. We came to love, and learn, and grow our capacities for living a purposeful life. And, when we reach a pre-determined exit point, we have the opportunity to return home to the spiritual realm, review our lives, and celebrate with our loved ones on the other side.

Michael took his exit. He left a trail of love and joy in his wake. The details surrounding his exit may leave us guessing and scratching our heads. Yet, I have made my peace with it, and whenever I think of his last few moments, I see him unfurling his angel wings and leaping into the waiting arms of love. I see him surrounded by those that went before him, and by his loving angels who brought him to us in the first place, and never left him for even an instant.

I had the joy and privilege of learning to be his mom, and am blessed by the 36 years he was here with me in the flesh. I feel a closeness and a connection to him now, perhaps even more than when we lived together under the same roof. I have immediate access to him, and I carry him in my heart wherever I go.

I treasure all of the writings I discovered among his papers. One that I treasure most is when he is talking about me in a letter to a friend. He writes, *"The one thing I have to say I am grateful for is my mother because she has always encouraged me and coached me to follow my dreams. It takes a lot of courage to keep going, very challenging, in a direction simply because your heart keeps asking you to. Like many, and perhaps most artists, I have been misunderstood, jeered and challenged in ways that have made me go on to appreciate and respect life's virtues more and more. We share a genuine positive concern and work for humanity."*

Now, I feel that he is encouraging me to follow my dreams. He is forever by my side, as close as a whisper or a song. The lyrics that he wrote on January 15, 2013, for a piece of music given to him by Stu are a precious reminder to me to pay attention. On Facebook he posted, *"Today I wrote a song and cried."* He called it *"When Angels Whisper."* I believe they were whispering to him as he wrote it for us, reminding us to laugh and be joyful.

Whenever I listen to it, my own tears flow. I know it was divinely inspired, and I know, whenever I ask, he meets me in the light of the rainbow bridging heaven and earth.

I've included it at the end of this section for your enjoyment, although reading it isn't nearly as wonderful as hearing him sing it.

When Angels Whisper

Such a mystery the world of music, never knowing what a song could bring.
Suddenly the simplest phrase turns into a ballad you could never dream.
Strange how it can summon old feelings, forgotten memories you left behind.

Funny how so vividly our past comes back to us in present time.
Suddenly the mystic and romantic wishes you'd try.
Suddenly your heart's wrapped in a basket wondering why.
Such a mystery the metaphysics, wrapped in love and wrapped up in between.
Funny how a love song nestles up to us like an angel whispering.
Funny how a love song nestles up to us like an angel whispering.
Have you ever heard an angel whisper? It's easy if you just open your ears.
Suddenly she's right there by your side if you should listen in and hear.
Have you ever felt your guardians watching?
Don't you know they'll always be right there?
All you have to do is trust and
Heaven is in you and everywhere.
I'll meet you at the end of the rainbow. I promise you this.
Anytime the rain comes storming, I'm there, you can't miss.
So fill your life up full of joy and laughter, laughter is a very vital thing.
Listen to your angels. They know why you're here
And what you've come to bring.
Listen to your angels. They know why we're here
And what we've come to bring.

Note: If you go to YouTube and search "When Angels Whisper" you can hear him sing it along with a video slide show we did of his life.

Michael and his proud Grandma Spengler
at one of her fund raisers for the Philharmonic

Thank You for the Whispers

"I'm right here, always in your heart.

Listen and know.

Feel the whispers, see the signs.

I'm right here."

I hear my beloved child reminding me to

Fill my life up full with joy and laughter,

With gratitude.

I'm listening, tuning in, remembering the love,

Reconnecting my awareness to the joy,

The laughter, the gifts of love in my life.

I am feeling your reflection all around me,

Hearing your voice assuring me I am never alone.

You are right here,

Always in my heart.

Thank you for the whispers.

Left Overs

Footprints of a life

Photographs and videos

Audio clips and recordings

Scattered documents—incomplete, yet finished.

No more live performances,

Creativity stopped midlife

Left-overs rich with memories

Dancing shoes and tuxedo shirts,

Guitars, harmonica and

A bandoneon tucked safely into its case

Sheets of music and binders full of songs

I am missing you, my son

Not ready was I to ever say good-bye

So I watch for you and see you in hummingbirds

I listen for you in the wind

And hear you singing to me

I feel you—is it my imagination?

I dance with you.

I hold you in the unwashed shirt-pillow

Filled with your smells

I love you always and forever

Did I tell you this often enough?

Could you catch it in my eyes?

You've cracked my heart wide open

You left a legacy of love

Of music

Of memories

Of beautiful images

Footprints on my heart

Footprints of a life

Left-overs

From a love that never leaves

My Heart Remembers

My heart remembers each mannerism

The way you walked, the tilt of your head

The lift of an eyebrow and the shape of your hands

My heart remembers all of the growing

From breast to bottle to big boy

From teen band leader

To entertainer extraordinaire

The smile that we all waited for

The joy of a great performance

My heart remembers

And it aches to have you back

My best friend, my beautiful son

My gift I shared with the world

My heart will never forget

Snapshot Moments

Snapshot moments

Moments of recognition

All is as it should be

All is well

More than well

Enjoying a moment of true connection

A smile, a phrase

Sitting in sunshine

Listening to nature chatter and sing to me

Catching a full moon

Or the fresh sliver of a new one

Precious snapshot moments

Mother and sons throughout the years

Not always caught on camera

Recorded forever in my heart

My snapshot moments

A Life Well Lived

What is the measure of a life well lived?

When it all goes back into the box

And what remains is how I played and

Who I became in the process

What is the texture and flavor and taste

The aroma and scent that remains?

When the cards are packed up

The flowers wilted and tossed

The shirts and pants and hats distributed

What is the essence, the gift,

The footprint of a life well-lived?

A Mother's Tears

Tracing back the times I've cried my mother tears

Each child so special

So delightful

Temptation to just eat them up

They were so deliciously precious to me

Crying at graduations and weddings

At their mushy cards for my birthdays and Mother's Day

Sentimental tears and big proud-Mama tears

Tears when they moved out and left the nest

Each time a flood of letting-go emotions

Relief tears when I learn all is okay

They are safe

And the tears of a broken heart,

Grief stricken

My child is gone tears

These tears come unbidden and flood me with memories

These tears are now blended with sadness and joy

And fill the crater in my heart

These mother's tears comfort and

Connect me forever to my child

RAW

FOOTAGE

Note: These entries are straight from my Facebook posts and personal journal entries, transcribed and organized in chronological order. There are some repeats from journal to Facebook, and I have pulled from some of these entries into the narrative. I removed surnames from most of the entries. Rather than repeat the poems, which mostly get written in my journal, I have made a note of the title of the poem that was written on a particular day.

FACEBOOK AND JOURNAL ENTRIES FROM
FIRST THIRTY TWO WEEKS

7/26/13—END OF DAY ONE

FACEBOOK: 1:00 a.m. This morning, July 25, 2013, I received the call no parent ever wants to receive. My dear sweet son Resh Michael was killed in a tragic auto accident. I have felt the love and support of those who knew him and many who only know me. I have cried myself dry and felt the numbness of disbelief. I have him home with me for a few hours which has been so healing. We have a service planned for Tuesday, 7/30, at 2 pm at Spiritual Life Center on Park Towne Circle.

Thank you for all of your prayers. I am so blessed to have been his mom for 36 wonderful, precious years.

FACEBOOK: 5:55 a.m. Thank you everyone. I'm surrounded by love and so is Michael and all of our family. If you see a real estate post, it's from a service I started using. Don't know how to stop it. Kind of like life—just rushes forward as I am stopped by sudden shock. Hold your loved ones close..tell them every day how much you love them. I am holding to my heart all of the sweet exchanges of caring I shared with Michael. They are precious memories to have.

7/27/13

FACEBOOK: 12:08 a.m. I'm tucked in for the night. Listening to the stillness. Reading all of the emails, texts, and Facebook posts sharing so much love with me. My heart keeps expanding and expanding to take it all in. I have never experienced so much love and so much pain all at once. The love is winning and I am so grateful and humbled by this outpouring. Michael continues to bless me in so many ways even as he moves along to his next big adventure. All of us left behind continue to celebrate his life even as we wrap our arms around each other and weep for our loss. Photos, stories, all the ways Resh Michael left his mark upon our hearts. I am so filled with gratitude for the gift his life was and continues to be to me. Thank you everyone for filling me up and helping the healing to begin.

7/29/13

FACEBOOK: 7:28 a.m. I awakened to a soft breeze and memories of my son Michael, wishing I could hold and hug him, instead I breathed deeply into one of his unlaundered shirts filled with the musky odor of his body and wept. I don't have a trail to follow on this grieving. Sometimes I'm doing the comforting, sometimes I'm the comforter What I am learning is to listen to my heart, to keep it open to both the pain and the joy, to stay with a wave and ride it through. I heard a recording yesterday of Michael chanting with the SLC choir "I am not alone. God is with me." I hear him singing it to me now on my inner soundtrack. This comforts me even as the waves of sadness rock my world.

7/31/13

FACEBOOK: 1:17 a.m. Words fail to fully capture the celebration of Michael's life we had today. What a tribute! I'm filled to overflowing with joy and gratitude for the ways he touched lives with his music and his spirit. After the service when we were gathered at home again, Sammie took out the angel cards that she and Michael loved to use. We all decided to pull a card and these are the ones that showed up: Harmony, Music, Signs, Divine Timing, Meditation, Spiritual Growth, Soul Mates (his brother Troy drew this one), Honesty and Integrity, and I drew Archangel Michael. The Archangel Michael card also jumped out of the deck into Sammie's lap the next day. He's definitely with us and having fun communicating from a different plane.

I am hearing his music even now in the silence. Big brother Troy leaves tomorrow at noon for Idaho. Sis will drive back to Los Angeles, as will niece Holland. Kurt and Thandi go back to Santa Rosa. I remain alone in a home that is filled with memories of Michael. I will be listening for his angel whispering. God bless us all.

8/1/13—ONE WEEK HAS PASSED

FACEBOOK: 12:50 a.m. Not quite an empty house. Minus two guests, last three leave tomorrow. I'm in no hurry. My nephew, Kurt, hasn't stopped contributing since he arrived. He and Resh Michael were best friends and created music together. They had big plans. Kurt produced all of the visuals for the memorial, worked day and night to make the musical slide show. Burned copies for myself and family today and then went through Michael's stuff for me. I keep telling him thank you, and he keeps going. Bless him and all the other angels with skin on who have done so much to help me through this passage.

FACEBOOK: 6:30 a.m. I find I am hungry for every story about Michael, every snippet of video or audio, and all the sweet memories which feel so nurturing to me right now. Taking time to savor each bite, seasoned with salty tears and the sweetness of laughter.

8/2/13

FACEBOOK: 9:24 a.m. I am moving slowly, ever so slowly. I have an image of having pulled over onto the shoulder of life, stopped completely, and now have my caution lights on as I consider pulling back into the slow lane. I am so grateful for all of the support I've received. Food and flowers and home baked muffins and apple pie, lots of chocolate cake, hugs and well-wishes, and sweeping and sorting, and my real estate clients being lovingly cared for by Patti. I could focus on honoring the legacy Resh Michael left in the short time he was with us. What a sweet blessing he was/is in my life. I love him so much.

FACEBOOK: 11:29 a.m. So many are asking about CDs of Resh Michael's music. His cousin Kurt and his dear friend Stu are working on that. Right now I believe there are only a few copies of a Christmas album he mixed for me and family members, another that has some of my favorite Italian songs, and a couple of CDs with his own compositions. He and Stu were working on a CD together. Ironic how his death brings his music to the fan base he was struggling to build.

8/3/13

FACEBOOK: 7:33 a.m. The house is very quiet. I'm grateful to wake up with Michael's voice in my head singing "when angels whisper." Kurt made me a looping CD of just that song and it's so comforting to play it and fill the house with his beautiful voice. Today I pick up his ashes and bring him home once more.

FACEBOOK: 12:32 p.m. Michael stories. Watch for hummingbirds. On the day he died, after finally getting him home to us, Cari drew a card for him from my Native American Medicine cards—hummingbird, the symbol for joy. Earlier that morning, within the first 15 minutes of me learning of his death, while my sister was contacting the home funeral director services, a hummingbird flew in her front door in Marina del Rey, circled for about five minutes, and left through an open window. At least four other people close to me or Michael had similar experiences with hummingbirds that same day.

8/4/13

FACEBOOK: 1:38 p.m. Today at SLC's church service, our music minister, Paula Mandella, selected "Everything Must

Change" as the meditation song. It was sung beautifully by guest vocalist Bajan. The song has a repeating refrain: "There are not many things in life you can be sure of, except ... rain comes from the clouds, sun lights up the sky, and hummingbirds do fly ... and music makes me cry." I did just that. Michael has filled my heart so full of joy that I just keep spilling over.

8/5/13

FACEBOOK: 9:00 a.m. Monday. I imagine Michael's on a tour, making people laugh and practicing his songs. He was working on a cabaret show of songs people on a cruise ship would love to sing along to. We laughed at some of the lyrics from the oldie but goodies like "flying purple people eater." Really? I am just the right target market for those oldies. I woke up today with him singing "Hey Mambo" in my head. I know I need to move back into work mode. Instead, I'm going for a cup of coffee and hope for a hummingbird sighting. So much love when I think of him...pretty much constantly.

PERSONAL JOURNAL: 10:44 p.m. Rotary. So much love for me. I feel strong and then tear up when I least expect it. Today Lev donated money in honor of Michael. So did Judy. I did as well. People want to take away my pain and also share their own sadness with me.

Louise visited me at my home, and we sat in the back room with Michael's ashes to visit for awhile. A hummingbird came to the window.

Spoke with Wendy at Hay House about writing a book. I know Michael wants me to use this energy he is feeding me to make a difference.

Pendulum time with Michael. He's very present. Wants to communicate with me internally, as he did when he told me how sorry he was for the pain of his death. He wants us to celebrate, not be sad and miss him.

8/6/13

FACEBOOK: 3:58 a.m. Middle of the night wake ups seem to be part of my healing process. I find myself being quiet so I don't disturb Michael. Then I remember it's just me and mini-schnauzer Chewie now. I hear Michael singing on my inner sound track and I check in with an "I love you." Learning to relate on a different level of awareness. Feeling my way through unfamiliar passages.

FACEBOOK: 8:03 a.m. I was sound asleep on the sofa from maybe 10 pm to 2:30. Made my way to bed trying not to wake up too much—but I didn't do such a good job of that. For several nights in a row, I've been waking up around 3 am from a sound sleep. Finding it's a great time to journal.

FACEBOOK: 12:51 p.m. I have ventured out for a pedicure. Realizing today is day 12. My ability to count has obviously been impacted. Two weeks this Thursday. Michael left some shattered dreams for those who were working closely with him on creating new songs and CDs—dear friend Stu, cousin Kurt, and girlfriend Sammie. Say prayers for each of them and send them love.

PERSONAL JOURNAL: 1:18 a.m. Sammie came over for dinner tonight and we put angel stickers on Michael's cremains container. I cooked and we talked. She has people telling her things they would never tell a mom. "You'll find someone else." "Give it three months and you'll be over it." They also

233

feel compelled to ask her for details about his passing and pressure her for information. She had such wonderful plans for the two of them.

I want to capture the essence of this process as I go through it. Day 13 and I'm out of what might be called the initial shock phase. I'm able to pick up some things where I left off. Others are of no interest. I think about doing some marketing for my real estate business. It has no appeal. I pick up my journal instead.

PERSONAL JOURNAL: 7:11 a.m. Not moving fast yet. Got a call that I can go and pick up the death certificate, but the coroners report comes from El Dorado county. Getting the house cleaned top to bottom on Saturday. I'm having a new refrigerator delivered today—the old one gave out. Life marches on. I get to choose the cadence that is right for me.

Noticing the distinctions between grieving as a mom, grieving as a fan or a friend, and what Sammie, Kurt and Stu are all experiencing—grieving as a partner in creating something beautiful together. All of us are experiencing the loss of a dream and the need to tread over shattered remnants and begin again. Many are feeling the loss of this vibrant, creative, fun energy we knew as Mikey, Michael, Naresh, and Resh. We all love you so much!

8/7/13

FACEBOOK: 1:05 a.m. I love the stories that I continue to hear about how much Michael impacted the lives of his friends. Today a friend of Michael's from high school said he had some tough times in his teen years and felt really different until Michael's total acceptance helped him accept himself. He worded it much more poetically. I hear similar stories even back to second grade about him befriending a new student and helping her feel welcomed. I love you Michael.

FACEBOOK: 6:40 p.m. First day back at the Coldwell Banker office today. Stayed about three hours. More hugs and gifts of love—flowers, a prayer quilt, a necklace, chocolates. Gradually getting back to business, but notice I am in no hurry. I'm grateful that I can take it slowly thanks to all of the support of friends, especially Patti and Holly who have picked up the transactions I was in the middle of. I picked up the death certificate in Roseville at the mortuary that handled the cremation. I saw another family entering into the process of saying goodbye to a loved one. On the way home, I bought some new bedding and sheets. All seems like normal, but there's a difference I can't quite describe. The reality of Michael's physical absence echoes in the background no matter what I'm doing. I've played his Christmas CD a couple of times today, plus two others that I love. Tried to copy a DVD so I could have it on my computer and share it, but find I'm not successful with it, and let it go for now. I pick Mom up shortly, and we are going to John and Michelle's for dinner and family time. Michael's long time friend Sean came by for a visit. We sat on the front porch swing where Michael used to play his music for himself and whoever passed by, and we talked about how Michael has touched so many lives and always lived with such honesty and authenticity. Two hummingbirds swooped down and hovered for a moment. We both smiled.

FACEBOOK: 11:51 p.m. Enjoyed the delicious dinner tonight made by my beautiful daughter-in-law Michelle. Asked each of my grandsons to tell me their favorite Uncle Michael memory. Isaiah hiked his pants up to his armpits and did a perfect imitation of one of Michael's goofier characters. Josiah and Judah both remembered when he was playing a mime, and they could not get him to say anything—he just kept acting things out. After dinner we found a few photos to share. No tears tonight—just lots of sharing. Love my family.

8/8/13—TWO WEEKS HAVE PASSED

PERSONAL JOURNAL: 6:48 a.m.

Two weeks ago today my life was completely different. Until the phone rang at 7:30 a.m. and my ex-husband's wife calls me and tells me my son is dead. I just interrupted my journaling to post on Facebook an important rule for myself: Do not go down the road of blame, regret, anger. Do not revisit the incident. No joy there. No healing.

FACEBOOK: 7:24 a.m. I'm just waking up and beginning to journal. Two weeks ago today, I was up, making some coffee, emptying the dishwasher, and at 7:30 am received the call that altered my world. One call—from my ex-husband's wife. Michael had been visiting his dad in Pollock Pines for a couple of nights. He had not slept in five days. Hardest part next to his death is feeling like if he had been with me, here at home, none of this would have happened. All the woulda coulda shoulda whyda howdas if-I'das in the world do not change the fact that he died and they only send me down a dead end road full of emotional land mines. No joy there. Blame, sadness, anger, regret just waiting for any attention to feed on. Staying in the present, paying attention to the thoughts that are healing, and keeping my heart wide open. This is what Michael's teaching me.

FACEBOOK: 7:27 a.m. I think I'm hitting a rough spot, exact time I got the worst call of my life. Right now. Revisiting the pain produces more of it. I see that so clearly.

FACEBOOK: 8:07 a.m. Facebook has taken on a whole new dimension for me. I would not have been able to reach so many to let them know of Michael's death. I didn't have his girlfriend Sammie's number, but found her on his Facebook friends list and was able to private message her to call me. I've used Facebook in the past to stay aware of what friends and clients are doing and to post what I thought might be helpful or inspiring. Now it's a way of sharing something so big that to carry it alone would be impossible. All of the love and stories and comments have made such a difference to me.

8/9/13

FACEBOOK: 7:55 a.m. Pizza and ice cream last night at Stu's. He was surrounded by the three women closest to Michael—his mom (that's me), his grandmother Barbara, and girlfriend Sammie. It was my first visit to the studio Michael spent hours in. Stu showed us the amazing complexity of how tracks are laid down, and I have even more appreciation for the talent of this man I got to call my son. We watched video footage of Michael's unfinished cabaret show with Sammie and Scott playing their parts to his central character, Giovanni. What a comedian! He had cut parts out of the video to shorten it for sending to booking agents for cruise ships. Even with the cuts, we could catch the one-liners he was dropping as he tried to woo the waitress (Sammie). Stu and Sammie are researching the best way to release his Broadway tunes album that was played at his memorial. We laughed and teared up and wished we could change what happened. We miss the physicality of you, Resh Michael. We want your finished cabaret show. We want your live laughter. We are all healing in our own ways. We love you.

FACEBOOK: 9:55 a.m. This morning I took all of the flower arrangements that were still at my home (I gave many away so others could enjoy them), pulled out the flowers that were still bright with life, and have three small arrangements now in vases. Live plants are doing well. I have much to learn about keeping houseplants happy. Some of the spent flowers are in a box lid drying out in the sun. Might make a potpourri of them, might not. Just want the option.

Yesterday my friend and fellow realtor, BJ, came over to show me plans for my back yard—a project we were working on and had an appointment to review when I got the news about Michael. The plans are beautiful and include a sanctuary for birds—now most specifically hummingbirds. We planted my Peter Pan camellia and hydrangea in a place near the garage (Michael's first studio) where hopefully they will thrive and remind me of how much Michael lives on.

My sister, Alorah Christina, wrote these words in her blog which I find inspiring and comforting: "Naresh was 36—an opera singer, a tango musician and dancer, an actor, model and magical man. He was never of this earth—he was always uplifted, he was always light-filled, he was always singing or playing his music. As I drove up from LA to be here with my sister I kept feeling inside—"He stayed with us as long as he could". My instincts kept saying that his exit was right. That he was one of those icons who was meant to die young. To never age. To never lose luster. To never endure the death of life's dreams. As we have processed the death of this dear one, we have all been inspired by the grace it contained. The grace of getting to handle his death through the natural death care project, to not have to turn his body over to some impersonal mortuary, to not have to pay exorbitant fees, to be able to hold him and love him and let him go slowly. The impossible perfection of how it unfolded has given each of us trust in the process itself. Forever desiring that it never had happened, we can each also feel its perfect design."

PERSONAL JOURNAL: 10:32 p.m. Hit a rough patch this morning. Wanting Michael here with us in his body, able to sing, and entertain, to love and to hug. Tried calling my mom, no answer. Troy, no answer. Kurt, no answer. Then I got a call from a dear friend and it pulled me out.

I had plans to do lots of errands today. I did zero. Homemade pizza and movie at Jeff and Jennifer's home. Eight-year-old Walker gave me a hummingbird coin on a necklace and told me a beautiful Native American story of the stars and hummingbirds. So sweet.

I had conversations eventually with Troy and Kurt, also Christina and Mom. Patti came by with more cards.

8/10/13

FACEBOOK: 7:29 a.m. Last night I had homemade pizza (we are talking even the crust) with my clients Jeff and Jennifer. She makes pizza once a week and I'm becoming part of the family. I had the joy of helping them find their new home and

239

sell their other. Walker and Phoebe (ages 8 and 11) came with their parents to Michael's memorial service. Our pizza and movie date was set up over a month ago, before the accident. Wouldn't have missed it. Walker tells me the story of the hummingbird and the stars, then delights me with the gift of a corded necklace bearing a coin with a hummingbird on one side and the tree of life on the other. The evening was magical. Life is very sweet even seasoned with tears of loss. I loved Walker's story and found it on Google to share. And, yes, as we were sitting on their deck, we were seeing hummingbirds sitting in the trees listening.

8/11/13

FACEBOOK: 7:33 a.m. At Southwest, waiting to board an airplane for a vacation planned months ago. Telling myself it's okay to have fun. I still feel cocooned and tender. Yesterday I took death certificates to close Michael's bank accounts. I cried. Showed his memorial slide show to a friend who just heard the news. Cried again. Took Sammie to B St Theater. We laughed and wished Michael was with us.

PERSONAL JOURNAL: 8:30 a.m.

I'm on the plane waiting for it to take off. Noticed as I stood at space B-1 in line, waiting to go on board, all of the children traveling alone were allowed to go ahead. I watched as a dad said goodbye to his daughter. I could feel the tears welling up inside me. Then a mom put her two daughters through the gate and sat for a moment watching them go down the ramp to the plane. More tears from me. I'm saying to myself, "Kiss them, hug them, you never know."

Yesterday I took the death certificate to Michael's banks. I cried. So many surprise tear triggers. Music in Chico's, hearing a song he would sing. I know he is present. I just want to hold him.

PERSONAL JOURNAL: 6 p.m. Charlene and Henry are Diana's friends who are in the cabin next door. Charlene is studying shamanic healing. She saw Michael in spirit standing next to me with his great big smile as we were leaving the dock on our Alaskan cruise. I shed tears of joy as I listened to her describe who she was seeing. When I pulled out a photo of Michael with his hair pulled back, she said, "That's him. He has the most beautiful smile."

8/12/13

PERSONAL JOURNAL: 6:45 a.m. Sitting up in the cruise ship crow's nest with Diana. Seas are smooth. Sunrise peeking through the clouds. Michael singing me awake, "Do I love you because you're beautiful, or are you beautiful because I love you." Peaceful, grateful for the healing time on the water. Quiet now as the crew prepares ship for a day at sea. Vacuums running in the background, clinking of cups, squeegees on the windows. Light changing the features of the water and the horizon. I see images of Michael and write down what is coming through me...

Wings unfurled
Leaping into the arms of Love
Protector and guardian
Hummingbird of joy
Peter Pan of wonder
Musician and song writer

Prince of our family
Thirty six precious years
Everybody loves you
Your light and sun have taken over my heart.
All is well.

8/13/13

PERSONAL JOURNAL: 7 a.m. Alaskan waters. Time change. Lots of tears yesterday. No Facebook connection. No posts. Learning more from Diana and Charlene about "seeing." I use my sense of feel more than I visualize with images. I have been using my pendulum bracelet to connect with Michael. I suspect I do not really need it—I call him to mind and feel him in my heart—it still brings tears to my eyes.

Cannot access email or phone yet. Not sure why. It's unsettling and I choose to let it go and be present to the beauty of the seas.

New beginnings for me. Life really without my favorite roommate and loving son. I miss you.

8/14/13

PERSONAL JOURNAL: 5:45 a.m. We are docked in Juneau harbor. Foggy up high but clear below. Three cruise ships here right now. One may be just arriving or leaving. It's moving ever so slowly and hard to tell.

Last two nights we've gone to the piano bar after dinner to hear a performer named Lee play. Very entertaining. Michael would have enjoyed his energy. Through me, I'm guessing he did. I brought a small container with some of his ashes so he can go with me to all of the places we visit.

I was quiet yesterday. We went through a narrow strait and saw a beautiful glacier up close. Ice blue has a whole new meaning to me. I haven't had Michael's CDs to play, so music is fading a little unless I consciously reach for it.

How do I communicate with you, my dear sweet son? What is the channel? *"Listen in your heart, Mom. I am right here. It's okay to cry. It's okay to laugh as well. You are still the best mom. I love you."*

8/15/13—THREE WEEKS

PERSONAL JOURNAL: 7 a.m. Sitka, Alaska. Took photos of sunrise this morning. In my quest to capture the beauty, I found a gentleman named Bob using his IPad in a most precarious pose standing on top of deck chairs and leaning on the railing. I passed my IPad to him so he could take some photos for me. We began to talk. Bob is recently remarried after losing his wife of 50 years. We talked about Michael.

I had just received a message through my tears as I was walking toward the back of the deck to catch the sunrise. *"Mom! Focus on what's here, all the beauty, not on what's missing and not on wishing it was different. I'm right here."*

So far a few teaspoons of his ashes have been scattered off the ship twice, in the sawdust at Red Dog Saloon, and to the whales when we were returning yesterday in Juneau. This has been a wonderful, healing trip.

Cell phone coverage—not so good. Just need to be relaxed about all of it. I love you Michael.

8/16/13

PERSONAL JOURNAL: 2:20 p.m. Leaving Ketchican, Alaska. Spent time on a pontoon boat and in the rain forest. Got an email from Mom sent yesterday. She says Michael feels very close to her and is her guardian angel.

8/17/13

PERSONAL JOURNAL: 7:15 a.m. Fog horn blowing. On our way to Victoria. Last day of our cruise. Tomorrow we are back in Seattle and I'll be able to use my phone again. Cannot remember going this long with no phone service since becoming so dependent upon cell phones.

Emails occasionally have kept me a little connected. I have longer spaces between the tears. Purchased several blown-glass and bone-carved hummingbirds. One of guides yesterday was a young man named Mike who is also a musician. The musicians on board ship are good. Michael was great. And, I need to let that all go. Diana and I both had bracelets fall off yesterday at different times and they were found. I believe my new guardian angel is watching out for me.

I woke up several times in the night. Ideas about taking Michael's teaching and publishing it. Taking his passion for supporting artists and creating a showcase for their work. Staying connected to Sammie, Ben, Sean and Kurt. Helping Family Directed Funeral Services grow and become a choice that is easy to make.

Staying in my heart space to make decisions. Coming from Love. Thank you Michael.

PERSONAL JOURNAL: 9:35 a.m.

Sitting in the Crow's Nest lounge and overwhelmed by memories of Michael. Him singing to Sammie with her balloon, totally a gift. Creating our Christmas album for the family. Singing "Mama" to me from our front porch when he put on a show for about 80 of my friends. Singing an Italian happy birthday to neighbor Jenny. Sitting next to me and just loving me. Kissing me on my forehead. How do I not weep? If I go down the sweet memory road, I weep. If I go down the blame road, I get angry.

PERSONAL JOURNAL: 2:25 p.m. Took two photo editing classes and learned quite a few tricks. Also learned from folks with Verizon that I should be able to make phone calls in all of the ports in Alaska. Tomorrow in Seattle, I hope to find out what's going on. Until then, I'm "off-line."

Charlene is telling me to put a white light around myself and call upon the angels who came in with me at birth for protection. I believe she is in touch with another realm and I am so far not accessing it the way she can. I know my path of the heart—when I am in that space. I felt it immediately when I was able to touch Michael after we brought him home. It's the place of total unconditional love.

When Charlene says talk to my angels, I don't know how. I have no experience to relate that to. I know I want to be able to remember Michael in all of the many ways he touched my life and, when I go there, I weep. I love each of my sons so much. Like Reverend Moran says, they were knit from my very body, formed in my womb. They have given me my greatest joy and now my deepest sorrow.

8/18/13

FACEBOOK: 12:06 a.m. Returning tomorrow after seven days at sea in the beautiful waters of Alaska. Very healing. Still finding my way through this. If I go to my sweet and loving memories of Michael, I get very weepy. Then I move through the wave of emotion to a place of peace. I've been cocooned by the quiet, slow pace of this trip and the loving support of Diana and her friends Charlene and Henry. I've had amazing support from my friends taking care of my business at home. I feel very blessed.

FACEBOOK: 5:21 p.m. Southwest is delayed four hours due to thunder storms somewhere. Seattle airport is not the same as a cruise ship. Looking forward to getting home.

8/19/13

FACEBOOK: 5:51 p.m. I've been collecting some of the treasured observations I've made since the event that rocked my world. Here they are:

- Feel what I am feeling—fully. Open to all of it.
- Joy and pain balance each other perfectly, if I am open to see and feel it.
- Numbness is a safe resting place—not a destination.
- Hugging and being hugged are essential to my healing.
- The salt of my tears mixes beautifully with the sweetness of laughter—savor each moment.
- Regrets, blaming, anger, shoulda's, coulda's, what if's, wish I'da's are all signs for dead end roads filled with land mines—do not enter.

- If I notice myself already on one of those roads, turn around immediately and grab a happy memory to hold on to and pull myself back.
- Say "yes" to helping hands. Let them feed, cook, clean, sort, and hug.
- Life marches on—I get to choose the cadence that I can handle.
- Revisiting the pain only brings on more of it.
- Capture the stories while they are fresh.
- The only right way to grieve, is the one that feels most right to me. My grief is as unique as my fingerprint.
- Give myself as long as I need. Listen to my heart.
- Choose which thoughts I want to spend time with. Healing thoughts lift my spirit.
- Stay in my heart space, listen to its wisdom. Let it guide all of my decisions.
- Some words carry more comfort than others.
- Watch for signs from my loved one—listen, feel, sense—serendipitous coincidences, alignment and perfection of timing—and especially hummingbirds.
- Sleep when I can. Time loses its grip and calendars are of little interest.
- It's okay to cry and it's okay to laugh—all at the same time.
- Focus on the beauty of what's here, right now, and not on what's missing or wishing it were different.

8/20/13

PERSONAL JOURNAL: 7:11 a.m. Way too tired last night to put two words together. When I did my check in at our Faith in Action book group last night, I was able to tell the story of bringing Michael home—the miracles that needed to line up—the way I knew he was orchestrating it from his side as well. *"Bring me home Mom. Bring me home."*

I told about him running and wanting to be free. I told of Charlene seeing him with me on the ship and Diana shared about how musicians kept weaving their way into our cruise—at the dinner table, the guide named Mike who is also a musician, and the piano man, Lee.

Lisa finally spoke through her tears that Michael had been talking to her the whole time Diana and I were sharing. He wanted her to tell us how hard he's been working to let us know he's present—all of the signs and coincidences. He also showed her how full of fun and life and magic he is—that he is enjoying the experience of not being tied to this three-dimensional world where he struggled with the day to day. He truly did need to go—to be set free. Now he can be with any of us whenever we think of him and call him to us.

I shared my 20 treasures on Facebook and have been told that I need to put these into a book. I will do this. I am the woman who is bringing forth a book on conscious grieving—a path to peace and restoration.

Someone said or I read that when I am moved to tears by a thought of Michael, he is communicating with me. I just remembered our last trip to fill his five-gallon water jug. We traded my giving him a ride for his walking Chewie. I love and miss you my sweet son!

FACEBOOK: 7:49 p.m. I've gone from a house full of family and friends to a cruise with lots to do to being at home all by myself. I've shared this home with Michael for the last five or six years. We joked that he came home for six months five years ago. He was a wonderful housemate. Messy and lots of music at all times of the day and night. Now I would love to see five towels hanging on door knobs and shower doors. Laundry piling up next to the washer. A few dishes in the sink. Would give anything to hear him practicing. I'm missing him. A lot.

FACEBOOK: 9:16 p.m. I'm missing him and I'm okay. Just getting used to lots of quiet and solitude. I'm watching TV which may or may not be the most productive thing to be doing. I know I need to build new patterns. I've lived alone before. Just seems so different now. I know I'll make it through this.

FACEBOOK: 11:49 p.m. I'm grateful for all of the support. It seems like writing down how I'm feeling helps me process and at the same time, I am also aware of how vulnerable I feel by sharing so publicly. There's that ego part of me that says to just suck it up and get over it. Thank goodness for the wisdom to know I need to treat myself gently. Not like a victim, but more like a newborn. This is new terrain in so many ways. So, again, thanks to all of you for swaddling me in your love.

8/21/13

FACEBOOK: 12:03 a.m. I believe I will eventually create a new normal that feels whole and includes all of the joy I still feel when I think of him and fills my hurt places with the love he is still sending my way. You are right about me needing to take as much time as it takes.

PERSONAL JOURNAL: 5:48 a.m. Wednesday   Just took Darlene to the airport and going back to sleep doesn't seem to be as important as writing. I want direct communication with Michael. I want to know he is here and present from my own recognition as well as from other sensitives being able to tell me about it. What is my channel? I have heard you, Michael, the day we learned of the accident. I heard you clearly over my right shoulder, *"I am so sorry, Momma. I am so sorry."*

I asked questions with the pendulum when you were here with your body. I felt like I was getting answers from you. All of the miracles that needed to happen to bring you home. I feel you had a hand in all of it. I need to stay connected and learn to recognize signs in this new place that I find myself in. Help me, sweetheart. Help me. I love you. I am listening. I am here and open.

FACEBOOK: 8:19 a.m. Facing my "I don't want to" energy right now. I don't want to leave the house. I don't want to go back to Michael's bank and re-do paperwork. I don't want to go stand in line at DMV and get his pink slip changed. I don't want to face the list of things that need to be done and I don't even know all of the things yet. Sooooo, I'm taking myself by the hand and heading in to my Coldwell Banker office where I will be surrounded by people who love me. I am promising myself that I can take as much time as I need to do the things I don't want to do. I intend to make it a great day! Grateful for the awareness that I get to choose.

FACEBOOK: 12:51 p.m. I want to stay in the flow of this process and see how I can help others find their way through. I believe there is a law about giving what you most need and it all returns to you. I think someone said it better than I just did, but I know being comforted and being the comforter are completely intertwined. Both bring me to that reservoir of love that sustains me.

8/22/13—FOUR WEEKS

PERSONAL JOURNAL: 1:57 a.m. Sammie came over tonight and we visited on our favorite subject—Michael. Then went shopping for ingredients to make her ratatouille, one of his favorites. We cooked that up together and talked more about Michael. Ate a delicious meal together. Kept up the talking, listened to Michael's Christmas CD and the Broadway CD, shed some tears and said goodbye.

She took a small container of ashes with her and the gifts of hummingbird and silk purse that I bought her in Alaska. We shared how our feelings are right there, at the edge, always ready to spill over. How we are each committed to seeing how this experience can bless us. She is drafting a book in her mind—a wonderful love story based on her experience with Michael.

I intended a good day and created one. Sammie shared how Michael showed himself to her with his Celtic symbol that he had given her as a gift. She pulled a temporary tattoo out of a vending machine just by "chance." It was the exact same symbol as the one on her bracelet from Michael.

FACEBOOK: 7:48 a.m. "Creating a new normal." I have found that to be a great response to the questions about how I am doing. It recognizes that my life has changed and I'm in a process for which I have no history. I do know I'm committed to having this experience contribute to me and to others in some beautiful way. Last night Sammie came over and we shared all of what we are each experiencing. We laughed, we cried, we listened to Michael sing on precious CDs that Stu is reproducing. I heard more stories of Resh Michael as boyfriend and entertainer and clown and philosopher. We shopped for ingredients and cooked her special ratatouille dish. She went home bearing left overs and gifts from Alaska and lots of love. We are helping each other with our healing and with creating that new normal. Today is a brand new day. I'm grateful for life and all the ways love shows up around me. And, I'm sure that list of "don't want to's" will eventually get smaller and cleared. I am relabeling the list to "ok—what am I willing to handle today—or not?"list or calling it "my permission to do it whenever I am ready" list.

PERSONAL JOURNAL: 2:08 p.m. I am still wanting to know the best way to communicate with Michael. Pendulum seems best right now. I may call JG for a reading. A working title of my book: Conscious Grieving: A Path to Peace and Restoration. What's next?

8/23/13

FACEBOOK: 12:33 a.m. Four weeks. Tried to listen in on a marketing call for coaching and had to hang up one minute into it. My brain refuses to move from its feeling mode to whatever mode matches marketing and sales and creating new business—real estate or coaching. I'm drawn to any opportunity to connect heart to heart, to listen when that's what's needed, to share my experience, to comfort, to be in the presence of the essence. I have not been able to listen to the news, preferring silence in my car during drive time, silence in the house unless listening to Michael's music, and long stretches of not doing much. Pre-recorded episodes of some TV favorites have entertained me. I'm picking up the edges of open escrows, finding out where I can take a step back into my business and appreciating all of the help I've received. I feel like a curious blend of open, vulnerable, strong, and tender—certain of my resilience and grateful for discovering a deep unshakeable core of knowing all is well.

PERSONAL JOURNAL: 12:55 a.m. I am drawn to conversations of the heart—deep resonant soulful experiences. I feel like a curious blend of open vulnerable, strong and tender.

Michael has gifted me myself! In his freedom from this world, he has loosed something me as well. I love you. I am grateful for our time together. Big hug to you Michael!!

FACEBOOK: 9:05 a.m. I never know what will bring up a wave of tears—this morning it was getting ready to cook an egg and looking at the pots and pans which Michael purchased when he was learning to cook on his own and brought back with him when he moved in for "six months" almost six years ago. He made such interesting concoctions beginning with garlic and onions and peppers, adding eggs, and whatever—usually in mid afternoon or midnight depending upon his entertainer circadian rhythms and when he was in creative mode. The wave has passed, I've eaten my egg, and played his song *"When Angels Whisper"* over and over until I was complete.

FACEBOOK: 10:02 p.m. I am certainly realizing that my heart is the best navigator through this process.

8/24/13

FACEBOOK: 8:27 a.m. I've been googling scientific studies on communication with people who have passed. Very interesting how many ways are documented and the percentages are over 50 percent which could be even higher if we were really paying attention. I find it comforting. I've been writing down the many ways Michael has made his presence known both to me and to close friends and family. I've heard his voice both singing to me and a couple of times clearly speaking comforting words. I've recognized unexplainable coincidences, especially when we were doing all we could to bring him home to us the day of the accident. Friends who can see energies have described his presence with me and given me messages. And then there's the delightful hummingbird sightings. I would love to hear others' experiences with connecting with loved ones on the other side.

FACEBOOK: 9:40 a.m. On board the cruise ship, I was having a particularly sad moment while up on deck to watch the sunrise. I heard Michael tell me clearly, *"Mom, focus on all the beauty in front of you. Don't miss it by being sad and wishing things were different. I'm right here."* He was a wise man. I immediately took in the amazing light of the sunrise over the ocean and was soothed.

8/25/13 ONE CALENDAR MONTH

PERSONAL JOURNAL: 6:34 a.m. Yesterday I went to soccer to watch the grandsons play, then to Modesto to a funeral service for Charlene's brother, then to clients Jennifer and Colin's open house, and then on to bed. Day before, lunch with Patti, hair appointment, visit with Christina on phone, a few phone calls to clients, a movie with Diana and Kelly, and then some TV and sleep.

I'm captive to Facebook as I want the feedback from my postings. Thought I would get all kinds of stuff done. Everything is still on my to-do list. Mom is noticing she doesn't want to be by herself as much.

I am feeling pretty good right now. The image of the huge pain landing in my timeline and me walking through it is very powerful for me. I believe I may be through the worst of it and can go and visit the memory of the process with mostly joy.

Just opened my emails and instead of deleting the one from OM Magazine, I scrolled down and saw an article on the book *The Afterlife of Billy Fingers*. I am sure Michael directed me to it. Billy's description of his experience when hit by the car is exactly what came to me intuitively about Michael—him unfurling his wings and flying into the arms of Love. This Billy that the book refers to led a much different life than Michael, and still he describes being in a most heavenly place with a way to see the earth and what's going on here.

Thank you my dear sweet Michael for connecting with me through this email so I could learn more. I love you so much!! What do you want me to do?

"Website; Write Books; Kurt—music; Stu—albums; Grams— comfort; John and Troy—connect; Sammie—love, love, love and enjoy and encourage and be there for her like you always were for me; Dad—forgive. Yourself—know you were the best, most loving mom I could have ever dreamed up. I did dream you up. Know we were a team and still are. I'm right here with you Mom. Never forget that. Listen and watch for me. You've been doing great so keep on listening to your

heart. *Do not worry about anything. All is provided for. All is well. Give that big gift of your love to all who need it. Let it shine, let it heal, let it teach. I love you so much, always and forever and we will meet again. I promise. And for now, I'm right here loving and supporting you!"*

I asked Michael tearfully if Aunt Betty was with him. I'd asked before with the pendulum and got a yes. This morning I was reading an article from Oprah's magazine sent to me by Diana about communication prior to death with those that have passed and it mentioned moms as being the ones to come most often. I had a moment of "I wasn't there for him" and asked if Aunt Betty was, then I realized I'm still here and still holding his hand if he needs me—on top of that relief came a line I then read directly from the article, "It's great that Aunt Betty is here with you." I had a good belly laugh with Michael.

I keep getting the message that he loves being able to be everywhere at once, with me or Stu or Kurt or Sammie or whomever calls him up through the loving connection they have with him—Troy, John, his Dad, me, Grandma, Michelle. He is no longer limited.

FACEBOOK: 6:58 p.m. Spent the afternoon with John and Michelle and my grandsons. Mom and Stanley were there too. We watched videos of the boys from when they were one and two years old. So much fun. So many memories. It's so cliche to say time moves so quickly, but it's true. The boys are seven and 10 now. Michael was in one of the videos from eight years ago and it stirred up memories. He covered a lot of ground in the past eight years. I'm so grateful for my sons—those that I can touch and the one that speaks to me from the other side. I have been cracked open by this experience and my heart feels bursting with love.

8/26/13

PERSONAL JOURNAL: 7:25 a.m. Going back through Facebook posts and seeing the trail—my journey and the love and support carrying me along the way. Beautiful. I was going back to find one particular comment by Sue that I have held on to. She wrote, "Grief is like an obstacle on your timeline. Many people try to climb over it or around it like it really isn't there. Others push it forward and take it with them for the rest of their lives. Both of these options take massive amounts of energy and leave little left over. Others step into it, become it, experience it, and then leave it on their timeline where it belongs. That's not to say you won't visit it occasionally, because we all do. But you are able to leave it and move forward."

I don't know if I've stepped all the way through, but I feel lighter and very much at peace.

Question: Does the length of time that one grieves a loss have any correlation to the depth of the love you felt?   Like the more you loved someone, the longer you will grieve?

FACEBOOK: 8:15 a.m. Yesterday was one month. I've been more aware of each Thursday marking another week, so almost missed 8/25 as a marker until John mentioned it. This morning I went back through my posts. What a journey this has been and all of the support that has carried me and held me and loved me is beyond my ability to capture in words. The emotions have been so intense that my normal ups or downs almost feel flat—not numb as in the early protective shock stage, but calm in comparison to the waves of the first few weeks. I had an interesting question come to me this morning. Is there any correlation between the amount of love you have for someone and the length of the grieving time you'll have? My sense is there are other factors at play. I see that I can extend the grief if I revisit the pain. Or I can speed the healing as I find ways to feel grateful and hopeful. I love waking up and tuning in to my capacity to feel love for Michael in his new journey, for myself on my new normal, and for my family and friends on this side. I want to notice and appreciate all of it.

8/27/13

PERSONAL JOURNAL: 1:29 a.m. Fell asleep on the sofa—not watching TV, just reading. Knew I should just turn in but kept turning over instead. At one point, I felt like Michael was sitting on the other sofa, just hanging out.

Amanda came over today. She missed his service because of living in Santa Monica. On her birthday, she went to the beach and had both a hummingbird and a dolphin sighting. The dolphin jumped out and pirouetted several times, much to her delight. Today, as we were sitting on the sofa, she looked up at my window and there she saw the crystal hummingbirds, the stained glass hummingbird, and dolphins dancing in the wind chime outside of the window, behind the hummingbirds. She also spotted a dolphin on a vase in Michael's bedroom. Amanda experienced a soft rain on the day she learned of his passing.

The video and especially the song Michael wrote, *"When Angels Whisper"* brought her to tears. I promised her a copy.

As she was leaving the house, she stopped at the street, then ran back and knocked on my door, handed me a copy of Carmichael Times newspaper, and said, "He's just messing with us now." The paper was perfectly folded so all you could see was "Michael" across the top. We laughed.

I got a bill from Marshall Hospital today. I don't think Michael lingered and the only way I can say it was instant is by asking him. He says it was instant, and I have my image of him leaping with wings unfurled into the light, into the arms of love. His death certificate says 5:10 a.m. and multiple blunt force trauma with aortic transection as cause of death— considered as "instant" when I looked it up. I know this is one of those roads filled with landmines. Spending any time there does not create peace in my heart.

Broccoli was a trigger today. Just going to the grocery store and knowing he shopped there too. Do people remember him? I'm sure they do and don't know he's my son or that he passed. I almost lost it at the broccoli aisle.

Spoke with Clayton at Rotary who had an El Dorado County chaplain call me. I spoke with him about Michael and my bringing him home. I was very fortunate to be able to do so. The laws are written to prevent this more than allow it. I really do see the hand of Spirit and Michael removing anything from the path of bringing him home. Thank you God. Thank you power of intention.

FACEBOOK: 7:24 a.m. Michael's friend and co-star from Jekyll and Hyde, Amanda, came by yesterday before heading back to Santa Monica. She had not been able to attend his memorial so I showed her the photo video with him singing. The final song, *"When Angels Whisper"* is one he wrote the lyrics to. Here are two of my favorite lines. *"I'll meet you at the end of the rainbow, I promise you this. Anytime the storm clouds gather, I'm there, you can't miss."* Hard to watch without crying, especially the first time. When we dried our tears, Amanda shared that she has had hummingbirds, dolphins, and soft rain show up clearly connected to Michael. On her way out, she looked down at an old paper thrown on my walkway. Only the letters "michael" were visible from the Carmichael Times. "Now he's just messing with us," she laughed.

PERSONAL JOURNAL: 11:11 p.m.

No tears today. Just a fairly normal day. I do love 11:11 and my sense of it being an opening in the veil. I always say "hello" to Michael if I catch it, which I just did.

I wrote some pages this morning for the book—a few each day is my goal. Listened to a Quantum Leap coaching call. Mary was coaching on communication. I listen to the things that upset people in relationships, and I see how insignificant most of these things really are. Try having a child killed—puts a lot into perspective.

Tomorrow I teach a class, and I have work to do to be ready for it. I'll get up early—for now I am going to relax. By the way, Love you Michael. Wish you could help with my back. It's tender.

8/28/13

FACEBOOK: 8:05 a.m. I'm preparing to teach a class starting today at Coldwell Banker on Blueprint for Success from the Inside Out. I didn't want to postpone or cancel as we've had it on the calendar for months. I have become even more attuned to the importance of listening and paying attention to our inner world of thoughts and feelings since Michael's passing. The cliche that we create our own reality may seem over-used. Yet, I have become acutely aware of how little control I have other than my ability to choose my responses, my focus, my openness...or not. Feelings come and I choose to feel them. I also try to pay attention to the triggers. Found out broccoli got to me at the grocery store. I always made sure Michael had broccoli in the fridge. Thought I was going to lose it on the vegetable aisle. Wish me luck on teaching today. Triggers abound and I'm with people who love me and understand. Life is good.

8/29/13—FIVE WEEKS

FACEBOOK: 11:25 a.m. Had breakfast with a dear friend this morning who told me of vivid dreams she has of her dad on the other side. I love hearing these stories. There is even an acronym for these communications—ADCs—after death communications. I feel so much joy knowing that we are never really separated from those we love. I envision Michael on tour making people happy with his music and his loving, mischievous personality. He's singing with the angels. Today is five weeks. Feels much longer. I'm so at peace.

8/30/13

FACEBOOK: 6:40 a.m. Last night Sammie and I spent time in Stu's studio working on some tributes for the set of CDs Stu is putting together. I know I've got that mom-thing when it comes to listening to Michael, but ohhh his voice ... it's so beautiful. I'm blessed to have recordings to listen to. What's hard right now is knowing the days of his live performing have come to an end here on this side. I love listening to him even though I know the tears will flow. It's a sweet sadness filled with love and missing his physical presence. Pretty sure he was right there with us in the studio last night.

8/31/13

PERSONAL JOURNAL: 3:10 p.m. Last night I was over at John and Michelle's for Isaiah's birthday party. So much fun energy going on. Laugher, swimming pool, mostly diving board antics. Brought back happy memories of my boys at that age.

Mom came over today for a moment and when she looked at the collage of photos of Michael on the wall, she was overcome with sadness. I seem to mostly be able to look at his photos with joy, and if I start to miss him and feel sad, I remind myself that he is right here.

Having read George Anderson's book and Dianne Archangel's book, I feel much more certain of his presence as real and not just my imagination. I love when I get clear signs and yet I am reminded that I see it when I believe it—not the other way around. I would love a vivid dream or an appearance. Perhaps those are also a matter of believing that's possible for me. I have no skepticism that it's possible for others. I believe souls communicate all the time. I just want to make sure I don't miss any of Michael's attempts to reach me. Here's my list so far:

- Hummingbird in Christina's home
- Me hearing him say *"I'm so sorry Mom. I'm so sorry."*
- Mom hearing his voice, *"I'm okay Grams. I'm okay."*

- Mom saying he's our Peter Pan and then having the label of agapanthus, the Peter Pan plant, on one of my gifts—also it's the purple lily storm cloud.
- Hummingbird medicine card drawn by Cari
- Timing for Christina and Jerri receiving my calls
- Jerri receiving her vision of Michael Naumer in her meditation that same morning before Christina called her
- Placerville not being Placer County—but mistaken as such so I would be connected to Cari and Richard
- Rabbi getting Michael released to us in two hours instead of two days
- Troy's storm cloud experience
- Sammie's cool breeze experience
- My pendulum asking questions of Michael and knowing when he wanted to be taken from the house to the mortuary
- Freddie and Joseph's hummingbird sightings
- My hummingbird card from Rachel
- Songs playing on John's phone, *Ripple* from Grateful Dead and *Little Wing* from Jimmy Hendrix
- Cari bringing me music box wrapped in same pattern of cloth as his massage cloth which we had wrapped him in
- Angel cards pulled after his memorial: harmony, signs, meditation, truth and integrity, music, diving timing, spiritual growth, soul mate, and my pulling Archangel Michael.
- Speaking to me on day 21: *"Mom, notice the beauty all around you. Don't miss it by being sad and focusing on what's missing. I'm right here."*

- Singer and guide named Michael on our Alaskan excursion.
- Singer at table and singer at piano bar—all saying hello to me.
- Finding dropped bracelet
- Charlene seeing him on board ship with me.

9/1/13

FACEBOOK: 7:26 a.m. Miracles and gratitudes have my attention this morning. Reading a book *"Meant to Be"* loaned to me by a dear friend whose miracle story with her husband after his passing is included in the book and was part of a TV story on angels. As I'm reading each story, I am so moved by the unseen Force orchestrating behind the scenes—a mystery I cannot explain even though I have my personal beliefs which sustain me.

I have been writing down my own list of miracles that I'm aware of and grateful for. Kind of like whale watching—I really have to pay attention or I'll miss them. First there's just a puff of a spout, then maybe a roll of the back, and then the flute as they dive. Little signs above that can be missed so easily in the vastness of the ocean unless I'm really paying attention. Spent time with grandsons and family last night. Appreciating everyone with eyes that are attuned to miracles. Loving and remembering the miracle of having Michael and his two big brothers, John and Troy. I feel closer to all three after Michael's passing. Technicolor love!

9/3/13

FACEBOOK: 10:48 a.m. I've been reading about ADCs (after death contacts) from several sources, some very scientifically documented and categorized, others not so much. These experiences really help those of us left behind when a loved one passes. I know I began to heal and my grief began to ease from the very first indication that Michael was just on the other side and doing his best to let me and others know that he's present and filled with joy. I am writing down all of the stories I have and love hearing from his friends many of the ways he's staying connected to them—dreams, hummingbirds, dolphins, soft rain out of nowhere, whispers, and always a song.

Friends have shared with me similar dreams of him hanging out with them and having very lucid, clear conversations. I would love a dream. So far that hasn't happened that I can remember, and this seems to be one of the key elements of being visited in a dream by a loved one, they are vivid and easily remembered. I still vividly remember when he came to me in my dreams nine-months to the day before he was born, so we are talking July 17, 1976. He clearly asked to be part of our family, running to keep after his two big brothers, but stopping at my side long enough to gain permission from me (I thought I'd prefer a girl). I still see that blond two-year old gazing into my eyes and feel my big "yes, of course." What a sweet and blessed journey it has been to be Resh Michael's mom. The journey continues.

9/5/13—SIX WEEKS

FACEBOOK: 12:06 a.m. Yesterday was 40 days. Forty is supposed to represent wholeness and completion. I am not feeling completely whole yet. Working on it. Rather weepy several times today. Between the tears, I was able to connect, teach a class, talk with clients, handle escrows, do all my normal stuff and even go to a favorite MeetUp group this evening. I haven't had a weepy day in awhile, so I just figure it's part of the healing process. Keeps me very connected to my heart. That's actually a good thing.

PERSONAL JOURNAL: 12:41 a.m. Weepy day today. Even as I'm writing, the tears are dripping off my cheeks onto the pillow. I tried sleeping. I keep thinking of my sweet Michael—wishing it were other than how it is—which I know does me no good at all.

Today I experienced gratitude for the fact that Michael went instantly and didn't suffer or survive with some horrible brain damage or paralysis. Seems like a far-fetched gratitude, but I was feeling it.

I saw police tossing a man like he was a bag of garbage today—in fact, I had to look twice to make sure I was seeing what I was seeing. His feet and hands were bound. The fire truck was just arriving. I think it brought up what could have happened if Michael had been captured and fought back because of his state of mind at the time of the accident. According to his dad, he was hallucinating that aliens were after him and had planted a tracking device in his ear. (He hadn't slept in over five days.)

I'm grateful for the ways I feel Michael has reached through and I must be feeling sad because I want more contact. What are the blessings I can see from all of this?

- Closer family connections
- Awareness of how precious life is

- Meeting Cari and aligning with her mission
- Tapping even deeper into my spiritual understanding
- Seeing how important certain processes are to healing
- After death communications (ADCs) and scientific evidence for contact
- Experiencing my capacity to open and experience love
- Realizing the amazing life Michael led and how much he was loved and appreciated
- People I care about care about me and appreciate my writing
- Maybe a book—not maybe, most definitely

Michael, I love you. I believe you are in a wonderful love-filled space and you can feel all of our love coming to you, enfolding you, from this side. Maybe it pales to the Love embracing you on that side. Is there anything you want to say to me as I write?

"Have fun with Sammie for me tomorrow. She can use some of your wisdom. Go to sleep, Mom. I'll see you in your dreams. I love you. You're the best mom. Take care of yourself. Trust that I'm okay and pay attention to my songs I sing to you. I'm forever with you. Forever and ever. I'll love you forever. Cheer up! All is at is should be. All is well."

FACEBOOK: 8:51 p.m. Luann treated me and Carolyn to a day in Napa with pizza and then lunch and then dessert. Luann loves to cook, so she was in heaven at the Oxbow Market. We told stories and remembered the people we love who are cheering us on from the other side.

9/7/13

FACEBOOK: 7:06 a.m. Woke up early and listened for my morning song from Michael. Today it was "they say that falling in love is wonderful." I also received a most beautiful poem in an email from Kathy, written by A. Powell Davies:

"When sorrow comes, let us accept it simply, as a part of life. Let the heart be open to pain; let it be stretched by it. All the evidence we have says that this is the better way. An open heart never grows bitter. Or if it does, it cannot remain so. In the desolate hour, there is an outcry; a clenching of the hands upon emptiness, a burning pain of bereavement; a weary ache of loss. But anguish, like ecstasy, is not forever. There comes a gentleness, a returning quietness, a restoring stillness. This, too, is a door to life. Here, also, is a deepening of meaning— and it can lead to dedication; a going forward to the triumph of the soul, the conquering of the wilderness. And in the process will come a deepening inward knowledge that in the final reckoning, all is well."

Those were the last words I had written in my journal as a note from Michael yesterday morning. He said, *"I'll love you forever. All is as it should be. All is well."* Wow again. All is well.

PERSONAL JOURNAL: 7:10 a.m. Received a poem in my email this morning from Kathy who said she was thinking of me. The last line was what I had just written in my last entry, "All is well." Michael must be really emphasizing this point to me. I was missing him yesterday as I watched the entertainment at Stanley's new place which is a retirement home for independent living. Mom and I helped get him moved yesterday. The entertainment was country western songs and the singer played the guitar. I could just imagine Michael wowing them with his live show. He was wonderful with the older crowd who really loved his voice. Not that he only appealed to that age group.

Today I am going walking with Vicky and this evening I go to a celebration of Michael's life at Sean's. Sammie is driving to Irvine today—eight hours. I'm going to miss her visits. Lots of changes.

9/9/13

FACEBOOK: 12:34 a.m. Should be heading to bed. Just checked in with Michael in a moment of silence and he's singing "Fly Me to the Moon" in my inner ear. This morning it was another Italian one I don't know the name of. I've been asking for his help to keep me tuned to a frequency of gratitude. I am tempted by thoughts of blame which I know better than to listen to. They do whisper though, and I find it helpful to remember the example Michael set of acceptance. I found this quote from him today on a yellow pad in his tiny writing: *"When you really love someone, it's unconditional. There's no such thing as flaws. We're all working on ourselves and everyday's a new chance to grow from mistakes with compassion."* Thank you, my dear sweet son, for being my teacher once again.

FACEBOOK: 6:13 a.m. Listening for his whispers now. Cousin Kurt says in one of his recent vivid dream visits with Michael, he was doing a stand-up comedy routine to a huge audience and having a great time. He could certainly light up a room.

PERSONAL JOURNAL: 10:53 p.m. Today I have listened to several hours of interviews by Bob Olson who created AfterLifeTV. Also went to Rotary. I've read eight books about after life and communications. I was talking to Kelly this morning and she feels I have wisdom to share with the world that Michael is to help me with.

9/10/13

FACEBOOK: 7:51 a.m. I'm looking for a good metaphor to describe my recent study behavior. Midday yesterday, I found myself listening to an online interview with Dave Kane whose actor/writer/musician son died in a Rhode Island nightclub fire in 2004. Loved the way his son keeps sending him signs. Interesting trying to retrace my steps as to how I found him. I start down a path that my heart is interested in exploring, another path takes off from there, which leads to yet another. I need to drop breadcrumbs.

I gave myself permission to follow as many openings yesterday as I felt like, and landed on a Bob Olson site called "AfterlifeTV.com" I had completed reading *"Hello From Heaven"* —a book filled with stories of ADCs—and googled the author, found a YouTube interview with him and landed on the Bob Olson website. Listened to him interview James VanPraagh, John Holland, and six others before sheer sleepiness had me turn out the lights close to midnight. Michael sang me to sleep. What a journey I find myself on— following the nudges of my heart.

8:03 a.m. My favorite was Dave Kane about all of the ways his son stays connected. I have to rein myself in so I get other things done, like work kinda stuff. I could spend another whole day exploring the interviews Olson has done.

9/11/13

FACEBOOK: 7:28 a.m. Today is 9/11. Remembering the many who lost their lives and all their families and friends who went through their own shock and grief a dozen years ago when the towers collapsed. I relate to the pain of it all from a much more personal place since getting that dreadful call on 7/25/13 telling me Michael was gone. Life altered in a second and there was no space in my heart to even comprehend what I was being told. I've been making space, feeling it all, and know I am healing and growing through this experience. Life is so precious and fragile. I saw a man scolding his teenage daughter yesterday for being late. He was thumping his wrist watch as he marched her toward his car. I thought if you only knew how lucky you are to be in her presence, that she is here with you, and you can give her a big hug! These are the things I notice.

PERSONAL JOURNAL: 8:20 a.m. Need to leave in 20 minutes and haven't showered yet. Where does the time go? I miss Michael. I know he's here, still singing to me, and I feel very connected to him. I miss his physical body—being able to hug him and watch him play and feeling so proud of how well he was doing even though the money hadn't shown up yet.

Sweetheart, I love you. I think and hope you know how much you are loved by me and everyone you connected with. From my studies and listening to people who contact the world you are now in, it seems you have more awareness of what I'm doing than I do of your world. Bob says you were at your memorial service. That's consistent with what I'm learning. I am here if you want to talk. Just tell me how, when, where. I'm open and available. I love you. I used to say that a lot when you were here. "Love you Michael."

9/12/13—SEVEN WEEKS

FACEBOOK: 9:27 a.m. Today Michael's singing "Hey Mambo" in my ear. I want to find the exact words because he does it so well. Always makes me smile. Yesterday I handed my friend Al the video tapes from Michael's memorial service. He's transferring them to a DVD for me. I'm blessed with wonderful friends. Stu is creating a 5-CD tribute album of Michael's work that will be sent to anyone who contributes to the scholarship fund that Ben set up in Resh Michael's honor. My sister taught me a phrase years ago that I feel has helped me walk this journey: *"Expand to include and have it contribute."* This has certainly cracked me wide open.

9/13/13

PERSONAL JOURNAL: 12:11 a.m. How have I changed since 7/25/13? Michael occupies much of my thoughts—I think it's more than before, although I don't know by how much. I feel more connected to my heart. I cry more easily and I listen more carefully, and I believe I love more deeply. I am present to the fragile nature of life, how precious it is. I am attentive to signs and very drawn to anything about the other side.

FACEBOOK: 7:24 a.m. I read a post this morning on my cousin Susan's Facebook wall about what a child of four should know. Great read. Reminds me that the most important thing for children to know is that they are loved no matter what and they have gifts to share. I remember explaining to Michael in the seventh grade that if the tests at school measured musical and artistic talent, he would be placed on the "smart track" like some of his best friends were with math and science. He had told me he was with the "dumb" kids. I was doing my best at self-esteem damage control. Right brain brilliance can be over-looked in a system focused on left brain measurement.

Michael memorized thousands of songs, in foreign languages, not only the words but then taught himself to play them on the bandoneon. I realize how truly brilliant and masterful he was and is. My good fortune was to be able to pour love on this child from the day he was born and watch him bloom. What a treasure.

9/14/13

PERSONAL JOURNAL: 12:24 a.m. Went through two boxes of Michael's papers today. Found another uncashed check, this one $500 from Cappola Winery. That makes $875 that I need to see if I can get reissued. Doesn't count the one for $50 from SLC. Was it my job to manage him? I felt that way at times, that I needed to help more, and yet I wanted to respect his privacy and not enable him.

So much of his writings deal with his desire for deep and lasting love. Maybe Sammie was becoming that for him. He also referred to himself as an angel, and I can see how he just didn't quite fit into a world that seemed cruel to him. Yet, he showed up, entertained, gave his heart, and did his best.

Seven weeks yesterday. Meeting with Cari and some others who are interested in moving family directed funeral services higher in public awareness. I know I want to help. Also, I have an interest in ADCs and in bringing those conversations to the forefront as well.

9/14/13

FACEBOOK: 7:34 a.m. Michael has been singing to me from one of my favorite songs he recorded with Stu on their Broadway album. I feel like he's singing to his own soul, and I see him locked in the arms of loving Spirit having answered a call to come home. Here's the part I keep hearing so sweetly, *"Hurry home, come home to me! Set me free, free from doubt, and free from longing! Into your arms I'll fly, locked in your arms I'll stay."*

Last night I was finally able to sort through another two boxes of papers from his room. Lots of music, some poetry written by him, and a flavor of such a good heart who wanted people to know they are loved and that there is a greater plan. He continues to inspire me.

9/15/13

PERSONAL JOURNAL: 6:43 a.m. Sunday morning. John came to see me yesterday. It was Yom Kippur and he walked the two miles from his house to mine. He shared some of his process with me and how this was the first time he listened carefully to a part of the Rabbi's service that speaks about people who have passed. John experienced Michael walking beside him. John's still sorting through his feelings and how to find his new normal. He loves his brother. I look at photos and Michael stuck to John like Velcro. He adored his big brothers.

It felt good to listen and share heart to heart with John. I love all three of my sons so much. Big gentle hearts, all three. Troy and John have each other and perhaps this passing of Michael serves to remind them of how precious life and brothers are.

I'm leaving tomorrow for a training with Mary Morrissey. I'm open and receptive and willing to see what's next. I intend to listen deeply to my heart and hear what is calling me. I know this experience with Michael cracked open some new areas for me to explore—death and life after, grieving and saying goodbye to the body of a loved one, ritual and ceremony and listening to your heart, being with family and friends and life after for those left behind.

Putting all of this into a teaching format. I will work through it and find a way to pull all of it together for a blessing to me and others. If I meet my resistance and fear along the way, I will befriend them both.

I have my angel on my side, at my side, on the other side, helping and loving me.

FACEBOOK: 8:56 a.m. I am mentally preparing for a week with Mary Morrissey and more training as a life mastery consultant. I've been a student of Mary's since first meeting her in 1998. She works with us from our vision statements, what we are consciously intending to create, and how to align with universal laws to bring an idea from the land of possibility to physical reality. Since Michael's passing, I have not wanted to visit my vision statement. Everything feels different. All dreams are on the table for examination and review. I make plans, life brings an unexpected life-altering event, my plans change. Mary teaches us to start always with "notice what you are noticing." This seemingly simple instruction continues to help me on this journey with Michael. I listen to my heart, in the moment, ask what I am to say or do, and act accordingly. I am willing to head for a week of training with my tattered vision to see what I am now going to create,

275

knowing that plans change. I get to choose how I respond and how I rebuild. I am not alone. Many walk beside me. I continue to look for and discover the gifts and blessings.

FACEBOOK: 7:14 p.m. Some days are easier than others. Friends tell me they're amazed at how well I'm doing. I'm grateful for that. I have nothing to gauge my state of heart and mind by, this event being like my own personal collapse of the 9/11 towers. Nothing I could have imagined or prepared for. I have learned which thought trails to follow and which to leave alone. Today seemed filled with more reminders and choices than others, and when they occur, I just keep telling Michael I love him. I'd rather feel the emotions than the numbness. I need to start packing. It's easier not to. I have until 6:15 a.m. when I need to leave for the airport. Resistance—not my first time on the dance floor with you.

9/16/13

FACEBOOK: 2:10 p.m. I'll be off of Facebook after this post and all week thru most of Friday at a training for Life Mastery Consultants. I need way more training before I feel like I'm even close to mastering life! Last night I hit a bump. In 36 years, I've never gone more than two or three weeks without seeing or talking with Michael. While he lived in Santa Rosa, we didn't see each other as often, but knowing he was two hours away made it not such a big deal. He moved home five or six years ago for "six months" and I so enjoyed him as a roommate and dear friend. Of course I'm his mom, but gave up the "mothering" role years ago. I feel his presence more sometimes than others. Really wanted an in-the-flesh conversation last night. Hugged his smelly shirt close to me instead and let the tears flow. Better today.

FACEBOOK: 2:45 p.m. One more post before I shut this down. I am so grateful for being able to hug and love on and talk to Michael's big brothers, Troy and John, who have stood by me and held me even as their own hearts were breaking. My mom, my sister, my niece and nephew, all of my friends—I appreciate and love each of you. Life is so precious.

FACEBOOK: 4:41 p.m. We are all moving through this together, guided by the love we all feel for Michael which has expanded to include so many others.

PERSONAL JOURNAL: 9:50 p.m. Great beginning to the training and cruise. Mary sat at our table tonight. She had each of us say which principles have made the greatest difference. I said, "noticing what I am noticing" so I can make choices that take me in a direction I want to go.

It feels good to be here. None of the coaches knew about Michael, so I needed to let them know. It was great seeing Barbara again and Pat and all of my friends made here over the years. I found myself speaking the words: "the bigger the impact, the bigger the impact." I have been given an opportunity to reach people from a powerful place of knowing about intention and choices.

Do I cry? Last night, before leaving for the cruise, I was holding Michael's smelly shirts like a baby, rocking us both. Realizing this is the longest we've ever been apart in this domain. I realize I need to learn new ways to be with him now. So I am.

9/20/13—EIGHT WEEKS

FACEBOOK: 5:46 p.m. Completing our Life Mastery Training at Sea and pulling into port at Long Beach. Last night Mary Morrissey honored my son Michael by concluding our group's time together with the playing of his song *"When Angels Whisper"*. She encouraged us to all sing our songs, not to wait. Life doesn't give everyone 100 years. Michael gave his gifts and sang his songs and played full out while he was with us in the flesh. I believe he was right there beside me as we all listened to his song. Thank you, Mary. And thank you, Stu, for writing the tune that inspired his lyrics: *"Listen to your angels, they know why we're here and what we've come to bring."*

9/22/13

FACEBOOK: Spent time with grandsons last night—three beautiful free souls that I feel good being around. Family time lights me up. I notice my tears well up around mothers and babies, like at the boys' soccer game yesterday. I relive how precious each of my own babies and grandbabies were to hold and rock. We still squish together in a blob on the sofa while playing "think of an animal" or watching movies. Just loving and being loved—learning to appreciate every precious moment.

9/23/13

PERSONAL JOURNAL: 9:50 a.m. Longer spells between journal entries. Committed to daily entries. Will forgive myself if I'm not perfect.

Yesterday, I learned that Michelle's friend Julie's mom lost her son when he was 21 and her husband when Julie was only three. I spoke to her of my experience and of feeling like

Michael is right here with me. I shared the writing of *Inside the Other Side* by Concetta Bertoldi about Mission Entities and Mystical Travelers and the gifts they came to bring. I believe we each experienced our sons this way and each shared the courage a mother needs to hold the center for the family. In my sharing, I blessed both of us. "Michael, I love you!"

FACEBOOK: 5:33 p.m. I was reading some of my journal entries this morning. I've journeyed quite a distance. Do I still tear up and miss Michael? You bet. Am I finding ways to honor his memory and see the blessings in all of it? Yes, that too. I wake up and still have a moment of needing to be quiet so as not to wake up Michael. Then I remember, and send him an "I love you" out loud. I used to do that daily when he was here in the flesh. We would exchange "love you's" throughout the day. I am so grateful that we expressed those feelings to each other frequently. Same goes for my sons Troy and John. We keep those love reservoirs filled.

9/24/13

PERSONAL JOURNAL: 1:26 a.m. Had a long conversation with Cari today. She is encouraging me to do grief coaching. I have a new working title for the book I am to write: *From Grief to Grace—a Journey of the Heart.* I believe the chapter headings have already been given to me. Cari and many others have used the term "amazing" about me. I am asking what that means so I can really ground it. Cari used the term "serenity" and I could relate somewhat. She also said I am really clear about what I'm doing when it comes to Michael. I think it has come from my heart and checking in moment by moment. I shared my 20 inspired points and she felt like I had downloaded such wisdom that she needed to process it all.

I've never felt stuck in this process—I've felt sad and my heart has ached for wanting to hold Michael and be with him for an in-person conversation, but I have always felt like I am moving forward and will help others to do so as well.

Right now I'm smiling as I remember hearing the car door, then the gate opening, then the slider and the instruments and cases piling up next to the banister, then Michael's footsteps up the stairs and the refrigerator door opening, then the cupboard and footsteps back down to fill his glass with filtered water. "How'd it go?" I'd ask. "Good," was his usual response.

I miss the messes—the little piles of papers, music stands, shoes, towels. "I love you Michael. I believe you know how much!" Is there anything you need to say to me or anything I need to do for you?

"Sammie. Call her tomorrow. ITunes—how to release the single. Work on the book. A little every day."

PERSONAL JOURNAL: 6:35 a.m. Woke up with a song from church in my ear, "My Soul is Welcome Here." I noticed a strong preference that Michael's voice be singing to me instead. Then I noticed this little thought, "If I am healed of this and create a new normal, Michael might go away. " Almost like a belief that if I stay sad, I stay connected—that hanging out in the grief is closer to hanging out with Michael and moving on feels like I'll lose him all over again.

What are my desires regarding myself and Michael? I can clearly see that I was guided in the beginning few hours by an intense need to be at his side. The strength of that burning desire brought him home to me. Next was a desire to connect and honor and tend to him—to allow others who wanted to speak with him and pray with him to be able to do so. Then, to send him off with his well-wishes written on his simple box and his body tucked in with all the love and tears and laughter we all were feeling. That it was all done here in our home allowed us to stay cocooned in our love for him and for each other.

Kurt began immediately to work on his music and photo video, on the artwork for us, and we began the next piece—a beautiful memorial. Lots of tears and laughter and connecting. We were still cocooned here even after Michael's body was picked up. We had our hummingbirds and each other. We had signs to share and memories to talk about and the energy was sweet and sad and joyful and painful all at once.

Next desire, go through his things and distribute to family. Kurt has most of his clothes. Sammie has some. Still very connected to him. Working with Stu on his tribute album, getting his service on DVD for my dad to watch. Still not complete.

Reading everything I can about ADCs and mediums, driven by my desire to know how to stay connected, how to recognize the ways Michael is here, and how to help others do so for their loved ones.

Here I am, 61 days later, feeling peaceful and knowing I have a book to write. If I take the steps—burning desire, bridging the gap, believing and becoming—I can see where I am and build on the foundation I've laid. My desire right now—stay connected to those I love—Michael, John, Troy, Mom, grandsons, sister, Dad, friends. Let the experience of Michael's passing grow in its gift so it touches millions with its beauty and love and possibility. Books, CDs, speaking—I am here to serve. I recognize a partnership with Michael that is powerful. "I love you Michael."

FACEBOOK: 7:58 a.m. I caught a thought this morning as it was knocking on my mind, and after a brief exchange in my journal, I got my blessing and then dismissed it. The thought was, "If I am fully healed of this grief and create a new normal, Michael might go away." Almost like a belief that by staying sad, I stay connected, and by moving on it feels like I'm distancing. I am glad I caught that one before it moved in and pitched a tent. I see clearly that holding onto the grief is not empowering and would not be an energy Michael wants to hang out in. He says *"Fill your life up full with joy and laughter."* I am learning to stay connected to Michael through the joy I feel when I see his pictures and hear his music and listen for his voice in my heart. Works for staying connected to those I love on this side as well.

9/25/13

PERSONAL JOURNAL: 12:16 a.m. Just received an email from a dear friend confirming much of what I've been feeling about Michael and his contribution to this next phase of my life. I am remembering a reading many, many years ago in which I was told he came to me to be my protector and care for me. I thought that meant he would be with me when I needed help as I age. Guess it will be in this new form. I am reading *"The After Life Experiments"* and already have this feeling that Michael is speaking to me from its pages. Rainbows, love that is eternal, ultimate earth lesson—I'm feeling bliss in this moment.

PERSONAL JOURNAL: 11:42 p.m. Two months—7/25—9/25. Facebook fan page for Resh Michael is up and I have much to learn. More songs and videos need to be added and I'm going to need Stu's help. He's out of town. Also want to get Michael's single out on YouTube and ITunes. The YouTube would be private, I'm guessing. Not sure. Found out 20 minutes is the maximum size for FB. I can learn to edit video, just need the right program.

How am I feeling? Just noticed all of that last bit came from the left brain side. My feelings seem muted right now. Not high or low, just normal range and sort of muffled. I haven't cried today. First time I believe. I received a beautiful gift from Clay of a hummingbird lamp. I felt gratitude and joy. Put it on the mantle and added two more hummingbirds. When I pass by, I smile and say, "I love you" to Michael.

9/26/13—NINE WEEKS

PERSONAL JOURNAL: 7:31 a.m. Woke up at 5:55 a.m. with Michael's angel song in my ears. I love that connection. Reading more about Gary Schwartz and his after life experiments. I have no problem believing all of this is true. Even more strongly now than before Michael's passing. I am desiring to develop my own abilities to communicate with the other side, even if it's just with Michael. That seems ironic that I want to ask him questions now, but was very mindful of his privacy while he was living here with me in the flesh. I think he's still here and also able to be anywhere else he chooses to be as well.

So, here's my experiment. I'm tuning into Michael and asking some questions. I'll write what comes through.

Surroundings? *"Mostly right here with you and Chewie. The colors are more intense and I have no need to sleep or eat. Just like I used to, I come and go, but I can be here immediately if you call me. I will always be able to hear you."*

Activities? *"Mom, the music is incredibly beautiful. All of the masters are here. I can hear and feel and even taste the music. Chopin, Strauss, Tchaikovsky, Beethoven, Bach, Jerry Garcia, Elvis, Jimmy Hendrix, Pavarotti, Puccini. I can play any instrument I want to. I love my bandoneon most of all. Thank you for always encouraging me."*

People? *"Yes, Aunt Betty is here and so is Uncle Ed. Grandma and Grandpa Ortego and Charlotte's little boy. I spend most of my time with family and you and Kurt and Stu and Sammie and Grandma, John and Michelle. I'm watching out for Troy and Riley. I get to be the big brother in some funny way now. I'll be there tonight with the family at John's to celebrate his birthday early. Dad isn't handling this as well as you are.*

Have to go now. Off to a concert. Love you Mom."

9/27/13

FACEBOOK: 7:41 a.m. Gathered at the Ortegos for a family celebration last night—early birthday for son John. I baked the same cake he's had for 40 years. Michelle refers to it as "the cake." Chocolate with split layers filled with chocolate pudding and iced with chocolate whipped cream. When he was little, John didn't like icing so this was my solution. Now it's become a tradition. Picking out a birthday card for him was a little more emotional than usual. I always let the right card speak to me. Some spoke to me of John and others were perfect for Troy or Michael. I love my sons.

9/28/13

PERSONAL JOURNAL: 7:44 a.m. Reading with JG went well. Confirmed my belief that Michael is very present, very aware of how much we all love and miss him. He uses the image of a rainbow to express how we are all still connected and there is no end to it. He said this was supposed to happen and the chaos was needed or he would have figured a way out of it. I'm not sure that's comforting to me. I would have preferred he stayed here, and evidently there is work for both of us to do that this is launching. My overall experience was of peace and recognition that the love I feel for Michael is matched by him and our souls are working together somehow. JG picked up that the energies of this world were very hard for Michael to be in. He is so sensitive and compassionate. He felt no pain in passing over and his guides were with him at all times.

Yesterday Cari and Richard came to visit with three women who met at Jerri Grace's training the day of Michael's passing. We are all connected through that event and they are creating a non-profit to promote awareness of choices when it comes to funeral services. I am speaking at Nandi's class at City College on 10/15 about my experience of bringing Michael home.

FACEBOOK: 8:28 a.m. Day by day I am learning about the nuances of joy and sadness and pain and healing. For awhile I couldn't bring up happy memories without threat of sobbing from the pain of missing him so much. And, I want to be able to celebrate and treasure all of these joyful moments we shared. I am helped by my belief and faith in life-after-life and am learning to talk to him out loud or in my heart whenever I need to. I love speaking to others about their memories of him and as I do a welling up of tears may happen. I am mostly able now to follow his direct instructions to me on Day 21 as I was weeping from missing him while an amazing sunrise was unfolding before me over Alaskan waters, *"Mom, pay attention to all the beauty in front of you. Don't miss it by being sad and wishing things were different. I'm right here."* Wise words. Focus on the beauty of the present moment. Part of that beauty is sometimes a sweet memory causing me to smile and be grateful for how many we shared.

9/30/13

PERSONAL JOURNAL: 4:08 a.m Reading more on ADCs and mediums. Learned there is a DCM-IV code related to a normal bereavement period. It's supposedly two months. How long does it take a bone to heal? How do you heal a broken heart?

10/1/13

FACEBOOK: 1:33 a.m. Sixty-eight days. Remember when you have a new baby and they are days old, then weeks old, and finally months old? I guess I'm doing a similar count. This Thursday will be 10 weeks. I'm the new baby it seems, learning to grow through this and making progress. A dear friend told me that it's not time that heals all wounds, but what you do with the time that makes the difference. This evening I gathered all of the entries I've made since 7/25 into a single word file so I could more easily read them. I also have a journal I've been keeping. It appears I've made it through the most intense part of the grieving. I still hear Michael singing to me when I tune in, and I still have one of his smelly shirts handy for a good whiff of his physicality, and I'm not triggered several times a day. I'm finding some blessings, and I'd still trade them all for turning the clock back and having Michael here with us in the flesh.

PERSONAL JOURNAL: 10/1/13 8 a.m. Love this quote from Cheryl Richardson, Debbie Ford's sister, on Facebook: "When we lose someone we love, the goal isn't to move on or get over it. The goal is to learn to integrate the new relationship into our lives. Talk to loved ones who have passed on. Ask them for support with your grief. Keep their spirit alive by talking about them. And allow the loss to keep you connected to what matters most—the people we love."

10/2/13

PERSONAL JOURNAL: 6:56 a.m. Noticing my thoughts. I'm trying to remember how much space in my thoughts was filled with Michael before his passing. Most of my time, I believe I was attending to my own life. Marketing for the business of real estate, attending Rotary and the board meetings, building a coaching business in the background. Michael was here and off to Sonoma quite a bit. I enjoyed watching him work on new material and was often thinking of ways to help promote him.

Now he fills my thoughts and I notice I am so used to it, that if I go awhile without him in the forefront, I feel an urgent need to call him in. Is he singing to me?   Do I feel him near?

Yesterday someone knocked at my door and ran. She had long hair and drove a dark colored compact car. I couldn't recognize either. She left flowers and a candle on my doorstep. Very sweet. I'm guessing they were as much for Michael as for me.

So now I notice my attention is on class and coaching and supporting Cari's work and having Michael's music available. Grief coaching is a path that I have some first-hand knowledge with. Intention, burning desire, reaching out, studying—baby steps.

FACEBOOK: 8:00 a.m. This morning Michael is singing "On an Evening in Roma" then switching to "Hey Mambo." It's an interesting blend. I am noticing a contrast in my thoughts before Michael's passing and after. When he was physically here, I was aware of his presence and entertained by his practicing, sometimes we would engage in conversation, and we would frequently fire off "I love you" to each other out of the blue. He had been spending three or four days in Santa Rosa the last few weeks and I missed him but didn't think about him every moment. Now I am learning to integrate him into my life in this new way. I imagine a time will come when I don't have him in the forefront of my mind so much. I've had glimpses of this. I notice I do love sharing stories about him with anyone who knew him, and I do notice how much more I am aware of those I love who are here in the flesh. "Life is precious—handle with care."

10/3/13 TEN WEEKS

FACEBOOK: 2:03 p.m. Ran into a friend of a friend of Michael's this morning at the grocery store. I could tell he was dancing around mentioning Michael, so I did. He wasn't sure it was okay to talk about him or what had happened. I reassured him that I welcome any chance I get to share about Michael and honor his life. I love talking about him. Makes me feel more connected. And, I'm finding that these conversations often go beneath the surface and create a heart connection, even for just a moment. Vulnerability and transparency—I find these to be good lessons I am learning about.

10/5/13

PERSONAL JOURNAL: 1:36 a.m.   John's birthday ended at midnight and it was literally a "poopy" ending. The store bathroom backing up from the restaurant next door and spilling raw sewage into his pharmacy caused a cancellation of his birthday dinner. He was, instead, babysitting hazmat people who were cleaning the mess up. He seems to be taking it in stride.

I have an appointment for a massage tomorrow here at home with Lisa. She is also going to see if she can contact Michael for me. I notice a little numbness setting in. Not like the disbelief numbness on day one, but a contrast to the intense emotions of the first few weeks. The tears don't come as often and I feel more peace than pain.

I was so vulnerable and my feelings were so intense that the breadth of joy and sadness I experienced expanded, leaving my middle range which used to feel normal, feeling a bit flat. I do still hear him singing and am wondering if the high-pitched ringing in my ears is due to his energy being present. I'd like to hope so. I don't remember it being so loud before. "I love you Michael."

FACEBOOK: 8:26 a.m. Noticing my appreciation of Facebook as a place where I have been able to share from my heart and receive such heartfelt messages of love and support in return. I know I could not have reached so many so quickly to let them know of Michael's passing were it not for Facebook. And the love and support have continued. Friendships have been strengthened, renewed, birthed, and my world is richer. Who knew! Who could have predicted this phenomenon when the site was created? I'm thinking of the power of our words and images to bless us all or cause incredible pain. We get to choose and Facebook is just our "telephone line" (to be really archaic.) How many have given up their landlines? But I digress. I'm grateful to all of you who have walked this path of healing with me and grateful for the latest form of tribal drumming we know as Facebook. Big virtual hug from me.

10/6/13

FACEBOOK: 10:46 a.m. Gentle tears, not the sobbing ones, but the gentle ones that well up and spill over from a sweet memory or the lyrics of a song. Woke up this morning and hearing Michael singing in my inner ear brought on the gentle tears. Also happened yesterday during my wonderful massage with Lisa who came to my house and worked on me in Michael's massage room on his table. I could close my eyes and imagine he was the one touching me. Quite a beautiful experience. She played the soundtrack from the movie with Travolta playing an irreverent angel named Michael. It was perfectly unplanned as background music and perfect to listen to the lyrics with new ears. I am learning to integrate new ways of being with Michael as I let go of the familiar ones which I so often miss. Gentle tears help. Thank you, Lisa, for your hands and your heart.

10/8/13

FACEBOOK: 1:49 a.m. I am noticing that since Michael's passing, when people ask how I am doing, I hear it from a place of knowing they are genuinely interested and care about me. It's different from the social exchanges to which we might reply, "Fine, and how are you?" and then keep on moving or talk about the weather. Instead, I stop to answer from my heart and most of the time my answer is, "I'm doing great." And I mean it. I have recently been adding that I am learning new ways to communicate with Michael and will ask if they have someone on the other side that they stay connected with. I love the moments of authentic sharing this results in. I am finding so many who love to tell me their stories and we both are blessed by the exchange. Another gift from Michael.

10/9/13

FACEBOOK: 8:02 a.m. "Luck be a lady tonight" are the lyrics being sung by Michael in my inner ear this morning. Came with an image of him entertaining, doing his cabaret show, still having a wonderful time doing what he loves to do. I'm beginning to call this frequency he uses my "love channel." I am noticing a similar frequency which feels like a "wisdom channel" that I can tune into more easily when I'm quiet. Then there's what Mary Morrissey refers to as "CNN—

constantly negative news channel"—which I do my best to tune out. Since our minds think in images, I find this channel metaphor helpful, especially as I am learning to tune into new ones from a higher dimension. Sometimes it's my gentle tears that let me know I've made the connection.

10/10/13—ELEVEN WEEKS

FACEBOOK: 7:17 a.m. "Our love is here to stay." Soothing words to awaken to. Day 77, 11 weeks. Just quietly reflecting on this passage and how I've grown as a result of it. Our love IS here to stay! Forever and always. Thank you, Michael, for teaching me this in so many ways, for expanding my heart and my capacity to receive all of the love flowing to and through me, for still singing to me, and for showing me new ways to stay connected. I am so blessed and grateful. Love you.

FACEBOOK: 8:39 a.m. This morning I'm hearing a medley of songs from Michael and when I opened my eyes the digital clock showed 7:11. Made me laugh out loud. Yesterday I saw a neighbor and past client in the grocery store with her preschooler. We stopped to chat and I realized she hadn't heard about Michael's passing. I notice I usually tear up when the news is fresh for someone else. I also shared how tender I feel watching parents with their children and how precious these years are. She hugged her son a little tighter as we headed off on our different paths.

10/13/13

PERSONAL JOURNAL: 7:31 a.m. Gentle tears this morning. Missing Michael's physical presence, his talent. Last night I was at Stu's to record my part of the tribute for the CDs. We played "This is the moment" and watching him perform so beautifully brings me that strange mix of joy and sadness that I am now learning so much about.

I buried my face in his smelly shirt pillow this morning, grateful for the fading familiar body smells. Will they fade too? Stu played a recording of Michael talking to the Three Stages manager in Folsom and it was so sweet to not only hear his speaking voice, but the way he was asking each question so he could truly learn about the other side of the music business.

I know better than to ask why—yet I'm watching Michael perform, then Josh Groban, and it's my haunting question. With such talent and motivation and beauty to give, why, why, why...no answers come. None that I am able to fathom.

In this instance,, "why" questions lead to a cul de sac of upset and not to any information I can make any progress with. Why progress? There's that why word again. It takes me into the logical side of my brain. So does "how." Who can I be, what can I contribute, who can I bless? These seem to be the questions from my heart that pull me through any darkness.

FACEBOOK: 8:12 a.m. Yesterday I watched the DVD of Michael's memorial for the first time and once again experienced this paradox of emotions—feeling such joy and pain at the same time—knowing that to try to dial down the pain will reduce my capacity to feel the joy. I am reminded of how much love was poured on me and my family to make that service so beautiful. From my heart to all of yours—thank you, thank you, thank you. The flowers have all faded, the visitors have scattered, we celebrated an amazing life together, and what remains lives on within each of us—the love we all shared. I felt it all over again as I watched the video and felt Michael's presence sitting with me, enjoying it all.

10/15/13

FACEBOOK: 7:21 a.m. Almost twelve weeks. When I put my head on my pillow last night and recalled my day, I realized it was the first "no tears" day. I spoke about Michael to friends several times, played his music, talked to him, wrote in my journal, revisited day one trying to fill in a block of time that is completely blank in my memory, and not even a gentle tear. In noticing this, I also noticed some concern that Michael would fade with the tears. Woke up with him singing "our love is here to stay" to me, so seems like he's given me a great answer to my concern. Last night I also finished reading my 19th book on life after life and on connecting with loved ones who have passed. I am speaking at a friend's class at City College tonight about my experience of bringing Michael home the day he passed and how sacred and important that experience was for me and those who were able to come and be with him. I will welcome the tears if they show up, and am okay if they don't.

PERSONAL JOURNAL: 8:55 a.m. I promised myself a page of writing per day—one yellow pad page. I'm on day two. So far so good. I also wrote on Facebook today. Noticed that yesterday was my first no tears day. I didn't realize it until I put my head on my pillow. Then I became concerned that my connection to Michael was fading, like the odor on his shirt.

Today I awoke to "Our love is here to stay," so I'm feeling okay that we're still hanging together. I believe he has the ability on the other side to be with many people all at the same time, so I'm not being greedy with his time. Today I go for a reading with Saireh. Mom saw her yesterday. I'm curious if she will also indicate I'm to write a book with Michael's help. Tonight I am speaking at a class on death and dying, telling the story of bringing Michael home.

10/16/13

PERSONAL JOURNAL: 7:55 a.m. Spoke last night at Nandi's class and can see the impact of this story of bringing Michael home. I spoke from my heart, answered questions, showed a few photos from my IPad, and flowed into the presentation as guided by my intuition.

I also saw Saireh yesterday for a reading. Flowing with my guidance seems to be my new directive. I am to follow, not lead, in this dance with life. I am being God with skin on, letting love use me, and allowing Spirit to flow through me. I'm finding myself conflicted, so need to step back and ask for guidance. Mary has us create a vision and energy flows where our attention goes. Is it my vision or Spirit's vision for me?

My heart's desire is to be a pure channel for love's presence— expressed through me as a mother, a friend, a realtor, a teacher, a coach, a writer, a sister, a daughter, and whatever other labels are mine to flow through.

10/17/13—TWELVE WEEKS

FACEBOOK: 11:15 a.m. Sharing a prayer by A. Powell Davies given to me by a dear friend early in my process. Just found it again and loved it even more this time.

10/18/13

PERSONAL JOURNAL: 1:17 a.m. There's a dullness I'm feeling, not always, just sometimes. What are the thoughts I'm noticing—the disempowering ones. About to hit 68 years of age and feeling fat and stiff, not lean and limber. Have a couple of listings, one brand new, one set to close end of month. Not much in my pipeline. Energetically, I'm on about a 4 or 5 out of 10. Shall I focus on my real estate or my coaching or the areas of my home that need attention?   I need not only a business plan, I need a life plan. I need to tap into gratitude and realize all is well.

10/19/13

FACEBOOK: 12:23 a.m. Seems like my days are arranging themselves into some kind of new normal. I'm used to the quiet of living without my favorite roommate. Still missing him and find playing his music is a way of connecting. Such a beautiful voice, and oh how I love the way he masterfully accompanies himself with the bandoneon. I miss his late night practice sessions which filled the whole house with sounds. And, I miss the smell of garlic and onions and whatever concoctions he'd get going in the kitchen late at night when I was heading for bed. There are no clothes piled up near the laundry and no towels hanging from doorknobs. Sometimes I pretend he's away on an extended tour. I'm grateful for my tour of duty as his mom. Such a blessing.

10/21/13

PERSONAL JOURNAL: 6:10 a.m. Kelly came by last night and we visited. Favorite topic for both of us—Michael. She calls on him for advice. She came over every day while I was in my most vulnerable place. Cooked, cleaned, sat with me. We have been through a lot in the years together as neighbors and friends. She watched Michael grow up and then he would, as a young man, enjoy some time in her hot tub—peer to peer. Great conversations and Michael's wise way of listening.

Shared with her last night my numbers discovery—"Nine" and "Eleven." Nine, in the numerology world, is considered to be the most conscious, most tolerant, least judgmental of all the numbers. Michael and Troy were born almost ten years apart and both are nines—5/17/67 and 4/17/77. So I began playing with some numbers related to Michael's time here in the physical world.

Born 9 months to the day after coming to visit me in a dream on 7/17/76. Age 36 = 9. Leap years = 9. Days from his last birthday to his passing = 99. 365 X 36 = 13,140 = 9 + nine leap years = 13,149 = 9, plus 99 = 13,248 = 9. Day of passing = 7 + 25 + 2013 = 2045 = 11. Now that I'm paying attention, whenever the numbers 9 or 11 show up, I say hello to Michael.

FACEBOOK: 7:12 a.m. I often will add up numbers for a calendar day and year or those on a digital clock. This comes from studying and playing with Angeles Arrien's Tarot book years ago, compliments of my mom and sister. My birth number is a six. Michael's is a nine. A quick Google of birth

297

number nine says it's the most conscious, most tolerant, least judgmental of all the numbers. That fits Michael. I started playing with more numbers. He was 36 when he passed. 3+6=9. He had 99 days here from his last birthday to his passing. He had 9 leap years. He was born 9 months to the day from when he appeared to me in a dream asking to come. And if you add up all the days he was with us in physical form, 13,239, it factors down to 9. Nine is also the number representing completion. Anyone else find that amazing? When I realized this around Thursday last week, I started getting little nudges to look at the clock—7:02, 6:03, 3:33 — all in the a.m. I've started laughing and saying hello to Michael when it happens. Feels like he's found another fun channel for reminding me of his presence, even in the middle of the night.

10/22/13

PERSONAL JOURNAL: 6:36 then 6:41 then 7:02 and 7:04 Michael arrived on a 9 and left on an 11. I believe he's using those numbers on the digital clock to say "Hello." This morning he woke me at 6:36 and next time I looked it was 6:41. So I went into meditation with those numbers and then felt this command: *"Now, open your eyes and look, now!"* Clock showed 7:02. I'm smiling and saying "Hello, Michael" and thinking 7:05 will be the eleven. My math needed help because I turned again to look and it was 7:04 which is what really adds up to eleven.

Writing at least a page a day and almost missed yesterday. Had my coaching class with Cari and Amanda. I am being blessed in every moment. I feel so loved.

10/23/13

PERSONAL JOURNAL: 12:33 a.m. Committing to writing a page a day on the book keeps it moving. I've not missed and it was a choice to write anyway, even if I'm tired, because I said I would.

I had great coaching sessions on Monday with Amanda and Cari. I can see that this time we are working with each other is very powerful. I am able to connect into guidance and ask questions that impact the patterned structures.

10/24/13—THIRTEEN WEEKS

FACEBOOK: 8:16 a.m. Hit a little rough patch last night of missing Michael and Sammie and them just hanging out here laughing and filling my home with joy. Texted Sammie in Irvine. Helped to share with her. Noticing the fear behind the tears was a feeling that Michael was slipping away. I wasn't as aware of his presence and didn't hear him singing to me. After texting Sammie back and forth a few times, I felt better and went back to my reading. I'm on book number 23 about life after life. This one is by Gordon Smith, *"Through My Eyes."* I looked at my digital time and it showed 10:44—adds up to 9. So I said hello to Michael, knew he was still there if I need him, and took a moment. Memories of him as a little child flooded me with joy. Today is week thirteen. He woke me with a song I cannot name yet heard him singing it often on stage. I opened my eyes and looked at the time—added up to a 9. He's teaching me about trust.

10/25/13—THREE CALENDAR MONTHS

PERSONAL JOURNAL: 12:36 a.m. Three months or 13 weeks or 91 days—my life is referenced around 7/25/13 and the events surrounding it. *"Listen to your angels."* I'm way more focused on that than ever before.

Noticing a flat feeling—not much inner motivation going on. My "light up switch" flips when I have an opportunity to help someone wake up to who they are and what's really possible for them. What would it look like if that was my life and it all came to me in a gentle flow that provided for all of my financial needs. That's an image worth pondering.

10/26/13

FACEBOOK: 9:47 a.m. Drama—the word popped into my head this morning. I noticed that throughout this experience of Michael's passing, I've felt extreme sadness and exquisite joy and no drama. Getting a pedicure last week and there was a soap opera on. I listened to these insane dialogues that could only produce upset and drama and thought "where's a modeling of another possibility." No drama, no television? Maybe that's why I love movies where someone wakes up. Give me *"It's a Wonderful Life"* or *"Scrooge."* Thank you dear Michael for being such a great entertainer, singer, musician and giving me the kind of drama that inspires. Loving you.

PERSONAL JOURNAL: 11:18 a.m. (11-9) This morning my first glance at the digital clock was 7:02—too early. Rolled over. Next opening of eyes was 9:11, so I wished Michael a good morning and gave him a virtual hug. I seldom sleep that late. Must have needed it.

An old friend popped by last night. We watched Michael's DVD slide show. It always makes me smile and tear up and appreciate my sweet, sweet angel of a son. I am so blessed. Life is sweet. Drama is optional.

10/27/13

PERSONAL JOURNAL: 7:27 a.m. Asked Michael what he can tell me about the best way for us to communicate. I sensed I had best grab my pen and journal. He's singing, *"Free from doubt and free from longing, come home to me, set me free…"*

"Hi Mom. You've noticed the way I use lyrics from songs I've recorded to send you comfort and love. I am always here and other places at the same time. Your thoughts include me and connect me. We are all connected through our love for each other. Our family knows how to love and be loving with each other. It's easy for me to connect in when there is so much love. Use joy and laughter to open the channels of communication with the angelic realm. It is the surest channel. Gratitude and joy carry the same vibration. Did you notice how often the Dalai Lama laughed in the film you watched? I was there with you. Yes, I loved the film and the director. I am teaching and learning and growing and feel none of the restraints from being incarnated. I know music in a whole new way and see how it can heal and align the very cells of the human body so they are back to their perfect pattern. Continue to work on your book about your process. It will inspire and help millions. We are a great team. I chose you as my mom and we grew together. I am always with you. I'll meet you at the end of the rainbow. That is for now and future and always—the rainbow—joy, hope, light in all its dimensions, primary colors, rain clouds storming. This is a

bridge of light to follow and I am always there to meet you in this present time. I promise. Take my hand. I'm guiding you now. I love you forever. You learned unconditional love. You gave it to me. I give it back to you and it grows for all of us to see and feel. Your way of coaching leads people to their own truth and holds them in love's truth as they open. You are learning to trust even more the Divine side of your nature to lead you and provide for you. Each day is a gift and you get to give your gift of unconditional love to the world. It makes a difference. I love you, Michael. I love you."

FACEBOOK: 8:24 a.m. Michael gave me a teaching this morning as I was journaling. I heard him say, *"Use joy and laughter to open the channels of communication with the angelic realm. It is the surest channel. Gratitude and joy carry the same vibration."* I wrote this down and he continued to teach. He spoke about the line in the song he wrote that I love, *"I'll meet you at the end of the rainbow, I promise you this."* I felt that to be a future promise for when I pass. He said, *"That promise is for now and the future and always—the rainbow—joy, hope, light in all of its dimensions, primary colors, rain clouds storming—this is a bridge of light to follow and I am always there to meet you—in this present time. I promise. Take my hand. I am guiding you now."* Powerful words for me to hear and take in. I'm in bliss and awe as I share this. It seems to be a message not just for me.

10/28/13

PERSONAL JOURNAL: 10:27 p.m. Came to bed last night and clock shows 11:09 p.m. which gave me a big smile as I said hello to Michael. Only needed two minutes for 11:11 to show up.

Got into my car to come home tonight and caught 9:09 as the time. I am enjoying the numerical reminders to check in.

I noticed this evening that there is an intensity in the attention surrounding the immediate loss and adjusting—then it all quiets down, less attention, less intensity of feeling—more "normal." I really experienced living from love and an open heart. I find moving back to more of the left brain activity is not as easy for me and I feel less connected when I do. I associate right brain with heart-centered.

10/29/13

FACEBOOK: 11:40 p.m. Saw a beautiful hummingbird up close today at a home inspection. It hovered right outside the kitchen window long enough for me to say "hello," and admire its green and red colors. Lit my fireplace for the first time this fall and remembered all the evenings Michael sat near its warmth to practice. I'm sitting there now myself. So many sweet memories. I can almost see him sitting with his bandoneon and practicing for his next performance. The things we take for granted, as if they will never end, I'm learning about these in a most up close and personal way. Moments I now cherish as memories. What am I taking for granted now? I must pay attention and not miss the gifts.

10/31/13—FOURTEEN WEEKS--Halloween

FACEBOOK: 9:38 a.m. Fourteen weeks. Thirty seven years ago today we purchased the home I now live in. Michael was six months old. Moved in when he was eight months old and it's the only home he knew. We had a fish pond that he would wade into and we tried fencing it. We did fence off the big pool and made sure he had floaties on so he could keep up with his big brothers jumping off the diving board. He learned to swim like a fish early on. John was seven, the age of his twin sons today. Troy was ten, John's oldest son's age. Seems not that long ago that I was juggling that full schedule most mom's have. Listening to Michael's CD this morning and missing him. He liked handing out candy if he was home for the trick or treaters. Feeling close as I am being flooded with memories. Love my boys! Three sons and four grandsons. Life keeps moving me along reminding me to be appreciating each moment. All of it.

PERSONAL JOURNAL: 10:08 a.m. (9) and 10/31/2013 (11)
My desire to connect and communicate with Michael grows stronger with each day. To dispel any doubt that this is possible for me—this is my mission. If others can do it, and I know this to be so, then I can do it as well.

Playing his music helps me tune into his voice in my ear. I hear his songs in my left ear, and when I feel he is speaking to me, it's on my right, almost over my shoulder. Right now I'm hearing, *"Our love is here to stay."* I know this to be true—the love I feel for all of my sons is so visceral. I remember each one as a baby and holding them and thinking how lucky I was. I see Michael's images on the blanket from Terra and the canvases on the wall, and I smile.

Michael, talk to me about what you are learning. *"The thought of fear and doubt that came to you this morning— when those are present, fear and doubt, your connection to higher frequencies is kinked or filled with static. I experienced fear and then when I ascended, it was instantly gone. Please know that I experienced no pain. I gave you the image of wings unfurling. It's the best description I can give. I am learning how to connect with you just as you are to me. We are on similar study programs. You are working for both of us on the lower plane. Fear isn't the big one for you. Doubt is where you've been stopped before, but not anymore. I'm here and we will conquer this together. Limit the TV. Increase the meditation. Get the CDs that work with brain waves. They will help. Keep studying and keep writing. Yes, I love to say hello through the images and energy of hummingbird. As you are teaching others about spiritual principles, I am helping. I love you Mom. I was ready for this new assignment. We were both ready. Listen to your angels. I am one of them."*

11/2/13

FACEBOOK: 12:32 a.m. Watching a Hallmark movie tonight and a background song came on for a romantic scene—an Italian love song Michael almost always included in his shows. I said "hello" to him through my gentle tears and looked at the time: 11:11. I am now so drawn to nines and elevens and see them way more than I ever did when I wasn't tuned in to them. I think that's part of the lesson—I can't notice something I'm not looking for. Received two hummingbird birthday cards today as well. Feeling loved. Here's to noticing all that is good and beautiful, and to listening and tuning in to our loved ones wherever they are calling in from.

11/3/13—MY BIRTHDAY

PERSONAL JOURNAL: 8 a.m. Today's date is both a 9 and an 11 depending upon if I include the 2 in the year. Just got started and Troy called. No journaling today.

11/4/13

PERSONAL JOURNAL: 1:04 a.m. Great birthday with so many Facebook birthday wishes plus Troy and John and Mom. I teared up a few times when I thought of Michael. He would run to the corner store usually last minute and find a mushy card and then write an even more mushy love note to me on it. I love you Michael. You are always here with us.

FACEBOOK: 9:32 a.m. I committed to writing daily in some way in my journal, on Facebook, on my yellow pad—each carries a different voice. Sometimes they overlap. Today I find myself looking at terms we use for speaking about death. Yesterday after church I was speaking with Christine and she used the term "change" in reference to her mom's passing. I liked it. I have noticed my hesitancy around referencing what occurred on 7/25/13 at 5:54 a.m. the official time on Michael's death certificate. "Death" has a finality for me that speaks of an event but not to the after death experience which I am learning about first-hand. "Passing" or "passing away" feels a bit like distancing, as does "leaving." "Transition" and "ascendance" are too formal for me, but the term "change" is simple. It captures all of it—his change, my change, and the change that occurred for everyone who knows and loves him. I get to choose how I work with change every day. Mostly, I notice I am not always quick to embrace it. I resist, deny, resent, and usually eventually accept it. Michael's "change" continues to teach me rather than torment me as long as I embrace it and choose how I relate to it and to him in this present moment. I'm reminded of the beautiful song Paula played at church dedicated to Michael— *"Everything Must Change."* I wept with joy and sadness—the topic on my yellow pad that led to this post.

PERSONAL JOURNAL: 9:45 a.m. (9+9)   Good morning my dear sweet son. Thank you for continuing to inspire my sharing on Facebook. I believe you and I are making a contribution. I also am seeing the desire to complete the first book and see what's next for us.

I am doing my best to notice your coincidences. Pulling my friends together at Piatti's—pretty great! Having "Sway" play for me overhead to add your special "hello"—very cool. I love and adore you. I appreciate my life and family even more since the change and I am grateful for all of the ways you are teaching me. You and me = love. The power of the heart. I love you so much.

FACEBOOK: 12:48 a.m. Thank you everyone for my birthday wishes. Went to dinner at Piatti's this evening and ran into fellow Rotarian Thom and wife Linda bedecked in face paint with friends celebrating his birthday dinner. Table next to them are clients George and Cathy celebrating her birthday. I then sat down with John and my adorable grandsons, my mom and her friend Stanley to celebrate my birthday. It was so delightful. Heard the song *"Sway"* clearly in the background and felt Michael making his presence known. It is one of the songs he sang in his performances and is on YouTube in a video called "When the Titanic Began to Sway." A little teary this morning and missing Michael when Troy called. He and grandson Riley will be here in three weeks for their visit. Received flowers and cards and hummingbird gifts and so many happy birthday wishes that I lost count. Feeling very loved. And that was just on actual birthday day. It started earlier on Friday with lunch and on to Saturday being treated to a fashion show. More lunches next week. Life is sweet. I am blessed.

11/6/13

PERSONAL JOURNAL: 12:51 a.m. (9)   Lunch with Annie today and got to talk about my favorite topic—Michael. Not so much about him, but about the process and how he shows up now. Speaking of which, I just heard knocking as I was dozing off between words here. Was it you Michael? I suspect it might have been.

11/8/13—FIFTEEN WEEKS

FACEBOOK: 8:22 a.m. I've been quiet on Facebook for a few days. It seems to reflect where I find myself, a quiet space of reflecting and grace. I look at the birthday cards and flowers and remember the lunches and dinners with little candle lit desserts for me to wish upon, and I am so grateful. The flowers wilt, the memories stay. Michael gave me so many memories, and the one I am drawn to share today came from him on day 21 of his passing.

I was on the Alaskan seas, top deck of the ship, watching the sunrise paint the horizon with reds and golds, and I was weeping with sadness and pain. I heard Michael's voice so clearly over my right shoulder saying, *"Mom! Pay attention to all the beauty in front of you. Don't miss it by wishing things were different or missing me, I'm right here and always with you."* Wise words. I felt an immediate shift, dried my tears, and took in the radiant beauty of sunrise. It's a practice to focus on the beauty and not be pulled into what's missing. Michael and this journey continue to bless me.

11/9/13

PERSONAL JOURNAL: 3:27 p.m. I have had a busy morning showing homes. Rare is the morning I skip some form of writing or connecting in. I've enjoyed playing Michael's CDs, especially his Broadway hits. Right now I hear him in my inner ear, *"Longing to tell you but afraid and shy, I let my golden chances pass me by,"* and it continues.

I spent several hours yesterday and Thursday working on a book of poems and getting them ready for publication on CreateSpace. Learned about it from a friend who recently published her book and thought this is how I'll publish the story of my journey through this process of change with Michael. I have 39 pages of yellow tablet filled, plus all of my Facebook posts. This journal is also two-thirds full and has its piece of the story.

11/11/13

PERSONAL JOURNAL: 8:10 a.m. (9)   11:11 speaks to me of gateways to heaven and my son Michael. My dear sweet son—I tear up just writing this. I love him so much. I am reminded of this daily, almost hourly, and learning to live with this change is my most important lesson.

Published my book of poems and ordered 50 copies. It's a breakthrough for me. And, I wonder where the poetry muse is sleeping. I seem to write only at special moments or in deep turmoil or deep joy. This experience with Michael seems like it would have qualified for all three. Have I not been listening?

What if I wrote a poem every day? Would the words run out? Could thoughts still flow unfettered? Would I succumb to a need for perfection? Could I just write and let Spirit lead? Would it matter? Could I just commit to write and charge the energy to flow, not waiting for inspiration to pick up my pen. What if I wrote a poem every day. Just because I decided to— for no reason. Only to engage and encourage the part of me that loves to share. Just because. Like an experiment. Maybe just a day at a time. Maybe. What if?

FACEBOOK: 1:24 p.m. What does 11:11 mean? I personally have related to 11:11 in many ways. Most recently very much connected to communication with Michael. I realize we make up our own meanings. Interesting that we ended a war at the 11th hour of the 11th day of the 11th month. Coincidence? For me it signifies a gateway opening into another domain— one I am just beginning to learn more and more about.

11/12/13

PERSONAL JOURNAL: 8:21 a.m. (11 and the date is 9 or 11) So, lots of Michael support as I sit down to write this morning. My printer is being serviced by Ryan from Steven's office. After yesterday's journal entry, I sat quietly and considered the muse question. I made a decision for writing a poem or an essay every day for 30 days, whether the work is profound, moving, or just plain dull and awful. I will write and charge the energy to flow through my pen. After doing this, making my commitment, four poems flowed right on through.

I learned something by virtue of that experiment. My creativity enlivens me, and the enlivened me is creative, and waiting does not create, so I'm unleashing the creativity muse.

I also noticed a tendency, if I don't stay alert, to drift back to old patterns before Michael woke me up, and they are dull and flat. He sparked up my life with his physical presence, and now he's juicing it up from the other side. Thank you my sweet, sweet son. I love you.

11/12/13

FACEBOOK: 10:11 a.m. I declare this to be a "wow" day. Synchronicity unpredictable in a trillion chances to one. Messages from the other side coming through to bless me and a beautiful young man who I thought was just here to fix my printer and computer. Spirit had other plans. A simple question from me, "What do you like to do when you aren't working?" opened a conversation that has left us both awestruck and filled with gratitude. I believe his dad and my son both reached through to affirm their presence and their love. We are forever connected. I am so grateful that I followed just the little nudge to ask a simple question. With Michael's beautiful photo shining on my monitor, this young man knowing I had recently been through a tragic loss, felt safe enough to share that his father had just passed less than two weeks ago. One bread crumb led to the next and we found ourselves profoundly moved and touched by both his dad and my son as we realized this "coincidence" was way too big to be just that. I declare this to be a wow day. And, it adds up to either a 9 or an 11 depending upon using 11/12/13 or 11/12/2013. Hello Michael. I love you.

11/13/13

FACEBOOK: 6:48 a.m. I did it! I'm a published poet! I learned about CreateSpace.com on my birthday Sunday and a week later this little book of my inspired poetry was complete. I've been so encouraged by my Facebook friends to write a book that I started with what I had—a collection of poetry. *"Moments of Stillness"* is now on Amazon. I call it my "training wheels" book. Now I'm ready for the big adventure that draws from my experiences with Michael. I'm in the process of transcribing all of my yellow pad and journal notes into digital so I can begin putting it together. Thank you all for nudging me along. Baby step one complete!

PERSONAL JOURNAL: Later in the day. Wow moments. Just had one. Turns out Ryan, who is working on my computer and printer, is a friend's step-son, but I didn't know that. I did know my friend's husband had recently passed. I took a moment and followed a nudge to ask him what he does when he's not at work. He shared that he's been watching the series "House" because his dad just died on the night before Halloween and it helps him cope. I began sharing with him about Michael and my hummingbird experience and asked if his dad had reached out to him. One moment led to the next and I began putting the pieces together. I finally asked him what his last name was, and my jaw dropped. This was a divine appointment. I feel Michael and Ryan's dad were engineering the coincidence from the other side. Ryan is now watching Bob Olson's interview with Bob Kane.

11/15/13—SIXTEEN WEEKS

PERSONAL JOURNAL: 1:26 a.m. Took an introduction to Aikido class tonight. Will it strengthen me and connect me to my body? I felt Michael's presence. He would have loved the class. $110 a month and recommend going 2-3 times a week. What would I feel like if I were thin and lean and flexible in my body?

What would I love? To feel free to sit on the floor. To welcome being tossed and rolling. To fly and drop. To feel energy flowing through my body freely. To feel muscles and strength. What would I do if I didn't believe it was impossible? They suggested I begin by taking tai chi.

11/16/13

FACEBOOK: 9:59 a.m. My freshly printed copies of my first ever published book arrived on my doorstep this morning. I opened the box, full of excitement and anticipation. Almost immediately I am noticing a familiar pattern—a temptation to see what isn't as I would like it—size of print, two repeated poems, not perfect—and I interrupt this pattern to say, "Excuse me, this is a wonderful little book, full of heart, and I will not have my joy robbed by any negative remarks from Ms. Perfectionism." So, I figure those repeated poems must have needed to be there twice and I'm grateful I didn't wait on perfection to move forward. Several new poems have come through this week and I'm feeling Michael nudging me along. *"Listen to your angels, Mom, we are whispering to you."*

PERSONAL JOURNAL: 12:35 a.m. A poem came through: *"Start with Saying Thank You"*

11/17/13

PERSONAL JOURNAL: 6:39 a.m. (9 + 9) *"Into your arms I fly,"* *"No other love have I."* Michael's song for me this morning. I am so grateful for his presence and my growing awareness of how to tune in. I notice if I'm not alert, I'll start wanting more and dismiss what I have received. These mental patterns are not new to me, just seeing them in a new light. How many times does the thought "Yeah, but..." come knocking?

Our loved ones are learning to break through the dense barriers to reach us and praying we'll pay attention. Celebration is what is called for. It's a sign because I say it is, and I give it a marker and a meaning so Michael can continue to use it. Like we are working out our own language of Spirit. When he was an infant, I had to learn to communicate with him. It's kind of like that now—some new channels to learn, and I am the infant. Inspired a poem: *"Learning a New Language"*

I'm missing your physical presence. I still weep for your loss to me here in the flesh. And, I've been finding the treasures that this change has brought. I love you Michael.

11/18/13

PERSONAL JOURNAL: 12:45a.m. My circuits were blown tonight listening to the CDs Stu has created with Michael's voice. So much love has gone into it. Mom was with me at Stu's while he played the tribute CD for us to hear for the first time.

On the way home, Mom was feeling upset again that Michael is gone. I so understand. It is not an easy adjustment. My forgiveness work needs to be directed toward my feelings about his dad and how his behavior contributed to the fatal outcome when it could just as easily have gone the other way if he had stayed by Michael's side. And, he didn't. And, when I go there, my energy drops. If my energy drops, I distance myself from Michael. I want to stay connected to Michael. I will learn to forgive my ex.

Went over to John and Michelle's for a quick visit this afternoon. I love watching John with his sons. He is looking forward to Troy and Riley visiting for Thanksgiving. Wednesday will be boys' and dads' day.

Missing my sweet Michael so much this evening as I listened to his music. Such a talent and such a gentle loving Spirit. Tears were flowing this evening. I don't think it's anything I will ever get over. I don't know how that phrase has anything to do with matters of deep love and swift endings. I don't even like calling it an ending. Really, it's a new beginning. Heard a poet on Oprah talk about abandoning the cocoon that has served us on our journey and honoring it but letting it go. Labels and roles and identities that no longer serve us.

PERSONAL JOURNAL: 10:05 p.m. Faith in Action book group tonight and we spoke of Michael and how he communicates to me from the "wisdom channel"—a high band width shared by my Higher Self. Carolyn put him into our prayer circle at the end and I felt his presence in his delightful, mischievous way.

11/19/13

PERSONAL JOURNAL: 7:53 a.m. Last night Stu finished the tribute CD set. It was 11/18, no accident there. I publicized the link today for donations and we'll see what kind of response we get. I'm also looking at how to publish Michael's little reluctant ghost storybook. I need to get the illustrations either scanned or reproduced.

11/20/13

FACEBOOK: 11:38 p.m. I changed my screensaver on my iPhone to a photo with Michael and his bandoneon. Big smile on his face and makes me smile whenever I see it. Starting to get ready for Thanksgiving and a visit from Troy and grandson Riley. It will be his first visit to meet and play with his cousins. Troy says Riley (6 years old) enjoys trying to play Michael's guitar which Troy now has in Idaho. John has his other guitar here in Sacramento. So many fun memories connected to music and Michael. I'm excited to get the CDs released soon. Stu's putting final touches on artwork and assembling the sets.

11/22/13—SEVENTEEN WEEKS

PERSONAL JOURNAL: 3:12 a.m. Woke up thinking about Michael. Remembering him as a newborn, looking at all of us with a Buddha-wonder-face just moments after being delivered. No crying—just taking it all in. I remember being rolled from delivery to our room and him lying on the gurney with me, sucking on my left breast, as I welcomed him.

When John would hear him cry, he would immediately run to find me. I have an image of him bringing Michael outside to me holding him like a rag doll, but wanting to make sure I took care of whatever was needed. I don't know how he got him out of the bed since he was not yet seven himself. I remember creating a mattress slide in our Las Cruces home when we first moved in so Michael wouldn't fall down the brick stairs from the kitchen to the family room. Also him standing in the middle of the fish pond outside. So many snippets of his life here with me have been flooding in.

The best thing about all of it is I feel no regrets—nothing between us left unsaid. I'm just wishing he was still here. Knowing we loved fully as a mother and son, that is priceless. I was his patron of the arts. He was my best friend. My life was so enriched by his being in it. So, no regrets. Poem coming through: *"No Regrets"*

Hi my sweet son. I am very present to how much love we share and how blessed I am that you are in my life. I have been cracked open from this experience of your death—this change of venue—this unexpected twist. I have made peace with our new circumstances. I do most of the talking. I listen for your voice on the inner wisdom channel, and your songs keep me company. I would love a conversation. We've had a few over our time together before you passed. I did my best to listen for your dreams and encourage you. I still find myself seeing opportunities you would shine in as a performer. I would tolerate no criticism of you or your path. I was your protector—and now I feel you protecting and loving me.

"I'm right here Mom. Right here. Always just a thought away. I love you. You will see the hand of God in all of this, I promise. And, I'll meet you at the end of the rainbow—full spectrum love. Always here, now. Kisses. Kisses."

Poem written: *"Notice What I'm Noticing"*

11/23/13

FACEBOOK: 9:06 a.m. "If we can feed into a highly charged state of emotion during our grief, we can both heal and learn about our inner selves," a quote from Michael Newton, *Destiny of Souls.* I just read this line and realized how true it is for me. Somehow I knew my way through this was to fully experience the grief and demand that it bless me. At Stu's home last night helping with some cover art, sharing homemade soup, looking at photos of Michael, listening to his music, knowing how many lives he is still blessing, I felt the healing and the beauty and perfection of it all. I am learning and expanding and the broken places are filled with light. Most of my tears come from joy these days, and I am holding onto it as I enter this holiday season. Baby steps.

FACEBOOK: 10:03 a.m. More from *Destiny of Souls.* I resonate with what Newton is writing. "Survivors must learn to function again without the physical presence of the person they loved by trusting the departed soul is still with them. Acceptance of loss comes one day at a time. Healing is a progression of mental steps that begins with having faith you are not truly alone." I am currently listening to Michael's Broadway CD so lovingly put together by Stu Boyer. He is singing *"This is the Moment"* and I know I am not alone. I love you Michael.

PERSONAL JOURNAL: 10:14 a.m. Grief has become an amazing teacher for me on life and living. Michael's passing has opened my channels of communication on all levels. My soul connection with him, my willingness to write publicly about my healing process, the poetry coming through. All of the blessings that I can see when I follow Michael's teaching me to *"Pat attention to the beauty right in front of you."*

Poems came through: *"A Temptation"* and *"Riding the Waves"* and *"Living from Love and an Open Heart"* and *"When Love Comes Knocking—Say Yes"* and *"When Angels Cry."* Fourteen new poems since 11:11—definitely a portal day for me. I am learning to let my heart lead. Right now it is leading me to my shower after I snag the leaves out of the pool.

11/24/13

PERSONAL JOURNAL: 7:36 a.m. Woke up this morning thinking of confidence and how mine comes from taking action. Before I act, I like a clear idea of what I intend to accomplish. I've wanted to write a book, publish my poems, and I've been stopped up until now, by not knowing how. At least that's my story. Once I went online and saw the ease of it all, I was unstoppable. I had the intention. I asked someone who had recently published. I got a resource to follow that was easy and free. I looked at what I could start with—my poetry I had already written prior to Michael's passing—and in less than a week, my book was complete.

When I got the call about Michael, all I wanted was to get to him. My intention was so strong and, I believe he was helping from the other side as well, such that in less than 12 hours I had his body home in his sacred massage space. So, I'm seeing it's a combination of clear vision, passion, commitment, collaboration and gratitude.

Wallace Wattles tells us to think in a certain way, apply gratitude, act in a certain way, be a person of increase. Mary Morrissey and Bob Proctor brought these principles into my awareness several years ago. I have studied for years all of the metaphysical teachings, beginning with Christian Science and class instruction. I have been laying the foundation for teaching these principles throughout my life. A door opened wide with Michael's passing, and I see that I have stepped through it to a new dimension of myself.

I heard the cricket choir this morning on a Facebook link. It had been slowed down to a vibration my ears could hear in a new dimension. It sounded like a heavenly choir. It is always there. I had to tune in to a different vibration. A poem came through: *"Cocooned"*

11/26/13

PERSONAL JOURNAL: 7 a.m. Troy and Riley arrive today. Very exciting to have them. Letting it unfold, not making lots of plans, trusting the spirit of love in the moment to show us and guide us to my intention that this be my best Thanksgiving ever. That Riley remembers this vacation as one of his favorite adventures. That he feel loved, and safe, and welcome. That the cousins he's meeting for the first time have a great time together. That we all experience the joy in our family and the presence of Michael joining us with favorite memories shared around the table.

Poem: *"Gratitude and Thanksgiving"*

FACEBOOK: 8:17 a.m. I am picking up oldest son Troy and grandson Riley at the airport today at 12:30. I intend to have my best Thanksgiving ever. I see the temptation to invite sadness to the table, and cancel that invite. Michael's joy will be present in the laughter of my grand kids, his music will be serenading us, his smile will be seen on all of our faces as we celebrate our love for each other and feast on delicious food.

His words remind me to pay attention to the beauty in front of me and not miss it wishing things were different.

So, while I acknowledge sadness, she's not invited to our table. Our seats are reserved for love and joy and gratitude and fun and wonderful memories and angels who are always with us. Learning to appreciate and find the beauty in all of life, especially when it changes.

11/27/13

PERSONAL JOURNAL: 11:29 a.m. From Robert Lanza— *Quantum Theory:* "The content of the mind is the ultimate reality and only an act of observation can confer shape and form to reality—from a dandelion in a meadow to sun, wind and rain. An observer determines physical behavior of 'external' objects. In all experiments, our mind and its knowledge or lack of it is the only thing that determines how these bits of light or matter behave."

This was pulled from a link sent by Cari regarding proof for life after death. It was interesting and I saved bits of what I read. I still cannot fully grasp what he is saying and the experiment's connection to proving life goes on.

I have faith that it does. I believe it to be true. I have a burning desire to know all I can about the subject in an experiential way as well as intellectual. I intend to pursue every way possible to stay connected to and to communicate with Michael. I know his physical body no longer exists here in my space and time reality. How are our two realms interconnected?

Troy, John, Riley, Isaiah, Judah and Josiah are all out on an adventure together today. Riley slept over at John's last night and had a wonderful time. They are all definitely bonding and I love the sound of their enthusiastic playfulness.

I rescued a black lab this morning. Got help from neighbors and a security guard to locate the open gate around the corner from which they had escaped over on Esperanza. Chewie also escaped this morning. It was a dog day. I thought of Michael as I was heading home and saw his hand in the solving of the situation.

Mellow, relaxed day. I still need to shower. Refrigerator needs to be serviced and two dogs rescued plus Chewie's escape kept me busy this morning.

Tri-tip and mushroom soup last night. Four boys hooting and hollering and playing hallway soccer—getting to know each other. John and Troy reconnecting. Michael singing in my ear, *"So in love, so in love, so in love with you am I."* What a sweetheart of a man he is, and so are his brothers. I am so blessed.

Poem came through: *"Am I paying attention?"*

11/28/13—EIGHTEEN WEEKS—THANKSGIVING DAY

FACEBOOK: 6:59 a.m. Quiet time before I get up and start making stuffing and getting the bird in the oven. Michael passed 18 weeks ago this morning, that's 126 days, both of which add up to nine. This completion number is not lost on me, and that today is a day of giving thanks. Michael's life continues to be a gift to us all as a family. Michael's selection to sing to me this morning, *"This is the moment,"* reminds me to cherish and be grateful for each moment. This is the first Thanksgiving with Troy and Riley since they moved away six years ago. Riley is loving being with his cousins and celebrated Hanukah with them last night. Troy and John have had some great brother time. My sister and niece just arrived at 5 am after driving all night from Los Angeles. Kurt is joining us along with Mom. We are gathered to celebrate the love of family and friends, just as we gathered 18 weeks ago to celebrate Michael's life. I am feeling blessed. We'll be watching for hummingbirds and seeing Michael's smile on all of our faces as we include him in this special day. Stu is bringing over the completed Legacy Collection this evening and Sammie is dropping by for dessert. I dedicate this Thanksgiving to Resh Michael, my precious angel tuning in from heaven and filling us with his joy and laughter.

PERSONAL JOURNAL: 11:42 a.m. Thanksgiving Day   Turkey is in the oven, dressing is made, potatoes peeled. Need to make pies, get rolls unrolled and ready to bake. I spoke with Dad this morning and as I did, my tears for Michael missing arose and spilled over. I thanked a client for calling and as I did, my tears for Michael arose again. I know he is here in Spirit, and I'm really missing him right now.

Poem: *"Some Days are Easier than Others"*

11/29/13

PERSONAL JOURNAL: 1:29 a.m. Everyone is tucked into bed. I spent quite a bit of time talking with Kurt about the house in Santa Rosa and what it might take to determine its value. I helped, but most of all, just enjoyed the time spent together.

Sammie came by for a good long visit and Stu was here for awhile as well. He delivered CDs that he labored over to have done by Thanksgiving.

We all enjoyed our time together as a family and there was a moment at the table where most of us were choking back some tears as we spoke of Michael and felt his physical absence from our table even though we were playing his music and feeling his love.

I noticed myself losing it around 2:15 p.m. just as I needed to get dinner completed. I think the stress of the meal prep and wondering when John was coming with his family all took me by surprise, and I sobbed into Troy's shoulder. It passed and we were able to get everything ready in perfect timing. No poem tonight, too tired to write.

I love you Michael. I'm glad Sammie came over and I was able to give her my published poetry book plus some of the new ones.

FACEBOOK: 7:17 a.m. My house is very quiet. I'm the only one awake and I'm reminded of how I would tiptoe in the mornings so as not to awaken Michael. His creative bursts were usually middle of the night occurrences and his deepest sleep often coincided with my morning wake up routines. Flush toilet, let dog out, make coffee, empty dishwasher, somewhere in there take shower, and hope I'm being quiet enough. Yesterday we all toasted Michael, listened to his music in the background, and shed a few tears. So, sadness did show herself, but didn't take center stage. I learned that I'm still capable of putting a big dinner together, and that my tolerance for stress has dropped. About 45 minutes before meal-on-the-table time, the tears started. Too many decisions, too much left brain required, and I stood in the kitchen and quietly sobbed into Troy's comforting embrace. The wave of grief passed. Needed decisions got made (when to carve, when to put rolls into oven, are the peas done, need to keep gravy hot, blah, blah, blah. Nothing earth shattering as you can see. Soon the rest of the family arrived, grandkids were laughing and looking for their toys, and joy took over. Favorite quote this morning from Facebook, "The root of joy is gratefulness." Thank you for a wonderful day.

PERSONAL JOURNAL: 11:28 a.m. Quiet for awhile. Everyone has gone. Gardeners have arrived and blowers are loud. I'm grateful that they are caring for my lawn. They have been with me for 18 years, half of Michael's life.

Yesterday was special and yet I truly missed Michael's playful antics with the boys, his laughter and mid-night raids on the leftovers, the banter among cousins who have all grown up together. Did I pay enough attention? Did I sleep walk through much of it, or work myself in the kitchen so everyone else could enjoy the feast at the end.

Wrote poems: *"Gratitude and Thanksgiving"* and *"Did I Pay Attention"*

11/30/13

PERSONAL JOURNAL: 11:12 p.m. Just missed 11:11 on night stand clock, but catching it on cell phone—11:11, my gateway to the other dimension. Nodded off and it's now 11:58, almost midnight. Shared my most recent poetry with Troy today and he was moved by it.

12/1/13

PERSONAL JOURNAL: 6:43 a.m. Michael is singing to me, *"So in love with you am I"* and earlier, when I had just awakened, singing another song that I cannot recall at this moment.

I received information from Troy and his visit to his dad's. Opened up my awareness that I have more forgiveness work to do there. I've been guilty of using my imagination to condemn him. When I think of him or his wife, it is not loving thoughts that arise.

Poem this morning: *"Imagination"*

I can see the story Michael's dad has spun around Michael's death and I don't believe it. I get so angry on the inside. My only sane option is forgiveness and compassion. It's what brings me peace, and I'm feeling anything but that as I write these words. I keep holding onto higher ground by a thread.

12/2/13

PERSONAL JOURNAL: 12:47 a.m. Taking Troy and Riley to the airport in about six hours. We've had a great visit. Riley playing with his cousins, soccer, hall ball, bicycles, basketball. Troy and John getting to really reconnect. All is good and feels like one of our best Thanksgivings, which was my intention.

I worked on the book some more today, so I could send Troy off with poetry and the yellow pages portion that I had finally transcribed. I started cutting and pasting the FB posts as well.

Poem: *"Sons and Grandsons"*

PERSONAL JOURNAL: 4:12 p.m. Waiting for my coaching students to arrive on the conference call. Both are late. Took Troy and Riley to the airport and Michael's backpack, which I gave to Troy, triggered tender tears. Who knew!

Called Troy on my way home to make sure he arrived safely. More tears. Missing him already.

Life presents me with questions. How will I respond? When I sum it all up at the end, what has been my contribution, my legacy? I used up resources, breathed air, engaged in conversation. Did any of it matter? My love for my sons and grandsons—all of the meals, gifts, time. I have to believe it matters.

12/3/13

PERSONAL JOURNAL: 8:53 a.m. Just opened some files on Michael's computer which Kurt returned over the holidays. I found his lessons he was recording on teaching guitar. Lessons on how to make money as a singer. Precious video that I haven't seen before.

I'm sitting in the living room and as I'm writing, I look up to see if hummingbirds are feeding. They are precious to me. I also notice my windows need to be washed. I see I can focus on the spots on the glass or look past that to the beauty of the park and the fall colors. My choice.

Today. What would make today a contribution day? I'm the one who gets to choose my thoughts and actions and declare how I will be. Michael's passing has made me so aware of my heart space and spending time there, wanting to contribute, to leave a legacy. Did I love fully? Did I leave the world a better place for my having been here?   Did I love well and live fully?

Poem: *"Looking Back—Looking Forward—Looking Within"*

FACEBOOK: 10:00 a.m. My nephew brought me Michael's laptop over the holiday. This morning I began exploring some of the videos he had made here at home. I discovered precious footage of him teaching guitar lessons and another explaining ways to make money as a singer. Last night I shared some of his Christmas album with friends—one of the CDs in his Legacy Collection. These last few days I've been standing in the question of: "When I sum it all up at the end, what has been my contribution? My legacy?" I've already used at least 3/4 of my time here—and that's if I live into my 90s. Did I live and love fully? Michael certainly did. He continues to inspire me.

12/4/13

PERSONAL JOURNAL: 6:42 a.m. I began writing in this journal in earnest on 8/1/13. Most of its pages are precious writings about Michael and a few conversations with him. I've tried to capture my journey. Tomorrow is nineteen weeks. The rawness has scabbed over and I have been very good about not picking at it. I feel its tenderness and feel the scar is a beautiful reminder of how much love we shared as mother and son. I found a beautiful card he had written to me from a Mother's Day—not sure the year, but I'm guessing about ten years ago. Very heartfelt and most treasured.

This is 126 days of journaling. Of course, that's a nine, and that also means I started this journal 18 weeks ago, another nine. I am on the last page. I am to write this book. I will continue to journal. This one is complete. I love you, my dear, sweet Michael.

Poems: *"Completions"* and *"Endings and Beginnings"*

12/5/13—NINETEEN WEEKS

PERSONAL JOURNAL: 5:51 a.m. Maria Nemeth spoke last night at our Speakers Bureau. She says to see monkey mind as a good thing, it means you're up to something. Make little promises at the border. Celebrate and acknowledge any progress. Align yourself with support. Say "yes" to life. Be willing.

How do I relate this teaching to my Michael journey? Monkey mind: "I'd turn back. Don't think anyone needs another book. You aren't really hearing him. Others can who have special gifts, but not you..." Because I'm aware of awakening these border guards, I can be assured I am at a gate. My little promises are to write everyday and be a strong expectation for a poem arriving. When I write and hear Michael, I say "thank you" and I celebrate.

Poem written: *"What Woke You Up?"*

FACEBOOK: 7:24 p.m. Nineteen weeks. If I were an infant, I'd be not yet five months old. I am birthing this new way of being with Michael. Tears today as I shared some sweet memories of him with one of his Tango friends. I've been considering how an infant learns to speak the language of its parents. We teach the child that this object means this word and this word goes with that thing. And I'm mama and this is dada.

Now I'm the infant and Michael is teaching me a new language. Quietly I listen and watch for signs and symbols so I can connect. I'm developing my skills of paying attention. I still awake each morning to Michael singing music in my inner ear. I watch for hummingbirds. I notice when he pops into my thoughts. Teacher is getting my attention.

12/6/13

PERSONAL JOURNAL: 1:31 a.m. Fell asleep on the sofa and now am awake. Just checked FB and watched a clip of Nelson Mandela dancing to a song by Clegg. Such joy and happiness emanating from him. He spoke briefly—just a sentence or two. He said dancing and music bring peace to his heart. Then he had Clegg do an encore and got the whole audience on their feet dancing.

Today Chooi came by to pick up her CD set and spoke of how Michael's arrival at their Tango studio would light up the room. Now he lights me up from the inside whenever I think of him. I'm grateful he chose me as his mom. Poem came through: *"Dancing and Song"*

12/7/13

PERSONAL JOURNAL: 7:02 a.m. Four wonderful Michael hellos on the clock this morning: 6:03, 6:30, 6:48, 7:02. Bring in the clowns is the song he's singing as he nudges me to write.

Last night Stu came over and we watched some of Michael's teaching video for guitar lessons.

Okay, now I'm hearing him say, *"Why are you speaking of me like I'm not right here with you?*

So, more correctly, Stu and I watched the video and I believe Chewie was actually seeing Michael in the room. Stu noticed first. I felt very connected.

So, Michael, what do I do with these lessons?

"Send them to Troy for sure since he has my guitar—the very same one I used on the teaching videos. Have them put on DVDs and a few friends will want them."

Troy wants me to order the canvases of you and the personal throw. He's rebuilding and can use all of our love and support. Mick says you showed up at his work site last week—a hummingbird actually landed on one of his crew's fingers for a rest.

Do you realize how many lives you've touched with your love and talent?   The number continues to grow as we share. My friends who never had a chance to meet you are getting to do so through my sharing on FB.

Poetry for today please. I'm listening. *"Ten Thousand Hours"* came through.

FACEBOOK: 10:59 p.m. Saw the local musical production of *It's a Wonderful Life* tonight. I thoroughly enjoyed myself, laughing and crying and boo-hissing Mr. Potter. I could easily imagine Michael in the lead role as George Bailey. At one point I felt him as a six-year-old sitting in my lap so he could get a better view of the stage. He used to watch live performances and say, *"I'm going to turn into that when I get big."* And he did! Anything musical called to him. We used to watch the Jimmy Stewart original together as part of our Christmas tradition. Just the two of us. He even wrote a song inspired by the movie. Tonight the temptation to feel sad showed up a couple of times and then I would realize what a wonderful life we both have. I replaced the sad by being grateful for all of the lives he touched, just like George Bailey, and I'm so glad to be one of those he continues to bless.

12/8/13

PERSONAL JOURNAL: 6:07 a.m. Michael woke me up at 5:04 and again at 5:24—9 and 11. This morning I leave for church really early so I can set up a table for my books and Michael's CDs. I need to create a few forms so my journal writing this morning may be brief.

Last night I went to see *"It's a Wonderful Life"* at Sacramento Theatre Company with my Rotary friends and Mom and Stanley. They very much enjoyed it as did I. I could imagine Michael in the lead role and even felt his presence as a six-year-old in my lap watching. Tears came more than once as I realized how many lives he touched. I wrestled with the suicide debate. I have no doubt that he was not in his right mind and did not intend to leave us—not his conscious human self. He was being called home. It was sudden and impulsive and I'm still not convinced he stepped intentionally into traffic, but it matters not in my knowing, he is still not physically here.

Poem written: *"Death and Dying and Passing On"*

FACEBOOK: 2:30 p.m. Listening to Michael's Christmas CD and noticing I am experiencing that strange joy/pain emotional concoction again. His voice is so exquisite and his Ave Maria did me in. So grateful to be able to listen to him and share his voice with others, and so sad that he's not here in person.

This Christmas album was his surprise gift to us two years ago. Another lesson to never take for granted that my loved ones will always be with me, or leave in the proper sequence—parents first.

12/9/13

PERSONAL JOURNAL: 8:11 a.m. Great visit with Kelly last night. She came over for about an hour and a half. I read her some of my more recent poetry and in my reading of it, I can feel the vibration of healing and love. There is for me a feeling tone to the writing as I check in with my heart and I listen for the words to write.

Poem written *"Tuning In"*

12/11/13

PERSONAL JOURNAL: 1:02 a.m. Missed a day of writing and I'm really sleepy now, so may not capture much tonight. Staying alert to how easy it is to let my thoughts wander over to the negative. Dinner tonight with Sue and Darlene.

PERSONAL JOURNAL: 7:35 a.m. Christmas is creeping up on me and I'm experiencing it from a new place—not a place I wanted—a child I adore and love no longer with me in the flesh. "What child is this..." I can hear him singing and I miss him. I thank God I have his recordings and video. Ronney just heard him for the first time driving home from a meeting Monday. She felt the joy/sadness concoction. I have this nudge to create a movie with a storyline of his life and his talent and the spiritual piece and the conflict it set up for him. The canary in the mine—his sweet spirit was dying. He couldn't sleep, he couldn't be heard by his dad or step-mom when he needed them. He was being called home. What does his life story have to teach me and us?

Media. Such a powerful force for good and for transformation. Movies and television, the internet, we have at our fingertips the power to generate and perpetuate whatever we choose. Like our thoughts on an individual basis, being able to choose our perception.

New poem: *"A Life Well Lived"*

12/12/13—TWENTY WEEKS

FACEBOOK: 12:12 a.m. Many joyful tearful moments today. Distributed several of Michael's Legacy Collection CDs and with each one I felt I was sending a little more of him out in the world to spread joy and love through his music. I received a photo taken of the two of us maybe three years ago. I have my mother beam going strong. I loved watching him perform and could just feel the joy beaming out of me. I get a little of that listening to his recordings, and it's not the same. Missing him and loving him and grateful for days like today when I got to share him with others that I love. Another big thank you to Stu Boyer who put together this amazing tribute collection.

PERSONAL JOURNAL: 12:30 a.m. Today I distributed over a dozen copies of Michael's CDs. I felt like each one was a bit of him going out into the world. Tonight I went to SLC for a tribute to Nelson Mandela and it was followed by candle lighting. Very beautiful. I have to wonder if Michael has access to him on the other side. I really am curious about what it is like and how he is doing.

PERSONAL JOURNAL: 10:01 p.m. Went to Bret's for our NBE pot luck. Great time. Played Michael's Christmas and Broadway CDs. Everyone is missing him. He was our live entertainment the last two years.

It's going to be a quiet Christmas. Wrote poems titled: *"Never Be the Same"* and *"Change happens"* and *"Wanting to Blame"*

Michael, your presence in my life from the beginning has been a blessing and a teaching. You didn't fit into any mold and you taught me so much about listening. Even now I'm learning to listen with new ears and see with new eyes. I want to explore the after-Earth, after-life-as-I-know-it realm. I want to sort out the facts from fiction, yet what is the difference really? Fiction often becomes fact when new information is revealed. Fiction that we could fly—and now we can. What if we could, I could, just as easily speak with you now as before? Is that possible? If it is, I dedicate my life to that exploration.

"Contact Bill Guggenheim. Okay? Also Bob Olson, okay? Let's get the book done soon and see what the next one will be."

Am I picking up on one of our channels? I can hear a prompting from within. I hear the hippopotamus song and realize how you lit up the room again last night. Everyone loves and remembers you. I love you, my dear sweet Michael—my angel of light and love—my teacher for what lies beyond. Help me give my gift.

"Listen to your angels, they know why you're here and what you've come to bring. I'm one of them Mom, my dear sweet mom."

12/13/13

FACEBOOK: 8:30 a.m. Last night my business mastermind group had its annual potluck and gift grab at Bret Rossi's and June's beautiful home. This group includes some masterful strategists for nabbing the desired gift by working in teams. Last couple of years it's been at my home with Michael as our live entertainment. This time I took him along as his CD collection, and he still lit up the room with his magical spirit. Grateful to have his music to share.

12/14/13

PERSONAL JOURNAL: 12:32 a.m. Tonight I met many of the people from Michael's Tango community. It was an opportunity to share some music and stories. He was very loved there. I read a paragraph to those gathered that Michael had written about his love of Tango and the community. I found it in his personal effects.

Here is what he wrote: *"I'm a very private person. I keep a very low profile; even my music has still remained unpublicized for the most part for the time being. This morning I woke up asking again, "What is it that I want, or what do I not want?" Thinking that if I knew exactly, life would be easier. They say it's especially important for an Aries to know what he wants, which I am, born April 17, 1977. I know that I want to surround myself with positive, healing people who really care about humanity and the planet. I want to feel hopeful for the future somehow, somewhere, with people who are creating this together. I believe there are many paths to unity. How does my background as a sensitive massage practitioner and musician come into play on a bigger level? For now the natural evolution of tango has been connecting me with different communities who all share a sense of refined taste in everything from wines to graciousness.*

Important to remember we are not stagnant fixed identities but a precious being in process that remains growing like a beautiful unfolding melody or whatever magical metaphor reminds one of who we might really be. I choose again to identify with greater divine presence in all of us and I share this with you from my heart. Your heart is my heart. Best love, Michael Ortego aka Resh."

When I sat down, it was 9:11, people were wiping their eyes. I smiled and thanked Michael.

PERSONAL JOURNAL: 10:59 p.m. Do not feel like writing and have no poetry tonight. Going to sleep. Went to Freddie's surprise party for his mom and dad's 45th anniversary. Rabbi spoke of it as a foundation number—one of commitment. It adds up to a nine. I do not particularly enjoy large crowds, especially when I know so very few of the people. I had a moment with John and could feel the tears coming. He put his arm around me. I was crying on the way there, feeling kind of raw. Left early.

12/15/13

PERSONAL JOURNAL: 7:14 a.m. Sunday, ten days to Christmas. No tree up yet. Still a possibility. Darlene has her home decorated top to bottom. I'm practicing my new rule— let my heart decide. So far the decorations remain packed.

PERSONAL JOURNAL: 11:25 p.m. Hi Michael. A friend from your Tango community came by today to pick up a set of your CDs. She had picked you out as her son-in-law for her

337

daughter. Plus, she misses dancing with you at the Tango events. You are so loved. I wonder if you realized it before. Surely you realize it now.

Today I enjoyed church and a visit to clients Susan and Steven's Christmas gathering. Then I dropped by John's and then stopped at Kelly's down the street. Last night was a big party. I'm looking forward to quiet solitude.

12/16/13

FACEBOOK: 7:24 a.m. Pain and suffering—not the same. Yesterday, Spiritual Life Center minister Rev. James Trapp spoke about joy and the difference between pain and suffering. He reinforced what I've learned for myself, that feelings of joy and pain are in-the-now-moment experiences. I can even feel them both at the same time. The story I tell myself and others about what happened is where peace of mind or suffering occur. It's a powerful distinction. Am I a powerless victim or a person with the power to choose my responses? Moment by moment I am strengthening my ability to choose peace of mind. Michael taught me this by example when he was here physically and now guides me from within. *"Look for the joy, Mom. Notice the beauty."* Quite the practice. I'm blessed.

12/17/13

FACEBOOK: 7:27 a.m. Reading *"Vibrating To Spirit"* by Kathleen Tucci. She confirmed my intuitive knowing that my ability to deal with and heal the pain of the physical void is linked to my ability to develop a new spiritual relationship with Michael. Paying close attention to signs and symbols, listening for his voice, building new channels for us to share beyond the physical dimension. This morning I could hear him singing *"listen to your angels"* so sweetly in my ear. This walk of faith and trust keeps my heart open and feeds me. I miss him even as I learn to recognize all the ways he is still here with me.

12/18/13

PERSONAL JOURNAL: 1:26 a.m. I've not written in the journal for a couple of days. I did post on FB. I am looking forward to spending this Christmas with Michael in spirit, in communion, connecting and writing.

I was calling forth poetry each day and hit a few voids. I certainly want it to be a pleasant and creative experience, not a chore to be checked off my list. Where is the balance in this?

I have been transcribing my journal entries onto the computer so I can publish the journey.

Just was reading more from Kathleen Tucci about being open to communication with loved ones and my guides and angels. My desire to connect with Michael even more is so strong. I had to laugh as I read within the next two pages of her book the words: "Uncle Mike" and "Ave Maria." I could sense Michael smiling at me. I continue to learn and stay open.

Kathleen had an experiment to see auras, using white paper and my own hand. I just held it up against the book page and could see the energy pouring from my fingers. So much for me to learn. *"And to teach,"* is the guidance I just received.

Who is my next teacher? My spiritual mentor? At times, I feel like I am complete with Mary, yet cannot imagine not seeing her each year. I will pray on this and see what my guidance is. I have really learned through Michael how important it is to trust my heart, my inner knowing, my gut and sensations.

PERSONAL JOURNAL: 7:42 a.m. Mom's 88th birthday today. She is dealing with irregular heartbeat and taking blood thinners so she can have a corrective procedure in January. She's still going strong and I'm thinking maybe 100 is in her stars. Who knows? Every day is a gift.

Poem: *"Every day is a Gift"*

12/19/13—TWENTY ONE WEEKS

PERSONAL JOURNAL: 11:39 p.m. Stu brought by 45 more sets of CDs. He ordered a canvas of Michael for the studio. He has devoted so much time to this project and I know he is missing Michael. I haven't heard from Sammie at all since Thanksgiving. I can see how when normal begins settling back in, I feel more distant from Michael. So I'm reading again and studying about ADCs and trusting that he and I are still very much connected by the love in our hearts. I want to talk with him daily. We take it for granted, the simple hellos and nods of awareness, familiar patterns and subtle nuances.

12/21/13

PERSONAL JOURNAL: 7:08 a.m. Awake to 6:36 and then 7:04. I always smile and say hello when I get a 9 or 11 combo. It's become a sweet way to connect. That and hummingbirds. So many, so cute. They are at the feeders and also land in the oak tree branches outside my office window. My morning songs are so important to me—that I awake with his songs in my heart and my ear. This morning was *"On this night of 1000 stars, let me take you to heaven's door, where the music of love's guitars plays forever more."* I was seeing his performance at the benefit when he took that song and really hammed it up. So much life and love in his soul.

I could feel the tears start and I could hear the dead end question of "why" begin to play. No joy there. It really is a moment to moment choice. So I went to some sweet memories of myself and Michael as a child. So much love. Skateboards, guitars, music and dance.

I was listening to my own inner guide about the difference between "refined and defined." I can see that the death of a child can define me and I could become that woman who labels myself as that, or I can see the many ways that the experience refined me, made me more aware and awake, added new dimensions of compassion, stripped away any layers of pretense. I am also much more aware of my desire to connect with the other side and develop those faculties within myself.

The song this morning, "let me take you to heaven's door" is perfect—let's go all the way through the door and keep it open so we can always visit. Michael's invitation to "fly away with me" makes me smile and recognize we are communicating. He has the vocabulary of all of his songs to sing to me of his life and love and presence here with me and also with others he loves. The story of the euros in his car and the meeting of Holland and Christina at a restaurant in Los Angeles where his friend Amanda was working—so sweet and so special. So like Michael.

12/22/13

PERSONAL JOURNAL: 7:52 a.m. Went to see *"Saving Mr. Banks"* yesterday evening with Mom and Stanley, my social life. It's the story of making Mary Poppins with Tom Hanks playing the role of Disney. An excellent movie and the music is playing in my head. This is messing with me. Michael's voice usually awakens me and it's his music serenading me. So, I'm remembering his formula which I reposted from my sister yesterday. Formula for a sacred life: Life minus fear equals Love (heart symbol). Thank you Michael.

12/24/13

PERSONAL JOURNAL: 6:42 a.m. Yesterday I didn't write. Wrestled with sciatic nerve pain all day on Sunday with two massages and an AI treatment yesterday along with the trip to a chiropractor who does soft touch network chiropractic. All of this pain in my body pulled my focus to such an extent that everything else seemed a big effort. I have much to learn about being masterful with pain of a physical kind.

Concluded my DreamBuilder class yesterday. I got an email from Maria Nemeth yesterday with her phone number and an invitation to call her. I've been drawn to her work and it may provide the structure I'm looking for next.

Made my airline reservations for January DreamBuilder. Lots of changes since Michael decided to leave this realm. Looking for my own clear teaching path. I know I am a teacher and a coach with a passion for the principles taught by both Mary and Maria.

Just noticed a string of metaphysical Marys in my life. Mary Elizabeth Commander, my Christian Science grandmother. Mary Morrissey, Maria Nemeth, Ave Maria—my mother energy. Greg sees me as the archetype of Mother Love—I can own that.

Poem: *"Mother Love"*

12/25/13—FIVE CALENDAR MONTHS—CHRISTMAS DAY

PERSONAL JOURNAL: 10:25 a.m. Christmas Day   Five months ago today, I received the worst news ever in my entire life—22 weeks tomorrow. I'm listening to his Christmas CD as I write this. Saw some hummingbirds this morning. I am feeling freedom from back pain and grateful for all the help I received.

How does this connection to the other side work? I'm told Michael is always with me. I have direct experience of hearing him loudly and clearly from behind my right side on two occasions early on—first day with *"I'm so sorry, Mom. I'm so sorry."* And then on day 21, *"Mom, pay attention to the beauty all around you. Don't miss it wishing things were different or wishing I was there. I'm right here."* I've spoken with him in my journal and I've heard him singing to me from within on my left side. So, what's my problem, I ask myself. Am I not grateful for what I have experienced, so I crave more? Or am I desiring to develop my ability and looking for evidence along those lines?

PERSONAL JOURNAL: 11:52 a.m. Here I am looking at the clock and it adds up to a nine and includes an 11. I find these numbers a comforting code for Hello—a wave to each other across the veil—and my doubting Thomas left brain logic wants to argue about it. So I notice that and say "hello" anyway. My heart connection to all three sons is so strong. I love each one of them so much. Spoke with Troy this morning, then had Facetime with John and his gang on vacation in San Diego. Mom called, Darlene called, I called Dad. Marj called. So many connections. My heart space is the receptacle, receiver, sender, transmitter, and place of authentic knowing.

PERSONAL JOURNAL: 12:24 p.m. Just hung up from speaking with Christian Science practitioner about treating my back pain. Comforted by her assurance and belief in our existence as spiritual ideas—not subject to ups and downs of the flesh and her reminding me, "Be not afraid, I will not fear what flesh can do to me."

She asked who would be left if all of my joy and love and compassion were removed—nothing—and these qualities are eternal and not of the flesh—so my connection to Michael is on that band width of joy and love that we shared.

I see him singing "Mama" to me and I feel the overflowing love from my heart to his. I remember his touch and his arm draped around me—his words of love and appreciation—his tender kiss upon my forehead.

Hi Michael. What can you and I create together now that we are connecting in new ways?

12/26/13—TWENTY TWO WEEKS

PERSONAL JOURNAL: 1:18 a.m. Enjoyed my Christmas very much. Time spent with myself and Michael, phone contact with Dad, Troy, John and Mom. Visit to Sue and Jerry's then back home with Lisa and then over to another friend's for dinner. Finished up with a visit from Sammie and a Hallmark movie. Michael's singing Christmas carols in my ear and I'm too sleepy to write anymore tonight.

PERSONAL JOURNAL: 7:27 a.m. Smiled when I looked at the clock. Double 9s. It is one of our waves across the veil. Today I have some work to attend to and also plan to work on more transcribing of my journal. Poems have flowed easily some days and not at all on other days. The way they seem to work for me is I'll get a line or two and it carries the rest. So many have been inspired by Michael.

Poem: *"Wonderment"*

12/27/13

PERSONAL JOURNAL: 7:11 a.m. 6:36, 6:56, 7:04, 7:11 all moments that called me to look at the clock and smile.

Last night it was 9:11, 9:45, and 10:44.

Lisa and I went to see "Saving Mr. Banks"—second time for me. Then we came back here for a sweet visit. She was asking me how I connect with Michael. His singing to me for sure, a hummingbird sighting, a voice in my head or an answer in my journal, an image with a strong memory, and the fun with numbers of saying hello. More often than not I will get a nudge to look or I'll awaken from sleep to a 9 or an 11 element. Even the mileage odometer has smiled at me when it turned 111,119 not so long ago.

This morning I was considering Saireh's reading and Michael as a WWII soldier/chaplain, which she said she was being shown. I could see why he would love entertaining at the senior retirement homes with songs that would have been his favorites as well as theirs. I'm feeling this deep emotion that I don't know how to name. I'm flooded with tears, my heart wants to sob, my chin and lips are quivering and contorting, and I am not making any sounds—like if I let go into the sound, the pain will grow.

Just before this wave of emotion, I was feeling this deep love for Michael. The wave is coming again. Deep love, sweet memory, experiencing the wave—the sadness/joy elixir.

John and his family are in San Diego having a great time. I know this. They did some Facetime and have some photos posted on FB. I can see that Michael is also on a new journey that it's not as easy to share with me since we haven't worked out the language quite yet. He can be in multiple places at once—this I do know. I get to be confined by time and space in my physical body, yet my imagination let's me go anywhere. I believe Michael now has freedom to express all of his talents and all of his healing and nurturing qualities as well. I can see him doing his comedy routines as Kurt saw him and clowning for the kids like he did with his nephews here.

So, how do I communicate with him? Multiple channels. I continue to develop them. Fishing pole, kite, floating inner tube for fishing—all left here as he moves on to new adventures—my Peter Pan.

Up in the atmosphere, where all the air is clear, let's go fly a kite, let's go soaring...childlike, not childish, playful and creative. Characters he would develop for stage and entertaining, like Giovanni. This alter ego ability, like Dr. Hyde—so opposite.

PERSONAL JOURNAL: 11:19 p.m. Still waving to me. Went to B Street tonight with Rebecca. Fun performance about relationships. I try to imagine myself in one and I don't get very far. Maybe if I picked the best parts of all the ones I've been in and did a collage. Not now, though. Will have to wait.

I am busy being grateful for my healthy back. That I can sit and stand and walk and bend. Don't want to take any of that for granted. Normal functioning, a good way to be. All systems working smoothly. So far so good.

12/28/13

PERSONAL JOURNAL: 7:20 a.m. (a nine)   For God so loved me that he gave me three beautiful sons and four beautiful grandsons and I am blessed. I learned to call forth my nurturing unconditional heart centered authentic love through them. I learned to deal with my need for control and to manage my anger. I learned presence and wonderment and I learned to listen from my heart. I've learned letting go and cheering on and biting my tongue. My dear sweet sons—and the lessons continue.

My first two sons were "accidents" and Michael was planned, yet he died in an accident. So I must relook at the idea of "accident." Either there are none or not...I caught myself in either/or thinking just now. I am recognizing that what I can call an accident is the unexpected. I did expect to have children, and I was irresponsible about conceiving them.

Michael, the reading by Saireh, it resonates as a truth, but how would I know? You would have been young and a man of spirit to be a war chaplain and lose your life in combat. To come back as my son with not an ounce of violence and a huge concern for our planet and trying to wake people up with your songs—this also makes sense. Where would Saireh pull this from if it didn't come from you showing it to her?

I'm thinking of the snow artist I saw on Facebook who creates patterns that need to be seen from high above to even know what they are. He has a vision and an intention and he begins to walk step by step with no way to step out and see how he's doing. I would love to interview him about the process. Maybe he is able to leave his body and direct his steps from a higher vantage point.

FACEBOOK: 8:28 a.m. Saw this quote today and it spoke to me: "Realize that with every sadness you are blessed to have your heart cracked wide open. One of the great mysteries in life is that by feeling our suffering we also invite in the possibility of feeling great joy. Suffering and joy are your partners in wholeness." I have been learning this daily as what I call the sadness/joy elixir shows up and I get to choose where I'll focus even as I'm experiencing both. So many Christmas memories of Michael singing to us, so grateful to have his music preserved and so sad he's not singing to all of us here in his physical beauty. I do hear him always in the morning when I awake. Such a path this is—one step at a time—Joy and Sadness holding my hands.

12/29/13

PERSONAL JOURNAL: 7:17 a.m. Woke up at 7:11 and didn't hear a song—asked and then went to the bathroom. As I returned, I am hearing *"When angels whisper"* and seeing Michael's face in my mind—the photo on the blanket as well as one I found yesterday of the three boys taken a few years ago.

Last night we went to see the Buddy Holly show and I know Michael would have loved it. I suspect he was right there with me. Holly died in a plane crash 1959 in his early 20s and his career was just taking off.

A dear friend named Al called me yesterday. I had sent him a Christmas CD of Michael, and Sue had given him one of my poetry books. He loved both and wanted to thank me. He said he keeps reading "Missing You" and crying. I am grateful I wrote and published what I did.

Yesterday I listened in on Mary's 2014 Dreambuilder call and creating that clear blueprint for 2014 is on my to do list. Prompted another poem: *"Plans and Goals"*

12/30/13

PERSONAL JOURNAL: 7:15 a.m. Whatever that attempt at a poem was, it qualifies in my mind as not so good. I can see what I was going for, but it feels flopped. My poetry really needs to flow out of an experience with emotion. Definitely it is a heart centered experience.

I'm wondering, as I'm seeing myself heal through the pain, if I'm leaving my heart space more than when I was in the midst of the pain. I prefer staying in my heart as a come-from place. What does that mean? I think Michael just sent me an answer.

"It's the sacred in life. It's being in touch with the love in life."

He showed me his formula *"Life minus fear equals love"* and that's the sacred. I just saw the shift that can follow depending upon where you place your attention and what you are "C"ing—saCred or sCared?

If I want to stay connected to my heart space, I pay attention to the sacred and the beautiful, the love all around me, the joy I feel, and I express gratitude for all of it. When I let fear in and get scared of losing something, my attention shifts and I create the opposite of what I want.

Yesterday I served clients as they decide what's next for them and their home. I love my life and all of the ways I am learning to serve.

12/31/13—NEW YEAR'S EVE

PERSONAL JOURNAL: 7:56 a.m. Last day of a year I'll never forget. One of those demarcation points in my life—7/25/13. Before and after. Can I see the gifts?

- Writing, poetry published
- Heart cracked open
- Softened and vulnerable
- After-death communications
- Closer to family
- New relationships with Stu and Sammie
- Willing to share my process

1/1/14

PERSONAL JOURNAL: 12:13 a.m. Happy New Year! Spent early evening with Kirchmans and watched a great movie called Hugo with them. Brought them Michael's CDs and my book, plus a couple of things for the kids. I just love this family.

Posted on FB today and received such positive feedback. Thinking about forgiveness and what it means to forgive myself—something that came up with Dr. Fisher working on my body's aches and pains. Forgiveness: To give another perspective, another meaning.

1/2/14—TWENTY THREE WEEKS

PERSONAL JOURNAL: 6:59 a.m. I just had a teary episode— woke up missing Michael. No song in my ear from him, no numbers on the clock. And, then I began to hear a song from years ago that I recently heard in Dr. Fisher's office, *"I will never leave you, on this you can depend...let not your heart be troubled."* Then I decided to write in my journal and got my 9 and 11—6:59.

This morning I was flashing on the accident and that whole period of time from when I last saw Michael to when I got the news—it's not a place for me to go and feel nurtured.

Popped out of my journaling to read more by Julia Assante on after-death communications. She says grief waves are one of the signs that we are connecting. What about joy waves?

1/3/14

PERSONAL JOURNAL: 11:45 p.m. Yesterday was a Thursday and 23 weeks from 7/25/13. Christmas day was five months. I'm the infant here. Today's date is an 11 or a 9 depending upon if you include the 2 in 2014. Twenty-three weeks is 161 days plus today adds up to 162 or 9.

01/04/14

FACEBOOK: 8:37 a.m. I'm retraining my brain to write 2014, tallying up the score for 2013, writing out goals and intentions because I know they are more fertile when written, and observing that part of me that resists it all. Life altering, knee buckling events occurred in 2013 that were not on my goals list. I am daily getting to choose my way of being with the sadness that shows up. So I am tender to the idea of setting big goals. I am listening to my heart when it nudges me. I pray to stay awake to whispers from Michael from beyond and to let my loved ones still here in this realm know how much I love them. I study and teach and learn and love and give it my best. I coach the power of visioning and using our imagination to design a life we'd love. I know it's powerful—and I feel the sadness that comes from shattered dreams as well. Here's to rebuilding, with a gentle loving appreciation of how fragile life is and how much our dreams need to include loving each other.

PERSONAL JOURNAL: 12:06 p.m. (9) Today I went to a friend's memorial at Spiritual Life Center—the same space we used for Michael's memorial service. I had some moments of tears and also experienced Michael's presence sitting between Mom and me with his arms draped over our shoulders, big smile on his face.

Yesterday morning I was very weepy, more than I have been recently. I was feeling some disconnect. I was also realizing how much Michael was my best friend and someone I could count on to listen and be there for me. So many of us are missing his sweet presence. Even though I know he's just a thought away, it's still an adjustment.

I had committed to a poem a day. I see it wasn't a real commitment or I would have kept it up. I have been pretty good about writing everyday and on Facebook as it calls to me. I am able to listen to my heart and make my decisions from there. I forgive myself for not writing poetry every day and commit to listening for and being intentional about inspiration.

Stu is caring for Michael's laptop right now, sorting through its files and gathering music and photos and videos. I asked if some day perhaps we could create a catalogue of all of Michael's music and images so I can enjoy them all in one place.

Poem came through *"My Heart Remembers"*

1/5/14

PERSONAL JOURNAL: 11:34 p.m. (Hi Michael)

I worked two open houses this weekend and went out to dinner both nights. Cari and Richard last night and Mom, Stanley and Garret tonight. Not much heart time, mostly head time. Makes me feel less connected to Michael. Shopping in Ikea with Mom and Stanley, watching TV with my house guest and friend Garret. No quiet time this morning because I got up right away and showered to be on time to take Cari and Richard to the airport. I really need my quiet time to go within, and early morning or late at night seems best.

1/7/14

PERSONAL JOURNAL: 1:15 a.m.

Poem: *"I Will be Blessed"*

PERSONAL JOURNAL: 7:51 a.m. Michael smiled at me at 6:39 a.m. and then 7:02 a.m. Woke me up singing *"Rocking Around the Christmas Tree"*—I need to tune into his Broadway songs and reload them.

"Wow, wow, wow!" said Steve Jobs when leaving his body. "It's all a hoax!" said Roger Ebert in his last breath of this life. Here's my question for you, Michael. JG says you appear to him as a being who is teaching children and there are rainbow lights all around you. Saireh has seen you as a WWII chaplain who was killed and reincarnated here with me and now you are helping victims of war cross over. What do you say?

"Mom, it's all possible at the same time—not limited, linear, singular reality. I know you miss me. I know this was a big impact experience and you signed on for it. You want to help people at the deepest, most profound level, and to do so from your own heart-felt experience. You and I, we are complete and one and always connected. I am here to help you help others. We are a team. The groundwork is being laid and you just need to listen to your inner voice for what's next."

1/9/14—TWENTY FOUR WEEKS

PERSONAL JOURNAL: 6:34 p.m. I have been knocked out with the flu and am on my third day of mostly bed rest. Today is better than yesterday.

It's Thursday, and I am missing Michael, and no amount of cheering myself up is working. I listened to Mary's call on self-image and I think I have a fairly good one—not that I couldn't improve it, but certainly better than what I grew up with and carried throughout my marriage. Mary asked us if we were to die tomorrow and knew it, what would we regret not having done. First thing that popped into mind was the book that I am working on. Second may be a deep and profound loving relationship with a man that lasts until one of us dies, and then continues after that. Third is a well-established coaching practice based on my own studies. I love Mary's DB CDs, but am not crazy about the workbook that goes along with them.

The idea of death no longer frightens me.

PERSONAL JOURNAL: 9:31 p.m. Still feeling puny. Have played solitaire until I am bored with it. There's a little voice nagging at me that it's not the highest and best use of my time.

Wrote a poem about it: *"Patterns and Mechanisms"*

01/10/14

FACEBOOK: 9:32 a.m. Listening to Michael's Broadway Hits CD and appreciating the mastery he achieved with his voice. Each song speaks to my heart in its own way. I always cry when I listen to him, missing him and feeling connected at the same time. I notice when my energy is low, such as when I've been dealing with a flu bug for four days, that I have more sadness and fear hovering in my space. This morning I am feeling better and watching the hummingbirds feeding lifts my spirits. No one can choose my thoughts but me. Today I choose to remember how much joy is in my life right now even as I embrace the reality that I am still grieving. Interesting mixture—joy and grief.

PERSONAL JOURNAL: 9:38 a.m. (9 & 11) Listened to Michael's Broadway CD this morning—wanted to hold him so much. Tears of sadness were flowing and I kept hearing *"I want to be free"*—the words he kept repeating to his Dad that fateful night. Chaos and confusion and then rebirth into a new dimension. I have to see it that way or I will perish. Any other thoughts take me down a road I don't care to travel.

1/11/14

PERSONAL JOURNAL: 7:49 a.m. (11 & 9) Woke up at 7:11 hearing *"Who can I turn to if you turn away?"* It's one of the more difficult songs for me to listen to. It brings up all of the what ifs and how comes that have no answers in this dimension and change nothing in the overall scheme of things. I know Michael doesn't want me to go there. It distracts me from what I am wanting to create for me—a now new way of being in communication across the veil. I say "for me" as that's where I need to start. Last night I was imagining speaking with Michael. Even now, I stopped writing to tune in. He's saying *"my romance doesn't need a thing but you"* and it feels like he's leading me with his voice down a path and showing me all of the beautiful places and faces that have ever been created—both urban and pastoral, old and new— with rainbow skies. He's tell me, *"I can see everything beautiful that was ever created in all of its glory—music, art, buildings, creatures."* He showed me the domain of dinosaurs. *"Mom, it's like a living beautiful museum—a mosaic of all the good we have created and that God has created and we are all part of it."* I could feel my vibration lifting as I followed his singing. *"It's like a living book of life and any page you pick has a story to tell and a gift to give."*

As I was speaking to him last night, I wanted to know that he hears me, that he is really present in my life. So I got out my pendulum and received a strong "yes" that he hears me. My intuition says yes, my heart feels the deep love we share. I love you Michael, now and always and forever into infinity and beyond. 8:55 a.m. (9)

PERSONAL JOURNAL: 4:02 p.m. Went into the back room to sit in sanctuary space and connect to Michael from there. I asked him to show me one of his favorite places where he is and he took me to the set of "It's a Wonderful Life" with Jimmy Stewart. He says he has the choice of seeing the movie being made or watching the debut of the film with Jimmy himself. There is a wonderful joyfulness to his energy. He is full of life and doesn't ever need to sleep. He says we need sleep over here so we can reconnect with heaven and be refreshed while we are sleeping.

PERSONAL JOURNAL: 10:50 p.m. Time to go to sleep. Wrote today, some poetic prose, but not a poem. I will be still a moment and see if my muse feels like gifting me anything. *"Feeling my Way"* came through.

PERSONAL JOURNAL: 11:07 I am picking up a message from Michael. He is showing me his dance moves—Fred Astaire style. He's understudying with the best and loves that he no longer needs to be concerned about making money—only with making music and learning all he can about music, art and entertainment in their best circumstances. Now he's showing me his jumping over his own foot trick that he did on stage.

1/12/14

PERSONAL JOURNAL: 7:59 a.m. Woke up at 7:20 hearing *"On this night of a thousand stars, let me take you to heaven's door."* Feels like Michael has been taking me on mini tours when I let my heart wander with his. So, I'm going to be still and see where we go this morning.

Beautiful ride on the avatar blue feathered bird holding tight to Michael, feeling the rush of wind in my face, then losing it all to left brain and beginning again. Losing to distractions and beginning again. Very patient is my guide.

1/13/14

PERSONAL JOURNAL: 1:44 a.m. (Hi Michael) Just a note before I turn out the light. I made progress today on transcribing my journal. Church guest speaker was Don Miguel Ruiz, Jr. He spoke about the power of our "yes" and our no, of life and of loving unconditionally, beginning with ourselves.

PERSONAL JOURNAL: 8:06 a.m. Taking time to tune in— inward to the still space of my heart, the portal where I knock and God opens, where I ask and it is given according to my faith. This inner tuning allows me to connect with heaven and if I ignore the inner and only focus on the outer, I see that virtual reality of my beliefs interwoven with seven billion others over which I have no control.

This morning I am hearing *"Stranger in paradise"* after my first song of *"Who shall I turn to."* Also getting an inner mental slide show of his studio shots. Such beauty.

PERSONAL JOURNAL: 8:47 a.m. Alone with our choices, our "yes" or our no, and we live with our yes's. We live in the truth of our lies to ourselves until we stop and listen and choose our true yes—the one that resonates with love and not fear.

Remembering the lines from PBS Downton Abbey show that I watched last night. Seeing how we have been trained to cover and pretend and swallow our truth, to say "yes" to what we don't want. It's the only way it can show up—with my "yes" being stronger than my no—for whatever I say a strong "yes" to gets to come forward into my experience.

Also was noticing the way they are portraying the death of a young father, the wife finally choosing life over death and the mom fearing to laugh because she will lose her connection to her son. How many of us deal with this when we have a loved one die? Believing we must stay sad to remember them? I'm grateful I caught that one as a seed thought before it had time to sprout.

1/14/14

PERSONAL JOURNAL: 12:04 a.m. Spent some time with transcribing my journal. Making some slow progress. My chest is tender and clogged and sore from coughing. I'm sleepy and will write more in the morning. Would love a poem.

PERSONAL JOURNAL: 10:15 a.m. Fed and washed and up to date on emails and Facebook. Michael woke me at 7:13 a.m. (11) and I smiled. Nudged me again at 7:20 (9) and at 9:09. I've been reading a Wayne Dyer post and enjoying a relaxing morning.

PERSONAL JOURNAL: 11:52 p.m. (9)   Hello my sweet angel Michael. I've had a full day. Dinner for Sue and Darlene this evening at my house. Seems like much of our conversation circles around illness, aches, and pain. Al isn't doing well. Michael, you may be seeing him soon on the other side. He really loves you (11:56 -11:11). I am requesting a poem. Can you help? I also found another medium site today. The more I am drawn to ADCs, the more I learn about them. Also, some beautiful rainbow images have been showing up.

1/15/14

PERSONAL JOURNAL: 7:26 a.m. *"Our love is here to stay"* awoke me at 7:11 a.m. (9). My Michael shirt pillow still smells, but not as ripely as it once did. Fading. So I stop and go within to my inner world of Michael. Are those memories fading as well? This thing we call death, how does it really work for the living left behind? Images and quotes and artifacts and none of it stays past a few generations unless your reach was wide and touched many lives—for good or ill. It becomes yesterday's news. Yet for me, this mother, Michael lives on in my heart—forever—our love is here to stay. It's the love that I'm feeling and the moments of love that we shared that live on and don't fade and I get to take with me.

1/16/14—TWENTY FIVE WEEKS

FACEBOOK: 12:31 a.m. Driving places—usually just me and my thoughts. Often in the quiet of my car, I'm aware of Michael singing to me. Better than the radio. It's like a private concert in my mind. I smile and say "hello" and tell him how much I love him. I try not to wish he was here, but

I'd be lying to say I don't wish it every day. We never spoke about the possibility of him dying. Our talks were full of dreams for life. As his number one fan, I still catch myself scouting out venues for him. Every day with our loved ones is a gift—a precious gift.

PERSONAL JOURNAL: 12:37 a.m. Need to get some sleep. Picking up Mom at 5:15 a.m. for a procedure at Sutter Memorial, where Michael was born. I remember walking in to the reception area for Lamaze classes and then for the big event. Also it's where three of my grandsons were born, so I also have wonderful memories of waiting for Isaiah and for the twins to arrive. It will be torn down soon. Another memory no longer present in the physical world.

1/17/14

PERSONAL JOURNAL: 8:49 a.m. Aunt Betty's birthday and she passed in 2000. Michael and John sang at her service.

PERSONAL JOURNAL: 10:18 a.m. Have taken Chewie to the vet and handled some business items. Now I am taking time to write. Well, actually, I need to interrupt and check in with Mom. No answer. She's off on errands, I suspect. Got her by cell phone and she's fine. Went to the doctor for meds and is off to Costco. I'm grateful for such a healthy mom.

PERSONAL JOURNAL: 10:33 a.m. I'm reading Mark Nepo's book, "7000 Ways to Listen." I find his writing inspiring. I know mine can be also, and I believe it's a matter of listening and being in the moment. My earliest good memory of school is of being celebrated for my writing in the sixth grade. I let my sister's writing talent dissuade me. I remember believing hers was better and not pursuing anything. I had a run at copy-writing which is so different in that it is writing with an agenda and a desire to influence. The writing of poetry and essays, when I'm still and reflective, comes from a different place inside of me.

My dear Michael. I miss you every day. I tear up often, flooding my eyes and my heart with love and memories, with wishes that I could have you here with me in the flesh. I'm so new and feeling unskilled with the after-life connection. Sometimes I feel right there and others quite distant or blocked. I love the silent, still moments. Garret is here and back in his room—no interruptions really, but a presence and potential for it. How do I tap in no matter who or what is filling my external space?

"Hi Mom. Be still and listen for me. I'm right here, right now." He's showing me an image of himself in the brown chair with his bandoneon and music stand. He's sitting erect and beginning to practice.

Nepo talks about the deep listening of the heart. You, my dear Michael, have taught me this with your passing. I have a new relationship with listening to my inner world of which you are a big part. It takes a moment of slowing down and dropping in, of noticing, and then listening. I want to share. I must find that place of writing while connected.

New poem, *"Missing You and Finding Me"*

1/18/14

PERSONAL JOURNAL: 8:04 a.m. Woke up at 7:27 (Hi Michael) and have two bits of song going through which are not from Michael's CDs. *"Mother Mary comes to me, speaking words of wisdom, let it be"* and the other I can only make out the *"for always"* at the end. It's a familiar one but is escaping me. I prefer Michael's voice and yet I'm learning to take his messages from whatever source. I made it through a weepy Thursday without realizing that it was an anniversary of sorts—each Thursday. Wednesday was actually weepier. All of it here to teach me.

Downton Abbey marathon watching yesterday. The story is like a fine novel and the pages keep turning. Having already watched this season premiere, I'm aware of what will be happening and am filling in the blanks. These characters become real and I find myself caring about them. Knowing one is going to die is sad. So, I'm also aware of my life as a novel with chapters and people who come and go—all of whom, including myself, eventually die.

1/19/14

PERSONAL JOURNAL: 8:10 a.m. (Hi Michael) Sunday   Michael woke me with song earlier and now the same one I can't remember the words to is repeating itself—ends in *"for always,"* so at some point perhaps I'll get the whole thing. (Found it ... song is *"Always...I will love you so for always ... can't find enough ways to let you know."*)

I count on him nudging me when the clock has a 9 or an 11 or both. I feel like he's tapping me on my shoulder saying *"I'm here."* Anyway, I notice like yesterday in the car that it opens my heart and I say "hello and I love you"—and the tears begin. Watching Downton Abbey to catch up and two of my favorites have died in the story. Brings up the emotion of loss. Makes me curious about where we get our beliefs about after-death.

Cultures pass them down along with how to hold your silverware—the etiquette of death. I've not been a good student of etiquette. Much prefer asking what feels right in the moment. Makes me remember trying to fit in when living in the deep South where I was so unaware of the rules.

1/20/14

PERSONAL JOURNAL: 8:56 a.m. Slept in to 8:30 with a nudge somewhere near 4 a.m. Really deep sleep with no dreams that I can remember. I remember very few or even recognize that I've had a dream. Several teary moments yesterday—church music and playing Michael's angels song. Stu has videos pulled from Michael's computer that I haven't seen yet. I wonder about what he's doing now. I want direct undisputed contact, not just for myself, for all of us who love someone who has passed and want to stay connected.

Looking at his photos on my phone—the one on my wallpaper with his bandoneon and the one on the river with rainbow light and angels all around him. Both bring me to tears of missing him and trying to understand. He began singing *"Stranger in paradise"* and I doubt he's a stranger anymore.

"Mom, I can pour myself into anything that brings me joy and I cannot begin to explain how easy it is to be anywhere, everywhere, all at once, without limitation. I love you. Write your book—our book!"

New poem, *"Anywhere Everywhere"*

FACEBOOK: 12:19 p.m. Sometimes poems come through me and one arrived after a journal exchange with Michael wishing he was here. I called it *"Missing You"*

1/21/14

FACEBOOK: 8:39 a.m. Reading more from poet Mark Nepo's new book, Seven Thousand Ways to Listen. No matter what page I open to, his words touch my heart. Listening from my heart, listening to my heart, listening with my heart—all are practices I have been deepening since Michael's passing. Stillness and nowness and presence amplify the sounds of within and I hear and feel deep channels opening—carrying me across the veil if only for a moment. Nepo's writing inspires and enriches me.

1/23/14—TWENTY SIX WEEKS

PERSONAL JOURNAL: 8:50 a.m. Twenty-six weeks today. Six months. *"I believe I can fly"* and *"Our love is here to stay"*— lyrics I'm hearing this morning. Still getting *"For Always"* and looked up the rest of the song. Very sweet message that love is for always. Tears yesterday and a hug from Patti, connected also with Bridget who lost her daughter a couple of years ago. Just really missing Michael and wishing he was here.

Need to pack this evening as I leave in the morning for Dreambuilder Live in Los Angeles. Michael used to drive me to the airport, half asleep.

Dr. Brian Weiss will be on Oprah this Sunday. What's my contribution to life? I know he made a huge contribution to mine.

FACEBOOK: 9:55 a.m. Twenty.six weeks today. A lifetime ago and just yesterday. I still weep, just not as intensely or as often. I was tender-hearted before Michael's passing and now even more so. Heading to Mary Morrissey Dreambuilder course tomorrow. I bring a beginner mind to this one even though it's the sixth time for me.

Rebuilding shattered dreams, finding my way from grief to grace, completing a book about my journey, these are the dreams that pull on me today. I listen for guidance and hold a vision of being of service and trusting what comes. "Trusting" seems to be one of my big life lessons. Today I am present to how much I love all of my sons and how grateful I am for my family here and on the other side. Trusting those connections never die.

1/24/14

PERSONAL JOURNAL: 12:24 p.m. (9)   Michael has whispered to me in numbers multiple times this morning as I traveled from Sacramento to Los Angeles for Mary Morrissey's DreamBuilder Live event.

A poem came through, *"Gentle Whispers"*

PERSONAL JOURNAL: 11:00 p.m. At the Marriott and ready to go to sleep. Taking a moment to check in. I always wanted to bring Michael to DreamBuilder. This was going to be the one, so I say, "He's here and enjoying it with me. Inspiring me to build my dream, to teach about life after life, to celebrate our connection."

1/25/14—SIX CALENDAR MONTHS

PERSONAL JOURNAL: 7:20 a.m. (9)   Good morning my dear, sweet son. Six months ago today, you slipped your earthly binding and thus began my new journey as well. I miss you, even knowing you are here with me. I miss your sweet presence, your laugh, your music, your messes. Our prince—

we all loved you so and still do—perhaps even more in some strange way. I carry you with me in my heart wherever I go. I feel your presence when I get still. I listen for you and see your wink when I have 9s and 11s. I weep.

"Mom, before I was here, I came in your dream. It's all a dream and we awake into such love and beauty when we drop the body. I'm here there everywhere. Teach yourself and others how to stay connected. Learn and teach and be the light you came to be. I'm your test pilot. We'll fly together. Hold the image. Edison was working on his next invention beyond the phone. Who else is on this path? Find them."

1/26/14

PERSONAL JOURNAL: 12:13 a.m. Enjoyed my day and catching a few sentences before sleep. Met an attractive man tonight. Spent some time getting to know him and could see myself enjoying many more long conversations and spending time with him. This or something better. It's fun to feel some energy about a man. It's been a very long time. Inspired a poem I called *"The Soul Knows"*

PERSONAL JOURNAL: 11:51 p.m. Back home. Tucked in bed. Didn't get to say goodbye to my crush in my rush to catch my flight. I feel like my vision is clearer now about what I am generating. In addition to my book about my journey with Michael, I am teaching myself and others the science and technology for connecting with their loved ones on the other side.

1/27/14

PERSONAL JOURNAL: 7:29 a.m. (9 & 9) *"Listen to your angels"*—Michael's one of my angels now, although I believe we felt his angelic presence when he was with us in the flesh as well. I am counting on his help with my vision. I will teach a system for opening new channels of connection with loved one who have passed, recognizing their presence, establishing ways to communicate, learning to listen from our heart.

FACEBOOK: 9:55 a.m. Back home after a weekend with my mentor Mary Morrissey. Dreambuilder Live filled me up as always. Connected with people who are passionate about possibility. Refining and energizing my vision of publishing my book about my journey of the heart with Michael. Did you know that Thomas Edison believed we could communicate across dimensions and was working on an invention to do so? I'll bet if he had lived into this century we would be having FaceTime with the other side anytime we wanted to. I'm in exploration mode about how we already do this without technology. I have a great teacher/contact on the other side.

1/28/14

PERSONAL JOURNAL: 6:03 a.m. (9) *"I Want a Hippopotamus for Christmas"* brought me a big smile this morning as I awoke. Felt good to have a tune from Michael in my ear again.

Watching Dr. Brian Weiss on Oprah and hearing the story of a woman and her sons being contacted by her husband, their dad. They each separately reported hearing their dad whisper in their right ear. He said to each of them, "It's more beautiful than you could imagine. I'm safe. I love you. I'm always with you." Very similar to what Michael has shared with me. Weiss says that somehow when we connect and are filled with the joy of that connection, we can find ourselves feeling even closer than we were in the flesh. I've experienced that.

Worked on my manuscript yesterday and also did more research on what currently exists in the field. There are trainings for self-guided ADCs. I spoke my intention to a couple of people at Rotary, that I would be teaching a system of connecting with loved ones on the other side—that there is a science and technology for this process that can be learned and used to heal loss and experience joy and laughter. Michael's gift to me and those I touch. I love you Michael.

Another poem, *"Snapshot Moments"*

1/29/14

PERSONAL JOURNAL: 7:42 a.m. Dinner with Annie last night. When I told her my vision of teaching a system for connecting with loved ones on the other side, she got God bumps all over and teared up. She could feel the truth in it.

Checking in with Michael. *"Mom, you've always wanted to touch people at the deepest level. This is your path to doing that. I'm right here with you, supporting you all the way."*

Did you just show me a piece of the puzzle? I saw that I'm here but my soul is also there with you as are all of our souls, and we are connected and communicating. *"Mom, you've always wanted to touch people at the deepest level. This is your path to doing that. I'm right here with you, supporting you all the way. Tell Sammie about it. Stay in touch with her."*

Did you just show me a piece of the puzzle? I saw that I'm here but my soul is also there with you as are all of our souls, and we are connected and communicating. Like in the movies

Avatar or The Matrix when we're in two places. I'm seeing a cord from spiritual being to human experience. You cut your cord for this chapter and I'm still here, but I am also there with you. We are never alone. God is with us. You are giving me the chant that you recorded for the SLC choir.

1/30/14—TWENTY SEVEN WEEKS

PERSONAL JOURNAL: 7:31 a.m. (11) Michael has winked at me at least four times this morning on 9 and 11 combinations. I smile and send him love when it happens. Dinner and Walter Mitty movie with Lisa last night. She spoke of being able to connect with her dad when she's in the stillness, that he will come and sit next to her. I believe the brain waves need to be tuned to a frequency that receives spirit. EMDR must take people to that frequency with bilateral stimulation. Lisa meditates. I go into my heart and deeply listen.

PERSONAL JOURNAL: 11:52 p.m. (9) Just thinking about Michael after a few hours of TV and solitaire—my mind numbing addictions. I saw another Realtor today and he was so sweet about remembering Michael and hugging me. I told him I talk to Michael all the time, and he said probably more than before, and we laughed because it's true, and he knew it.

Wrote a poem, *"The Club"*

1/31/14

FACEBOOK: 10:25 a.m. Last day of January already. Yesterday was week 27 or 189 days, lots of 9s in those numbers. I see combos of 9s and 11s numerous times throughout my day and I always smile and say an "I love you Michael." Often I well up with tears. I notice I cry less often, yet welcome the tears when they come. They are filled with a Mother's Love, blended with joy and sadness and gratitude for my learning a new language of connection—moments when I feel his presence and hear his heart and feel his words of comfort. When I tune in, he is always there. I miss him and yet he's with me. Still working through this new territory of my heart.

PERSONAL JOURNAL: 11:00 a.m. Enjoying the dancing rainbows from Barbara's gift to me. When the sun is shining it rotates a small crystal and radiates rainbows all around my living and dining room.

Wrote a poem: *"A Mother's Tears"*

2/1/14

PERSONAL JOURNAL: 7:12 a.m. The month of love. Such an all encompassing word—Love. I love my children, my family, my friends, my clients, my home, my neighborhood, my work in the world. I love watching the birds in my back yard, the children playing at the park, the YouTube laughing babies.

So what's the common experience here that I'm naming as "Love?" A soft space opens in my heart, a feeling of connection. Stillness, wonderment, appreciation, grace. 8:19 a.m.

Michael's recording of *"Oblivion"* is playing. Tears flowing. Such a talent gone from our sight and our physical world, never from our hearts.

2/2/14

PERSONAL JOURNAL: 7:15 a.m. "Somewhere over the rainbow" singing to me last night and this morning. Not his voice, since it's not a song he recorded, but it reminds me of his promise to meet me at the end of the rainbow. I listen to the words and they speak of a higher vibration—way above the clouds and chimney tops—a frequency that melts troubles like lemon drops "is where you'll find me." Not in this lower range, but in the higher one, what I've called the Love Frequency—the place I know to tune in for guidance and wisdom.

So when Michael sings "listen to your angels" he's telling me to go to the angel frequency. The rainbow points out heavenly beauty and light and a presence always with us—a source of light, refracted through transparent, clear crystals or rain drops, and then we see the full spectrum of color always present yet hidden from our human eyes.

2/3/14

PERSONAL JOURNAL: 7:33 a.m. Michael woke me—7:11 a.m. and I began imagining myself on a large stage and he is standing next to me. We are speaking (I'm doing the talking) about our journey and my learning to stay connected. I ask to have the house lights up so I can see faces. I take them back to the phone call day—the knee-buckling news. I have them live it in their own mind with a loved one—not so they feel sad, but more so they recognize the fragility of life and the importance of tuning in to the presence of love.

I've changed the tagline for my book to "a mother's journey." Title stays "From Grief to Grace." I took a course last Saturday on writing, publishing and marketing your book.

Instructor was quite helpful. Scenes, chapters, rewrites, humor, romance, drama, flyers, book signings, book plates, speaking engagements—all pieces of the process.

Today will be gone in a blink. Curious about where are my most productive energy vortexes in my home. Living room, office, bedroom, maybe the sanctuary—definitely not on the sofa in the family room where the TV lives.

2/4/14

PERSONAL JOURNAL: 8:48 a.m. I can see the connection between Michael being able to reach me through his musical lyrics and my playing his CDs on a regular basis.

Today is fairly wide open and I can make good headway on transcribing from my journal to digital.

2/5/14

PERSONAL JOURNAL: 8:16 a.m. 7:04, 7:22, 8:03 all 11s this morning accompanied by "let me take you to heaven's door" which to me the 11s represent—gateway number. I hear Michael singing and I smile. Making progress on my (our) book and Saturday's class was quite helpful.

Writing my book pulls me back through my journal entries and into emotions and memories still quite fresh.

2/6/14—TWENTY EIGHT WEEKS

PERSONAL JOURNAL: 6:21 a.m. 5:31, 5:44, 6:03 Michael was nudging me awake. I've shared with several people my analogy of how I feel as far as being driven to achieve. It's like I'm an old fashioned car that required a crank to turn over the engine and get it started. That was the level of my drive before Michael's passing. Now, it seems my crank is completely missing, tossed to the side on the road of material success. My firing up cannot come from any sense of being driven from the outside. I've gone into an attraction or drawn-to-me mode, and relaxed trusting. I am here to serve and to express grace and serenity.

PERSONAL JOURNAL: 11:54 p.m. (11 & 9) Just turned on AfterLifeTv.com to listen to interview with Paul Selig. So I'm taking a moment to listen and take notes. Selig is a channeler.

2/08/14

PERSONAL JOURNAL: 8:15 a.m. No writing yesterday. I was at the Masters Club Educational Roundtables and home for awhile midday and then off to the theater with Mom and Stanley. Home at 10:30 and didn't open my journal to write. I see that mornings and evenings are best—not midday. I've noticed this from transcribing my journal.

Existential crisis—what am I doing here? To serve and to love. Just wrote those answers a few pages ago. To serve and express grace and serenity.

Yesterday I spoke with a couple of fellow realtors about my book and that I am learning the science and technology for after life communication so I can teach it. I saw Ron light up. He remembered an experience with his grandmother at her grave when he was speaking to her in prayer and experienced her presence. I said when you take yourself to the frequency of prayer you are dialing in to a higher realm and that's where the communication occurs. It's not in our heads but in our hearts that the vibration occurs.

FACEBOOK: 9:31 a.m. Writing my book pulls me back through my journal entries and into emotions and memories still quite fresh. Reflecting on my journey as a mom and what I've learned. My three precious sons, as we have grown up together, each have given me lessons in loving and letting go. I've learned to listen and not lecture, to watch and not hover, to celebrate wins and soothe disappointments. They taught me to be curious about the male side of the species, to honor their space, to ask and not intrude, to appreciate and not baby them. My oldest two have shown me how much I love watching them take on parenting, how proud I am of the love they express with their own sons, and have given me the gift of being a grandma.

And my youngest showed me the path of the gentle artist, the dedication to a love for creating music, for never giving up on his dream, and now, with his passing, he's teaching me the deepest language of the heart that bridges the dimension of physical time and space. He's guiding me through grief and feelings of loss to embrace a new way of being connected—a letting go and holding on and staying open to joy and sorrow and to trusting that all is truly well. "A mother's journey"—my subtitle to the book.

2/9/14

PERSONAL JOURNAL: 7:50 a.m. "Stranger in Paradise" playing this morning. I can't imagine Michael remaining a stranger anywhere for anytime at all. We all love him. Feeling his presence this morning as I take time to write before breaking my silence. One of the perks of sleeping alone—my precious silent time. This morning I was practicing a breath concentration that brings the breath in from the heart toward the back and up through the nose, over the crown chakra front to back, and out the front of the heart, forming an infinity loop. Feels like a way of harmonizing heart and mind. When I turn the loop horizontal and see it sending love out into the world, it comes rolling back in to me—expanding the love field I can generate.

Planning a spaghetti dinner for family tonight. It's been a month and that's as long as I ever want to go. Michelle connects with her family every day. It's the mother to mother lineage connection. I understand and catch my moments when I can.

PERSONAL JOURNAL: 4:33 p.m. Everyone will arrive around 6 p.m. for spaghetti. I've got the sauce cooking and brownies made. Just went through the toy box and crafts box to sort what I have for the grandsons to create with if they want to. I also have a movie, Hugo. I could go out and get a few more things so they can make Valentine cards. We'll see. It's a lazy rainy day.

PERSONAL JOURNAL: 10:56 p.m. Great evening. Mom, Stanley, Stu, Garret, John, Michelle, Isaiah, Josiah, Judah and me—all chowed down on salad and spaghetti and wine and great company. Michelle remembers handing Stu notes at Pizza and Pipes. Michael would have enjoyed the evening and probably did. We just couldn't see him in person. Stu brought me a DVD of Michael's performance at Del Webb.

People handle grief in such different ways. Mom says she can't listen to Michael's music because it makes her miss him more and she starts to cry. I think Michelle is similar. I find the more I listen to him, the closer I feel and the sadness comes with lots of joy to balance it out. Do I miss Michael—so much. I'm just insisting upon my blessing. If I choose to live my life trusting that I am being loved and guided and protected, then there has to be a blessing in all of this.

2/10/14

PERSONAL JOURNAL: 7:44 a.m. "On this night…let me take you to heaven's door." I shut the lights down at 11:11 last night and this morning the times of awakening were both 11s. I just kept turning over and going back to sleep.

Yesterday in church we did a meditation on being at peace, wishing peace to someone we don't feel so at peace with. I still have work to do. Three showed up and all are very difficult for me to love, to extend a blessing of peace to. So, I do my best and know it's for my own inner peace that I do it anyway. Interesting that their behaviors I find hard to deal with are all connected to my sons and not to me. I don't condone their actions and behavior. I see that's not what's being called for. That they are all doing the best they can with the belief systems they have, and I can see them as children of God. I don't have to like them, just send peace.

Wrote a poem *"Peace in My Heart"*

2/11/14

PERSONAL JOURNAL: 7:49 a.m. (11,9)…..Woke up with Michael singing Music of the Night to me.

FACEBOOK: 4:52 p.m. This afternoon I needed to go to DMV to take care of the last bits and pieces of having Michael's car transferred out of his name. I created an intention as I was walking up to the building that I would have a positive experience and leave a blessing with whomever I had helping me.

When my number was called, I went to station 17, and the most wonderful young man awaited me, wearing a Fedora hat just like Michael loved to wear. I told him I loved his hat, that it reminded me of my son, and asked if he was a musician. Turns out he plays guitar and his band plays gigs in San Francisco. What are the chances that I get the only musician in DMV who is wearing a Michael-hat? I love it. This young man is named Nicholas and he and his band have created a new kind of music they call Folkadelic.

By now I'm beaming at him and telling him all about Michael, we are having a great conversation, and when I go to write my check, there's a rainbow on it. I reached over the counter and held his hands for a moment. I could feel Michael so present, and all three of us were certainly connecting in spirit. Very sweet. I could hear Michael say "Good job Mom."

2/12/14

PERSONAL JOURNAL: 6:53 a.m. Had a great conversation with Maria Nemeth and am going to see a woman named Nancy who specializes in EMDR. I told her about Michael and my intention to teach the science and technology of afterlife communication.

2/13/14—TWENTY NINE WEEKS

PERSONAL JOURNAL: 5:44 a.m. Michael woke me with "Soon it's gonna rain." Took some time with the pendulum and dialed in to connect with him. It was 5:51 a.m. when I picked up my pen again to write.

Last night Mom and I went to see a psychic medium named Blair Roberts and I was hoping to get a reading. Didn't happen. Enjoyed myself anyway. Mom kept making faces and comments indicating she thought he was a phony. I didn't have that experience at all. He was picking up information from the other side and when he mentioned Frank Sinatra, I thought for a moment we might bridge to Michael and music.

I asked Michael again about suicide and I got another strong "no." I also get that from the readings I've had as well. He was running and frightened and in a chaotic state of mind. He also acknowledges that it was time. This is the part I have a tough time with. Seems like he still had so much living to do and so many gifts yet to give.

2/14/14

PERSONAL JOURNAL: 7:40 a.m. Happy Valentine's Day—a day for celebrating love. I love you Michael. I love you John and Troy, Mom and Dad, Isaiah, Josiah, Judah, and Michelle. I love you Riley, Christina, Holland and Kurt. Darlene, Sue, Kelly, Sammie and Stu.

Michael loved singing love songs especially to couples at their table. I hope you are singing for loved ones all over the universe today my sweet son.

2/15/14

PERSONAL JOURNAL: 1:16 a.m. Just a note before going to sleep. Great evening at B Street and dinner with Christine. Such a blur the first few weeks after Michael passed. She came to visit me and remembers sitting in the sanctuary and I barely recall it. I am glad I kept a journal of my feelings or they would be gone.

Had lunch with my friend John and he gave me a photo promo of Michael from about 10 years ago that I hadn't seen before. He says my energy is softer. I think he's right. He feels like whenever we think of our loved ones, we bring their energy to us. I recalled my experience of bringing Michael home to me and it brought me to tears. Tears are welcome. I feel my connection through the tears.

1:26 a.m. (9) and I hear Michael singing "On the Night of 1000 Stars." I love you Michael.

10:39 p.m. Cari and Richard are here and going to church with me tomorrow. We always have very interesting conversations about death and burial. I notice I can talk freely about these topics.

I just flashed back to having Michael here and the difference of him alive and well and playing his music as contrasted with him in his cremation box—yet I was so grateful to have my private time with him. Those moments were precious to me and healing for all of those who needed to have closure and communion with his spirit.

Hi Michael. I'm learning that your Mount Madonna silent monk who gave you your name of Naresh is making his transition. You will be able to greet him. I'm thinking of how tenderly sweet your own spirit is and how you received your name of Naresh from him. I found your precious piece of paper that you wrote your request of him on and then received your sacred name printed on the back. I feel so grateful that you and I were connected at that heart level. I miss you and your sweet energy. I'm receiving so much as I write our book. I love you.

2/16/14

PERSONAL JOURNAL: 7:15 a.m. "I will love you so, for always." My thoughts are drawn this morning to others who have lost their children. Paul Newman came to mind. MADD was founded by a mother who lost her child. The Newmans created a foundation and folded their energies into those efforts. I notice my energies are drawn to afterlife connections and exploring those. How much does this help with healing of grief. Seems to be a major piece. If I feel myself losing my connection to Michael, I begin to go into my head and then doubt and worry and fear start talking to me.

I don't worry for Michael. Some deep knowing says he is happy, growing, being his delightful energy for many on the other side. It's my life that begins to feel dull without him in it. My children and grandchildren light me up. I can hear myself saying, "that's an inside job." So let me rephrase. It's my love for my children and grandchildren that lights me up and I delight in their company. I still delight in Michael's company and if I begin to feel he's missing, the sadness descends.

2/17/14

PERSONAL JOURNAL: 9:20 a.m. (9 and 11) Hello Michael my love. I've been reading *The Untethered Soul* again so I can work with Cari on it. You are in my heart and my thoughts and my desire to complete the book about our journey. If you were writing the introduction what would you say?

"This is a story about the love between a mother and a son, and more than that, it's a story of moving through grief and staying connected at the Soul level where the connection began, always was, and always will be.

It's a story of dreams and possibilities, of love and support, of holding on and letting go. It's a story of wonder and mystery and trusting and sharing.

It's about a voice—a most beautiful voice—and music and healing. It's about joy and sorrow and expanding to include it all.

It's about contribution and reaching out with a light into the darkness. It's about gifts hidden in tragedy and lives forever changed.

It's about commitment and persistence and courage and life-everlasting. It's about you and me and us."

Michael-Angel-O

2/18/14

PERSONAL JOURNAL: 7:06 a.m. Woke up at 6:59 and smiled at my 11 and 9 hello from Michael. Had a great phone call from Kurt yesterday. He just returned from Uruguay and plans to move there. We talked about how Michael dreamed of going to South America and that he was probably with Kurt watching over him and enjoying the people and music.

I read him a couple of my poems yesterday and cried. Heard a song from Les Mis on Olympic ice skating and wept. Revisited the morning of 7/25/13 and cried my way through writing about it for the book.

"Who can I turn to" is my inner song this morning. I carry the image of Michael's dad leaving him and going home and haven't been able to process it through so I don't carry a harsh judgment of his behavior and mental capacity.

9:09 a.m. I have been working on the book this morning. I played Michael's Broadway CD and trust he's here to help me. I can do this. I'm good at fitting things together.

2/19/14

FACEBOOK: 12:40 a.m. Spent much of the last several days writing on my book about my experience with Michael. I have been revisiting the details of those first few days and can do it only in bits and pieces. So many memories to process through. Brings up the tears. My commitment to completing it keeps me going—one phrase, one page at a time. I can hear Michael encouraging me.

2/20/14—THIRTY WEEKS

PERSONAL JOURNAL: 6:41 a.m. Yesterday was 30 weeks. Four more days and we're at seven calendar months. Numbers and music are my strongest channels, that and my continued experience of deep love for him.

I've been pulled by errors this week—mine and a lender's—about $7000 worth. Working with my mind and the principles I've learned through the years. Fretting about it lowers my vibration and that is not where abundance resides. It also affects my connection with Michael. I notice I now come from a perspective of having news that was gut wrenching about Michael's death which makes anything else pretty easy to handle. No one wants bad news, and each situation has a lesson to be learned and a chance to forgive myself and others.

Working on the book with a strong desire to have it contribute to others. Today I have an EMDR experience and learn more about its connection to communicating with those who have gone before us.

11:30 a.m. Listening to Michael on CD and having a lunch. Just came back from a session where I experienced bilateral stimulation with headphones—not EMDR. Not sure about the sounds in my ears being the best for me. Distracting somewhat.

Received confirmation that I am being supported through this process in a way that works for me. Michael has been holding my hand and guiding me, which gives me my strength to go on.

Keep writing. He helps me to know what to say. My purpose is to share our experience for whoever wants to share it.

2/22/14

FACEBOOK: 10:36 a.m. Making progress on the writing of my book. Trusting that somehow I will pull it all together in a comprehensive format. Staying in my heart space to write, listening for encouragement from Michael, gathering the stories and poetry and weaving them into a tapestry. I really appreciate and admire those who write our books. I love reading. My writing, up until now, lies safely stored in boxes of journals privy to my eyes only. This naked vulnerability from sharing my thoughts publicly both calls to me and scares me at the same time. I listen for my "Good job, Mom," and keep on putting words on paper.

2/23/14

PERSONAL JOURNAL: 12:46 a.m. Forgot to write about the "hello" Michael did at my EMDR session. I'm coming to the end of the process of the bilateral stimulation and I can feel myself being urged from within to tell the therapist about my DMV experience. As I mention Booth 17 and the guy with the Fedora, she stops me and says, "The angel at the DMV?" Turns out she was there last week and Nicholas helped her as well. What are the odds?

Worked more on the book today. I'm thinking it will be three parts—my writing on the things I've noticed, my poetry, and what I'm calling "raw footage" from my FB and personal journal entries. Something for everyone. Narrative, poetry, and a peek into my journal. I still think the poetry will be divided as I have it, but not sure. I look forward to meeting the woman I'll have become when this is published.

I feel like Michael was stroking my arm earlier, using my own hand to do it. I felt his presence and tenderness. Heard his songs several times during the day and caught him digitally saying hello with 9s and 11s. I love you so much my dear Michael.

PERSONAL JOURNAL: 6:57 a.m. Heart meditation this morning and strong connection to Michael. He showed me presence. How I can recognize his energy and essence without his physical body. He related to the body like a familiar outfit—something to be worn but it's the wearer of the outfit who matters. I can reach him on my heart channel. I told him I want to learn and teach this. He just showed me masses of people in comas, and those on the other side are trying to get through to us and only a few are awake enough to pick up their signals.

"Keep trusting yourself and our connection Mom. I am here and this is our work to be done together. Keep writing the book. It is the first of many. Listen to your angels Mom. I'm one of them. Always was, and I tried to stay as long as I could before going back home. You are here with me. Someday you'll understand.

Right now you just need to trust and listen and write. I love you Mom. We're a team. Always have been. You can let go of any worry about your real estate business. It is solid and will flow to you. Just stay in grace and receptivity. Let go of worry. Make the phone calls and visits you get nudged to make. You have a whole team over here supporting you."

2/24/14

PERSONAL JOURNAL: 6:39 a.m. (9, 9)   Have been awake since 5:45 a.m.—just being still in a form of meditation. Michael singing Phantom's Music of the Night and then 1000 Stars, alternating them even now in my inner ear. I am feeling his presence within my heart so strongly. Images of his last night and confused state of mind were presented to me. Do I need the coroner and police reports to put this to bed? Poem today: *"Bringing You Home"*

2/24/14

PERSONAL JOURNAL: 11:32 a.m. Mark Nepo again tonight at book group. His words, so moving and encouraging to me. Immersion and art—writing, creating, music—losing myself to find myself. Writing to listen to and learn about myself, to capture a feeling and experience. Very sleepy right now. When I close my eyes to drop deep inside listening mode with myself, I fall asleep.

2/25/14—SEVEN CALENDAR MONTHS

PERSONAL JOURNAL: 6:12 a.m. This morning the thought "what if I had known" was so strong in me. Could I have stopped it? Everyone tells me to know it was his time. All the mediums say similar things. I still want to turn the clock back, bring him home, not leave him at Al's, drive him myself, stay by his side until I know he's okay. I weep with this pain of missing him and wishing I had known or asked or intuited or somehow tuned into this trouble.

He sings of angels whispering and guardians watching and I have to turn to a higher view of all of it or I know I will drown. Swim towards the light I can see. He tells me to listen for my angels to whisper. That it easy if I just open my ears. All I have to do is trust and heaven is in me and everywhere.

Who am I? Who is Michael? We are both points of awareness, bubbles of consciousness, seeds of love sown by creation, little mirrors of the whole. Awareness trumps it all— has a body but doesn't need one.

Poem written today: *"If I Knew It Would Be the Last Time"*

2/26/14

PERSONAL JOURNAL: 7:15 a.m. Michael is singing to me and I love him for this sweet way of awakening me each day. I was reading my most recent entries and feel the vibration of creativity contrasted to that of numbness or hypnotic trance. I remember the first few weeks after Michael passed and how I didn't watch TV or play Solitaire or Sudoku. I wrote and I read and I spent time in the stillness with Michael and strengthened my new inner channels.

2/27/14—THIRTY ONE WEEKS

PERSONAL JOURNAL: 7:06 a.m. Woke up at 6:03 and have been hanging in the silence for a bit listening to Tango Fire sung by Michael on my inner airwaves. Appreciating and loving him. My morning quiet time is so important to me. I ground myself for the day.

3/1/14

PERSONAL JOURNAL: 6:57 a.m.   Michael's musician friend Scott is visiting me. Picked him up at the bus station last night in the pouring rain and we went over to Stu's for pizza and studio time to see his latest video productions of Michael. Stu has edited Jekyll and Hyde as well as the Del Webb performance so they can be included in our tribute cases. Stu says he has lost eight family members recently and none of those have been as hard as losing Michael. This gentle spirit we had with us for thirty-six years gave such joy to those he touched. Now he knows the breadth of his "fan club." To a person, he was kind, accepting, present and gentle.

3/2/14

FACEBOOK: 2:46 p.m. A friend at church today said she knows I'm working on my book but misses my posts on Facebook. I'm kind of wondering myself why I post less often about my journey with Michael. Healing doesn't have to mean silence, yet there is a peacefulness in my life that is quiet. I'm still very aware of his presence in my life and the many ways he winks a hello to me during the day.

I watched his performance on video of Jekyll & Hyde Friday night with Stu and Scott, a friend of Michael's from San Francisco. They were collaborating on a cabaret show and auditioning for cruise lines together. Scott didn't hear about

Michael's passing in time to come to his celebration of life service. So, yesterday morning we sat in my family room and watched the video. I am so touched even now by the many comments about how Michael showed up for life—so full of light and love and so gentle.

I see his smile easily in my mind's eye because so many photos captured it even from the time he was tiny until he passed. My heart remembers him so clearly. Tears flood my eyes often and they are mostly from those sweet memories and my gratitude for the new ways I am learning to stay connected. I love the photo that shows his delight in doing Tai Chi by the river. I believe those are his guardian angel orbs surrounding him.

PERSONAL JOURNAL: 11:02 p.m. I feel like I have less to say in Facebook these days. I seem to be through the intensity of the loss and now I'm learning to be with Michael in a different way. I did get a poem coming through from doing all of the revisions requiring me to revisit the first day. Wrote *"What is the Sound of a Heart Breaking"*

3/4/14

PERSONAL JOURNAL: 6:56 a.m. Almost complete with a second journal. I can feel the back cover through the few remaining pages. In a journal, I can see the end arriving and, to keep writing, I just buy another journal. Not so with a life— write until it ends and others are left to tell your story.

Thirty six years—such a short life. Yet Michael didn't waste time. No TV for him. Nothing held more interest for him than his own practicing or writing or reading or meditating. He tended towards worrying as I look back. He was working on that, but fear could certainly get a grip on him—fear that something had happened to me or his dad or his grandmother. I'm not sure he ever felt completely secure except here at home. Most kids cannot wait until they are old enough to leave home. Not Michael. He worried about that when he brothers left. He was only 10, but he really didn't like the idea of moving out at all.

3/5/14

PERSONAL JOURNAL: 11:45 p.m. Found a beautiful new journal at Barnes and Nobles today since this one is a wrap. I am also going to declare it a wrap for what is going into the book. Otherwise, it becomes a never ending story. Tomorrow will be thirty two weeks. I have filled two leather journals given to me by Mary Morrissey at training. They are now my "Michael Journals" and have been a great source of strength as I've shared my process and connected with him throughout. Seems appropriate to close with one of his messages to me....

"Hi Mom. You're doing great. I catch you when I can. Good job working with Scott on Saturday. Help him keep his dreams alive. You and I have the same tender heart. It's what makes you a good mom and grandmother. Look at all the people you help.

I couldn't really grow up in the traditional sense over there and here I am able to just be me and it's perfect. No stress. Earth school filled with the dark and the light—duality—good and evil—it's all shadows and we learn to love and add our song to a concert that never ends—and when we drop our bodies—our love stays. I love you." Michael

Thank you my precious son for all of the love we share and all of the ways you continue to show me how connected we still are. Thank you for my songs and my hummingbirds and my 9s and 11s. Thank you for your promise to meet me at the end of the rainbow. It's raining hard right now and I'm sure there is a rainbow somewhere in the world. Keep spreading your joy.

Author's Note

Before I published the first edition of this book, my father, Charles DeLong IV, passed on May 23, 2014 at his home in Katy, Texas, just eight days after his 91st birthday. He had struggled with Parkinson's for over ten years and had reached the point where he could no longer swallow. He was ready to go and was in hospice care. When I was speaking to him on the phone the day before he took his final breath, saying my good-byes and my "I love you's," and wishing him well on his new adventure, I asked if he had seen anyone from the other side. My brother and sister-in-law both heard him whisper, "Michael." I am positive that Michael was there to greet my dad and welcome him home. I had told Dad a couple of days earlier that if he saw Michael, he was to take his hand and not let go. I think he did just that!

Michael and his Grandpa DeLong at a rehearsal

About the Author

Robyn DeLong has been a successful top-producing Realtor in Sacramento, CA, since 1999. She is a former college professor with a Masters in Interpersonal Communication and multiple certifications as a personal development and life coach. She has appeared on the Sacramento cable network and has been trained by some of the best, including Mary Morrissey, Wayne Dyer, Jack Canfield, and Joe Dispenza.

Robyn lives in Sacramento with her poodle-mix Moxie. Her oldest son, Troy Ortego, is a builder/contractor in Hailey, Idaho, and has a son named Riley. Middle son, John Ortego, is a pharmacist and owns Parkside Pharmacy and Wellness Center in Sacramento with his wife Michelle. They have three sons, Isaiah, and identical twins, Josiah and Judah.

Robyn's mom, Barbara Spengler, lives in a granny-flat connected to Robyn's home. Every Sunday they can be found seated together at their local Unity Church, Spiritual Life Center. Robyn loves volunteering as a member of the Rotary Club of Sacramento where she has served since 2001.

Robyn's first book *Moments of Stillness*, is an inspirational poetry book written prior to Michael's passing, but published afterwards.

This is the second edition of From Grief to Grace...a Mother's Journey. Mostly minor changes since its first publication in 2014. Since then, Robyn has written two other books which share her journey and the tools which have helped her heal and create a joy-filled life. She has also created a personally guided, in-depth healing program for those who want support as they take on this journey through grief.

If this is something you would like to learn more about, just email Robyn and she will set up an appointment for a free consultation.

Comments and emails are always welcome.

Email: info@GrieftoGrace.com

FREE GIFT: Visit Robyn's website GrieftoGrace.com to download your free gift: *Transforming Triggers into Treasures*...plus a bonus 30-Day Inspirational Journal *Beyond the Stages of Grief*.

~~~~~~~~~

Books by Robyn

Moments of Stillness

From Grief to Grace...a Mother's Journey

Finding the Good in Unspeakable Sorrow

Tilling the Sacred Soil of Sorrow...Tools for Living Joyfully from a Broken-Open Heart

Available on Amazon and in some bookstores.

Many of Michael's performances have made their way to YouTube and can be found by searching under Resh Michael or Naresh Michael. To hear "When Angels Whisper" go to: https://www.youtube.com/watch?v=w6MRC7_VPis&t=5s

~~~~~~~~~~

Facebook has been a wonderful way to stay connected and reach out to the communities of people who loved Michael. Robyn created a Facebook page dedicated to Michael at
www.facebook.com/ReshMichaelMemories

~~~~~~~~~~

A scholarship fund to send young musicians to the music program at American River College has been set up in Resh Michael's name by his close friend and music teacher Ben McClara. The URL for making donations is:
http://tinyurl.com/reshmemorial

~~~~~~~~~~

For information about green and loving family-directed home funerals, go to
Thresholds.us
FinalPassages.org

~~~~~~~~~~

Acknowledgements and Gratitudes

How do I thank everyone who contributed to the writing of the first edition of this book, the process of moving along on this journey, and the healing that I've experienced since first publishing it in 2014. Many are mentioned in my journal entries. Special recognition to the following:

My three sons, Troy, John and Michael...your love sustains and strengthens me. My greatest joy finds expression in being your mom. My sister and mother, Alorah Christina and Barbara...you've been there for me through all of my life's lessons—three women finding our way together as a family and as best friends—what a gift.

Girlfriends holding me and nurturing me as my world shook— Darlene, Sue, Kelly, Annie, Vicky, and so many others. Rabbi Taff, Cari and Richard for helping me bring Michael home. My friends from Spiritual Life Center who, in just five days, pulled together the most beautiful celebration of life service ever. Stu Boyer, Rev. Michael Moran, Louise Bezark, Paula Mandella, and all the helping hands bringing food and setting everything up.

Michael's cousin Kurt who worked tirelessly on the musical slideshow for the service. My Coldwell Banker friends who organized food and drinks and took care of my clients, especially Clay Sigg, Mary Grebitus, and Patti Delgado. Another shout out to Stu for creating the legacy CDs and for creating the cover for the first edition of this book.

Thank you to all of Michael's friends who came forward with their stories and their love—Ben, Sean, Winko, Jamie,

Sammie, Amanda, Terra, and so many, many more. Thank you to Mary Morrissey for her spiritual coaching over the years, installing deeply in me the power of noticing what I'm noticing, and of making choices for expansion and aliveness.

For all of the friends who encouraged me to write this book, helped me with proofing it, and looked forward to its birth...here's a BIG HUG of gratitude. The journey continues and many have already been blessed by the first edition.

Roly